New Ways
of
Paying for College

NEW WAYS
OF
PAYING FOR COLLEGE

Arthur M. Hauptman
Robert H. Koff

AMERICAN COUNCIL ON EDUCATION

MACMILLAN PUBLISHING COMPANY
NEW YORK

Collier Macmillan Canada
TORONTO

Maxwell Macmillan International
NEW YORK OXFORD SINGAPORE SYDNEY

Macmillan Publishing Company
866 Third Avenue, New York, N.Y. 10022

Collier Macmillan Canada, Inc.
1200 Eglinton Avenue East, Suite 200
Don Mills, Ontario M3C 3N1

Library of Congress Catalog Card Number: 90-20222

Printed in the United States of America

printing number
1   2   3   4   5   6   7   8   9   10

Library of Congress Cataloging-in-Publication Data

New ways of paying for collge / [edited by]Arthur M. Hauptman, Robert H. Koff.
    p. cm.—(American Council on Education/Macmillan series on higher education)
Includes index.
ISBN 0-02-897183-3
1. Student aid—United States.   2. Student loan funds—United States.   3. Finance, Personal—
United States—Planning.   4. College costs—United States.   I. Hauptman, Arthur M.   II.
Koff, Robert.   III. American Council on Education.   IV. Series: American Council on
Education/Macmillan series in higher education.
LB2337.4.N49   1991   90-20222
378.3'0973—dc20   CIP

Contents

Preface

Surely one of the most interesting trends in higher education in the latter half of the 1980s was the remarkable growth of various new and remolded plans for helping students and their families pay the costs of attending college. After a decade or more in which virtually nothing new was introduced in this area, we have seen a virtual explosion of ideas, proposals, and programs. Following on the heels of the Michigan Education Trust, more than half the states have adopted some form of college savings program in the last several years. State and private loan efforts have blossomed as alternatives to the beleaguered federal student loan programs. Hundreds of philanthropists have followed Eugene Lang's I Have a Dream model of providing tuition assistance and support services to elementary school or junior high classes of disadvantaged students. And the decades-long discussion about the merits of linking student aid to the performance of national or community service has now assumed a prominent place in the national policy debate.

We believe this volume does an admirable job of addressing these important developments in the financing of higher education. The editors have assembled an impressive group of experts in the field, each one bringing a particular viewpoint and expertise to the topic at hand.

The John Ben Snow Foundation, the Teagle Foundation, and other foundations generously provided financial support for the conference and the papers that led to this volume. We are pleased that all proceeds derived from the sale of this book will be provided to the Minority Initiative of the American Council on Education.

The editors would like to acknowledge the contributions of a number of individuals who helped in the development of this volume. Alan Wagner, before he left for a position with the Organization of Economic Cooperation and Development in Paris, played a key role in the initiation and conceptualization of this project. James D. Carroll provided key logistical support at the Brookings Institution. Paul Wolman edited each chapter, working with each author in the editing process. Pauline Piekarz supervised the production of the volume. Carm Colfer helped prepare the manuscript for final publication and assisted in the process in a number of invaluable ways.

FRANK NEWMAN
President
Education Commission of the States

ROBERT ATWELL
President
American Council on Education

Contributors

Richard E. Anderson
Washington University
St. Louis, Missouri

Robert H. Atwell
American Council on Education
Washington, D.C.

Sandy Baum
Skidmore College
Saratoga Springs, New York

Theodore L. Bracken
The Consortium on Financing Higher
    Education
Washington, D.C.

Joseph M. Cronin
Massachusetts Higher Education
    Assistance Corporation
Boston, Massachusetts

Lawrence E. Gladieux
The College Board
Washington, D.C.

Janet S. Hansen
The College Board
Washington, D.C.

Terry W. Hartle
U.S. Senate Committee on Labor
    and Resources
Washington, D.C.

Arthur M. Hauptman
Washington, D.C.

Peter J. Keitel
New York State Higher Education
    Services Corporation
Albany, New York

Robert H. Koff
State University of New York at
    Albany

Martin Kramer
University of California at Berkeley

Ernest A. Lynton
University of Massachusetts at
    Boston

Aims C. McGuinness, Jr.
Education Commission of the States
Denver, Colorado

Jamie P. Merisotis
Washington, D.C.

Kathryn Mohrman
University of Maryland at
    College Park

Frank Newman
Education Commission of the States
Denver, Colorado

Robert L. Payton
University of Indiana at Indianapolis

Susan Stroud
Brown University
Providence, Rhode Island

Timothy R. Warner
Stanford University
Stanford, California

Introduction and Summary

As the cost of college skyrocketed in the 1980s and as public aid subsidies fell in real terms, new strategies for accommodating the growing financial burdens placed on students and their families emerged and began to gain favor. New tuition savings plans, a multiyear assessment of the ability of families to pay for college, alternate financial aid packaging strategies, expanded use of institutional funds for student aid, more employer-provided tuition benefits, and differential pricing policies all were advanced as ways to facilitate paying for college. As pressures for innovative financing strategies continue to build, it seems appropriate to investigate what the possible roles and responsibilities might be for all participants in the system—students, parents, the federal and state governments, philanthropists, employers, and the colleges and universities themselves.

In 1987, Vernon Snow of the John Ben Snow Foundation met with Robert Koff and Alan Wagner of the School of Education of the State University of New York at Albany to discuss the ramifications of these trends in financing higher education. These discussions led the Snow Foundation, in collaboration with the Teagle Foundation and several other foundations, to provide funding to the School of Education for the purpose of investigating new financial arrangements in higher education.

Subsequent to these discussions, Alan Wagner, who had played a key role in establishing the general direction of the project, took a position with the Organization of Economic Cooperation and Development in Paris. Following Alan's departure, Arthur Hauptman agreed to assume the responsibilities that Alan would have had in the subsequent development of the project.

The thrust of the grant was to bring together federal and state policymakers, institutional and foundation officials, academics, and others to discuss innovative financing approaches and how their use might be expanded. To do this, a conference was held at the Brookings Institution in December 1988. Most of the chapters in this volume were first prepared as papers to provide a basis for discussion at that conference, but several of them grew out of the discussions at the conference.

The December conference followed another held at Brookings in June 1988 at which a similar set of issues was discussed. The first conference led to the publication of *The Tuition Dilemma*, by Arthur Hauptman, which was published by Brookings in February 1990. Although both conferences

1

addressed the evolution of new financing mechanisms for higher education, the two differed in emphasis. The first conference and the publication that resulted examined the trends that led to the development of new financing approaches and provided a broad-brush analysis of the different plans that had been developed. This volume focuses more on the specifics of the various approaches and engages a number of authors, many of them advocates of a particular point of view, to discuss how each plan might best be implemented. We believe the two books together form a useful basis for understanding why innovative financing plans for college have become so popular and set forth concisely the merits and drawbacks of the different financing approaches.

Structure of This Volume

This volume is divided into three sections. The first addresses the historical development of the traditional student aid programs and the trends in financing that have created a situation demanding alternatives. The three chapters in this section identify stresses in the current student aid system, trace the evolution of alternative financing mechanisms, and describe a number of the new plans that have been developed.

The second section focuses on the various kinds of new financing plans and how they might best be implemented. The plans addressed include savings incentives, tuition prepayments, alternative loan programs, programs designed to assure access for disadvantaged students, and proposals to create a stronger linkage between service and the receipt of student aid.

The chapters in the third section examine what the appropriate roles and responsibilities should be of the various organizations that might involve themselves in new financing plans. These organizations include the federal government, the states, colleges and universities, and the private sector, including philanthropy and employers.

This summary reviews the chapters in each of these three sections and concludes with a distillation of the commentaries that were made at the conference.

THE DEVELOPMENT AND DESCRIPTION OF NEW FINANCING
APPROACHES

Martin Kramer, in "Stresses in the Student Financial Aid System," traces the consensus built around the concept and practice of needs analysis over the past thirty-five years. He begins by suggesting that the place to start looking at new ways of financing is the current need-based aid system and its several improvements over the previous arrangement, whereby institutions bid for students by offering aid packages. The need-based approach ended these bidding wars and introduced a great deal more equity into the system. Kramer also asserts that another strength of the need-based approach is that it is flexible enough to allow for integration of governmental and nongovernmental aid.

Yet, for all the strength of this consensus on the use of needs analysis, Kramer indicates that four critical assumptions which underlie the existing system are less valid today than they were when it was first established in the 1950s. One assumption is that the primary source of aid would be in the control of the colleges themselves. But the viability of this assumption has been called into question by the fact that federal and state governments have now become the primary sources of aid.

Second, the growth over time in the proportion of students who receive aid is somewhat contrary to a system aimed at helping the neediest students. Today over half of all students receive some form of aid, and it seems reasonable to assume that this puts a strain on a system designed to help at most one-quarter of the student population.

Third, the growth over time in loans as a proportion of all aid is not consistent with a system designed primarily to determine eligibility for grant aid. Grants were the predominant form of aid when the needs-analysis concept was formulated, and the notion of family contribution is not nearly as compatible with loans as it is with grants.

Finally, Kramer argues that the increasing proportion of aid recipients who are financially independent of their parents plays havoc with a system that was designed primarily to measure the need of students who are financially dependent on their parents. On this last issue, Kramer suggests that there should be a second system of financial aid for the growing numbers of students who are financially independent of their parents, a system that would more accurately reflect the realities of how these students are financing their education. He concludes with suggestions for how any new financing mechanism should take cognizance of these changing realities.

Terry Hartle, in "The Evolution and Prospects of Financing Alternatives for Higher Education," provides historical perspective on how higher education has been financed in this country all the way back to colonial times. He points out that innovation in financing is by no means a new phenomenon: colleges and universities have shown a great deal of creativity over time in how they are financed. For example, some colleges in the past were financed through toll road fees and lotteries, and in the nineteenth century a few individual colleges offered perpetual scholarships similar to recent tuition guarantee programs. He notes that current tensions in the form of reduced funding for student aid, greater uncertainty about aid availability, and the growth in students' indebtedness have all contributed to the recent intensified search for financing alternatives.

Hartle also draws a very useful distinction between plans that help current students and those that are designed to help future students. He suggests that a number of the new financing proposals and plans, including various loan programs and proposals to link service with aid, are aimed at helping those students who are currently in school, but that other alternative financing approaches are designed to help future students, including savings and tuition-guarantee plans and assured-access efforts such as Eugene Lang's I Have a Dream concept. Included in the Hartle paper is a matrix that indicates how the various financing plans might be divided according to which type of organization sponsors the plan and whether the plan helps current or future students.

Jamie Merisotis, in "An Inventory of Innovative Financing Plans to Help Pay for Higher Education," describes the essential elements of each type of new financing plan. This chapter provides a great deal of information useful for quantifying the scope of these new financing approaches. For example, the chapter includes the results of an informal survey which suggests that two-thirds of the states established alternative loan programs in the 1980s, but that the total volume of lending is roughly a half billion dollars a year, a small share of total student lending. The chapter also indicates that by the end of 1988 more than 100 sixth grade classes had been adopted in programs similar to Eugene Lang's.

One difficulty in writing a chapter like this is that the pace of change in new financing plans has been so rapid that some descriptions rapidly become out of date as existing programs change and new plans come on the scene. Merisotis nonetheless provides a very good background for understanding what new financing plans are all about, a framework that will for the most part accommodate continuing innovations in financing.

THE DIFFERENT TYPES OF INNOVATIVE FINANCING APPROACHES

SAVINGS PLANS AND TUITION GUARANTEES. Ted Bracken, in "Developing a National College Savings Agenda," focuses on the objective of encouraging more savings by the families of traditional college-age students, particularly those of more moderate means. He points out that most of the discussion about savings has been targeted on how to help more-affluent families afford college. He also predicts that it is unlikely that the federal government would create any additional savings incentives over and above the provision that allows for a tax exemption on the income earned on U.S. savings bonds if the proceeds are used to pay college expenses. Thus, he suggests that the best course is to develop savings incentives that build on what already exists.

Bracken makes an important and often overlooked point when he notes that a successful savings plan need not meet a student's total college costs. Plans that encourage parents to start saving for college when a child is young and to put aside a substantial portion of the total bill represent a big improvement over the situation in which little or no savings have been put aside. Moreover, whatever parents do save could also be used as collateral for loans that might make up the difference between the costs of attendance when the student is ready to enroll and the amount saved up to that point. This kind of savings plan would provide reasonable assurance to parents that they would be able to pay without invoking much of the administrative and financial complexity entailed in a tuition-guarantee arrangement.

The savings model that Bracken advocates would build on the provision that exempts from taxation income derived from U.S. savings bonds. He would expand the use of these bonds to meet college costs through a variety of mechanisms, including possibly a savings-stamp program for children. Corporations could contribute through promotions such as providing a bond to new customers who open up accounts or including a bond when new parents buy a supply of diapers. Bonds could also serve as payment for some forms of community service, thereby also advancing the concept of voluntary service.

Bracken would take savings incentives a step further by creating an educational savings trust fund that would provide additional flexibility for those families for whom bonds are not the right vehicle for college savings. Such a fund, which might be modeled along lines of Teachers Insurance and Annuity Association (TIAA) as a nonprofit organization started by a foundation, could offer a variety of investment products to its customers to meet their particular needs.

Richard Anderson in "Prepaying for Higher Education: Why It Works" begins by asking why parents currently do not save enough to pay for college costs. His response is that too few incentives exist to save for college. In addition, he points out that timing is critical for small investors who cannot diversify their holdings and maintain sufficient liquidity to meet their financing needs when their child is ready to enroll.

In response to these shortcomings of the current system, Anderson suggests a prepayment model that would have as its principal objectives investment security and an ability to keep up with the growth of college costs over time. He further suggests that such a system should adhere to the principle that those who bear the risk should share in the benefit.

To meet these criteria, Anderson proposes the creation of a nonprofit foundation by colleges and universities that would serve as a financial intermediary to presell tuition contracts well before children are of college age. The fund would issue prepaid tuition certificates to investors and have a diversified investment strategy that would provide both security and liquidity. The crux of Anderson's argument is that a historical analysis of the yields on different financial instruments suggests that a reasonable investment strategy will outperform the growth of tuitions as long as investors are willing to share in both the benefit and the possible shortfall in performance. Anderson also argues that although the issue of whether and how such a fund's proceeds might be taxed should be discussed, the creation of such a fund need not, and should not, hinge on the provision of a tax advantage.

Sandra Baum, in "Issues of Equity in College Savings," begins by asserting that encouraging savings for college is a good thing. For higher education to survive as we have known it, parents must begin to think of it as an investment rather than a consumption item.   More savings is a big part of such a philosophy. She goes on to say, however, that although savings as a general matter should be encouraged, some plans are better than others. Some will lead to increased savings overall, rather than shift savings from one form of asset to another, with little or no increase in overall savings. Some of the plans currently being discussed—particularly tuition-guarantee plans— serve to limit choice of institutions, while others will expand choice.

This chapter includes a very helpful suggestion that borrowing and savings plans should be considered at the same time rather than separately, as has traditionally been the case. Under a simultaneous approach, policymakers could compare the amount of subsidies in the loan programs to what incentives are provided for savings and then consider which approach might be more effective in influencing behavior.

Baum then suggests a set of criteria that might be helpful in choosing from a variety of savings incentives and borrowing plans. One criterion is that it is better to have a plan that leads to increased overall savings than one that leads to a change in asset mix with little or no increase in the amount saved. The other principal criterion is that the plan should embody basic fairness in the distribution of benefits, both in terms of horizontal and vertical equity. In terms of vertical equity—students from lower-income families should receive larger benefits than those from more-affluent families. Most savings plans do not fare too well on this standard because they do not help the groups most in need, such as older, nontraditional students, those from lower socioeconomic circumstances, and minorities. The regressive nature of tax subsidies for savings is a critical point in detracting from the vertical equity of most subsidized savings plans. In terms of horizontal equity—the principle of treating similar students alike—Baum points out that under the current system borrowing is highly subsidized, whereas savings is not. This introduces horizontal inequities in that students will receive large subsidies if they borrow but the same students will receive little or no subsidy if they save.

ALTERNATIVE LOAN PROGRAMS. Martin Kramer, in "New Varieties of Student Loans," starts with the assumption that not too much can be done with the existing Stafford, or Guaranteed Student Loan (GSL), program if it continues to be comprehensive. As long as the program is viewed as a subsidized loan for needy students, a loan of convenience for students from higher income families, and a major source of funding for students in graduate and professional schools, it will be difficult to have a consistent and effective student loan structure. Kramer also suggests that most students care more about loan availability and affordability during repayment than they do about interest subsidies. The loan structure should reflect this set of preferences, especially when money is tight and we can no longer afford a loan program that is all things to all people.

Kramer indicates that the current structure could be revised along several lines. One is to shrink the program by restricting eligibility for subsidies for middle-income students and not allow borrowing by groups of default-prone students. Or there could be a massive restructuring of student loan programs, for example, by creating a full-blown income-contingent student loan structure to replace current loan programs and grants. This could, however, have the untoward effect of greatly increasing the use of loans as a means of financing higher education when many observers are concerned that too many individuals are already being overburdened by their student debts.

Kramer comes out on the side of turning GSL into an umbrella program of several types of guaranteed student loans in which different groups of students would qualify for different terms and conditions. A number of options might flow from such a "boutique" approach to student loans. For example, there might be an unsubsidized loan plan for students attending expensive institutions whereby the parents assume the repayment obligations for the first few years and then pass the responsibility on to the student once he or she has joined the work force and is able to repay. For students in professional schools, a different kind of loan plan could be made available, whereby large amounts might be borrowed with repayment of the principal deferred until the student had entered the work force and had established a practice. There might also be an option of repayment insurance for students with catastrophically low income, with repayment obligations geared to a percentage of income.

ASSURED ACCESS EFFORTS. One of the most highly publicized college finance efforts in recent years has been Eugene Lang's I Have a Dream concept, in which a philanthropist adopts a class of elementary or junior high school students and promises to pay the college expenses of each student who completes his or her high school education and goes on to college. Several of the chapters in this volume address the assured access concept.

Robert Koff, in "Philanthropy, the Public School, and the University," discusses the research that the School of Education at SUNY—Albany has embarked on in examining a dreamers' class in Albany. Koff explains that it is "vital to examine these programs, as they evolve from impulse to systematic policy, to help us refine this model for educating students at risk."

To help in furthering the examination of these efforts, Koff describes the arrangement that has been made between the School of Education at SUNY—Albany and the Yulmans, the philanthropic sponsors. He indicates that there were three guiding principles in structuring the agreement between the university and the Albany school district. One was that there would be an individual assessment of the needs of each student. Another was that sensitivity to parents' and students' needs and concerns would be of paramount importance. The third principle was to ensure nondiscriminatory policies in the development of the program.

The university's role in all of this is to coordinate the range of services provided to the children, to maintain continuing-education programs to both parents and teachers, and to design and implement the evaluation of the effort.

For the Yulmans', the project sponsors, their role was that of funder of the tuition payments as well as many of the support services that are to be provided while the children are in high school.

Koff has several suggestions for others who may seek to develop programs along these lines. One is that money alone does not ensure success. Another related theme is that support services are critical in making sure that the students complete high school; such services may be even more important than the promise of tuition. Koff also talks of the importance of creating an ethos to protect the students from the world from which they come and into which they may return. It is important to involve the parents as much as possible, to not allow them to be passive bystanders in the experiment. Finally, the efforts must be repeatable in other locales; it will do little good to have a successful experiment that cannot be repeated elsewhere. Koff suggests that there will be little comfort if the operation is a success but the patient dies.

Peter Keitel, in "New York State's Liberty Scholarships Program," describes the effort there to translate the Lang concept into a program at the state level. He makes the very useful suggestion that Liberty Scholarships should be viewed more like an incentive program to reduce high school dropout rates than as a program of student financial aid, although clearly the New York approach uses student aid and support services as a mechanism to reach the objective of dropout prevention.

Keitel asks rhetorically why the state should become involved in an effort like this and responds that it is because of the tremendous costs to forgone income and reduced tax revenues, on the one hand, and higher government expenditures, on the other. Employers also have a tremendous interest in seeing the dropout problem sharply reduced. Much of the paper is devoted to what the costs of dropout are to society and how a program like Liberty Scholarships can reduce those costs.

This chapter also provides a very useful description of the process by which Liberty Scholarships were enacted into law and how the program will work. The New York State legislature made a number of key changes in Governor Mario Cuomo's initial proposal. For example, legislators did not want to wait for six years until the first class of sixth-graders became eligible for benefits until the program bore results. In addition, the legislature added the Liberty Partnerships program, which will provide support services at the high school and college level as well as community-based organizations to improve the chances of students to enroll and complete a postsecondary program.

Joseph Cronin, in "Corporate Support for Scholarships: A Tale of Two Cities," reviews the business, foundation, and public-sector efforts in Cleveland and Boston that have helped to assure access to higher education for low-income inner-city youth. He also provides a great deal of useful information on similar efforts in other localities across the country. This chapter was not one of the papers prepared for the conference, but grew out of the discussion of the Koff and Keitel papers.

One of Cronin's basic points is that the recent emphasis on the I Have a Dream concept and its translation into Liberty Scholarships tends to obscure other efforts along these lines, some of which predate by a number of years what Eugene Lang and New York State have done. Much can be learned from these other efforts, which Cronin well demonstrates through the very useful background information he provides on how the public/private partnerships in both Boston and Cleveland have gone about trying to help at-risk students enroll and complete a higher-education program.

The chapter describes what kinds of services are provided through these programs, including last-dollar scholarship assistance, information centers, and counseling and tutoring services. It reviews the steps that were taken to build and maintain support for the programs within the community. The chapter concludes with a review of the evaluations that have been done of these efforts. In short, officials of any community who are considering such an effort would be well served by reading this chapter.

Linking Aid with Service. Kathryn Mohrman and Susan Stroud, in "Public Service and Student Financial Aid," trace the linkage that has long existed between the performance of service and higher education, and examine the different suggested ways in which service and student aid might be connected.

They note that over time there has been a shifting balance between the competing goals of rewarding service and achievement, on the one hand, and providing equal opportunity, on the other. They suggest that proposals to link aid to service should be judged by the same criteria as other aid efforts in terms of access, choice, and equity. They argue that service should be part of a multifaceted, multiprogram approach to student financial aid, and stress that a stronger service component in student aid should go beyond economic values to address concerns about moral and spiritual values as well. They also suggest that service should be encouraged at various times in the life cycle. Aid could be provided as a reward for service prior to going to college, concurrent with college attendance, or after students have completed college.

The chapter addresses a number of questions that might be raised over service-based aid. For example, should all aid be need-based? Their response would be no. Should all aid be linked to service? Also, no. They also ask what can be done to ensure that service-based aid is made available to older nontraditional students as well as those of more traditional age.

The second half of the chapter examines a number of the plans and proposals for linking aid and service at the federal, state, institutional, and foundation levels. This is a very helpful guide to understanding the many different ways in which service and aid might be linked and the arguments that are used on both sides. The authors conclude that selective expansion of aid-and-service linkages would be very beneficial, but that an aid system entirely devoted to such a linkage may miss the mark.

ROLES AND RESPONSIBILITIES

The chapters in the third section of this volume describe what might be the roles and responsibilities of the various organizations that will be involved in the development of new ways of paying for college. The purpose of this section is to provide some guidance to policymakers and others who might be interested in establishing one of these new mechanisms but do not know which is the best one for the organization they represent.

In "New Ways of Paying for College: Should the Federal Government Help?" Janet Hansen and Larry Gladieux examine what the appropriate federal role might reasonably be in developing new financing mechanisms. They base their discussion on the notion of burden sharing, asking how much of the burden of paying for college should come from parents, students, taxpayers, and institutions. They point out that the United States is unusual among industrialized nations in that the burden is shared fairly equally by the four sources; in most other industrialized nations taxpayers foot most, if not all, of the bill. They also note that the relatively equal sharing of the financing burden is useful in explaining why access to higher education is so much greater than in other countries, where the expectation from the nontaxpayer sources is so much lower than in the United States.

Hansen and Gladieux make the point that changes over time in the share of who pays for college in the United States have contributed greatly to the growing pressures on the whole system. In this context, the apparent increase in the parent and student share of financing may be a primary reason why new financing mechanisms are being so hotly debated.

Given that new federal resources are likely to be scarce as a result of the large federal deficit and the many other competing needs for federal funds, the authors argue that if the federal share of the financing burden is to be most effectively utilized, it needs to be spent selectively so that it will do the most good.

In this context, the authors argue that what the federal government is presently doing in the area of savings through the tax exemption on U.S. savings bonds used for college is probably as much as it should be doing. They suggest that increases in Pell Grants and providing greater assurance that the funds will be available to the most needy students should have a higher priority than increased savings incentives. They indicate that subsidies in the student loan programs should probably be reduced, not increased, and that help in the student loan programs should probably come in the form of some kind of insurance that protects borrowers against the risk of low future earnings. To translate the Eugene Lang concept into a broader reality, they suggest an expansion of funding for Upward Bound, Talent Search, and the other federal support services programs. As for a larger service component in student aid, Hansen and Gladieux are skeptical about a service requirement in order to receive aid, but they are open to the possibility of a smaller, more experimental approach that would not involve wholesale replacement of the existing student aid system.

Aims McGuinness, in "The States' Role in Financing Higher Education: A Perspective," makes the point that the financing debate is undergoing fundamental changes. He suggests that the focus should be as much (or more) on education issues as on dollars and cents. He lists five points that he thinks should be considered in developing a state policy with respect to new financing mechanisms:

- There must be a greater emphasis on the importance of the quality of the education received.

- There should be a greater recognition of the role that states currently play in the financing of higher education, including the fact that the state investment far exceeds the federal.

- There continues to be a need to reduce the complexity of the student aid system and to lower the barriers that deter many students from enrolling in postsecondary education.

- Perceptions about the growing costs of higher education and their impact on whether and where students enroll have to be addressed.

- There should be a greater awareness that each of the various financing alternatives being discussed here may help to reshape the nation's system of higher education.

Much of this chapter traces the history of the Michigan tuition-guarantee plan and the response by other states to the publicity over the Michigan plan. McGuinness makes the interesting point that the majority of the study groups formed in other states to study the Michigan plan were designed to respond to perceived shortcomings in how higher education was being financed within the state.

McGuinness concludes from all this that in the future the financing of higher education will require greater partnerships between the federal and state governments, the institutions, and the private sector because no one group can do it alone. McGuinness also suggests the need for an integrated financing mechanism that, for example, melds issues of savings with those involving more traditional student aid programs. He, like Hansen and Gladieux, indicates the importance of equalizing the relative burdens borne by the various groups who help with higher education financing. He reiterates the need to strengthen the connection between educational and financial objectives. He concludes with a plea for a broader framework in which to discuss these issues, one in which principles of action are agreed to before technicalities of programs are discussed.

Tim Warner, in "New Ways to Finance College Costs: An Institutional Budget Officer's Perspective," suggests that the role colleges and universities have played in the development of financing alternatives has generally been a marginal one. While a number of programs have been initiated and implemented by institutions, for example, the Penn Plan, he also suggests that in this arena educational institutions have been more reactors than initiators. He speculates that one reason for this reactive stance is that the marketplace, with applications continuing to rise at most elite schools, has not yet indicated the demand for greater institutional intervention.

Warner suggests four principles that might govern institutional decisions regarding whether to involve themselves in one of these new financing approaches:

1. There should be an ability to leverage funds, so that the institution will not be committing only its own funds in this endeavor.

2. The amount of internal administration should be minimal, suggesting that outside organizations should be recruited for the effort.

3. Institutions should maintain maximum flexibility and control over the programs and should therefore resist plans that entail long-term and large commitments and thereby ultimately limit their control.

4. Institutions should be somewhat entrepreneurial in their approach, leaving to others the more traditional aid programs.

These four principles of action in turn lead Warner to suggest four concerns that institutional officers should consider before involving themselves in financial alternatives:

1. Institutions have limited resources to meet the many needs that confront them, and alternative financing plans should have to compete among other priorities.

2. Institutions should keep in mind their reputation and most cannot afford to enter into a financing plan that might flop.

3. Institutions should be careful in their analysis of financing alternatives to establish whether there is enough demand for the type of plan they are considering.

4. Plans that are put forward by institutions should not be seen as self-serving.

Using these principles and concerns as a framework for institutional decision making, Warner reviews the process that Stanford University has used in deciding whether to pursue any of these alternative financing mechanisms, including supplemental loan programs, public service opportunities (in which Stanford has been a leader among institutions), differential aid packaging, and tuition prepayments, guarantees, and savings plans. It is very instructive to see the process by which Stanford decided whether to pursue each of these four alternatives and which type of approach was chosen. Warner concludes by suggesting that institutions must think through their positions on the role of middle-class subsidies, sit down together to see whether consortial approaches might be worked out, and be clear on their own priorities.

In "The Role of Employers in Financing Higher Education," Ernest Lynton provides a very useful introduction to the role that employers currently play in the financing of higher education and how that role might reasonably be expanded to include some of the alternative financing mechanisms discussed in this volume. This chapter was not included in the initial set of papers prepared for the conference, but grew out of some of the comments that Lynton provided there.

He begins by noting a shift in the reasons why employees takes college courses. More and more, they take courses for the purpose of refining or changing career paths as the interweaving of careers and education becomes much more common.

The chapter describes the variety of employer assistance that is currently available, including the traditional reimbursement of employee tuition and fees payment, in-house training and instruction, cooperative education and paid internships, apprenticeships, scholarship support, and loans to employees and their children. There is a great deal of useful information in the chapter on participation and expenditures for employer-related training and education. Lynton makes the insightful point that these expenditure levels are all the more remarkable when one considers the relatively low levels of employee participation, therefore suggesting that there is much room for expansion.

The chapter concludes with a list of questions about possible future policy directions, including whether employer contributions should be increased, whether there should be greater governmental encouragement of employer-related assistance, and whether there can be greater recognition of the realities of lifelong and recurrent education in student aid and other policies.

Robert Payton, in "The Role of Philanthropy in Higher Education," begins by asserting that the role of philanthropy in financing higher education is both "insufficiently recognized and poorly understood. As a result, there is overemphasis on governmental ('public') solutions, on the one hand, or on marketplace ('private') solutions, on the other." He goes on to say that in higher education, as in most other areas of society, too little attention is paid to the third sector, philanthropy, which is increasingly being displaced by a new and self-serving breed of professionalism.

Payton insists that the issue is educational, not financial, and that philanthropy has the best chance of convincing students of the importance of helping other people, a belief and a spirit that most students do not currently possess. Payton devotes most of the chapter to exploring the history of the third sector and the reasons why it can contribute in ways that the other two sectors of government and business cannot. He also speculates that if the primary objective were to avoid educational failure, it is likely that resources would be allocated in a much different way than they are today.

This historical and philosophical approach serves as a guide to what the role of philanthropy might be in developing new financing mechanisms for higher education. Payton stresses that moving in this direction will require a consensus effort. It also will require considerably less emphasis on money issues and a great deal more attention to moral and spiritual issues.

THE CONFERENCE DISCUSSION

Several themes emerged at the conference that are helpful in providing an overall context for the discussion of new approaches to paying for college.

First, several conference participants indicated that the developers of new financing approaches should focus as much (or more) on educational issues as on financial ones. Put another way, efforts aimed at trying to help students and their families pay for their education should not obscure the importance of maintaining the quality of the education that is received.

Second, in developing new approaches to paying for college, it is important to look beyond the nuts and bolts of the traditional student aid themes of equal opportunity and choice of institution to a broader set of societal goals. These broader goals include restoring American economic competitiveness, encouraging greater public and voluntary service, and encouraging more saving.

Third, it may be worthwhile to consider whether the combination of traditional and alternative student aid programs should be tailored to meet the needs of subgroups of students—what Martin Kramer has described as the "boutique" approach to student aid. Or would it be better to aim instead for a supermarket approach, in which one program meets the needs of all students? The boutique concept leads to the notion that it may be appropriate for there to be a division of responsibility among the various organizations that provide assistance to students, whereby each provides a different program or set of programs designed to serve the needs of target groups of students.

Michael McPherson, economics professor at Williams College, served as a discussant on the first set of papers prepared for the conference. He began his remarks by asking whether these new forms of aid should replace or supplement the traditional aid programs of grants, work-study, and subsidized loans. In doing so, he raised the issue of whether it would be better to dismantle the current structure or simply tinker with it. His response to this issue is that we could do a lot worse than we do now, and thus, tinkering seems more appropriate than wholesale change. In this context, he pointed out that the resources of the current programs have not been exhausted and that one reason that they may not have worked as well as expected is that funding and commitment have not always been sufficient to meet the aggregate financial needs of students and their families.

McPherson also made a very useful distinction between two types of aid: one that meets the lifetime needs of students and one that helps to meet more temporal financing needs. He argued that the availability of grants might best be geared to the lifetime needs of students, thereby reflecting the socioeconomic status of the student's family. Loans, on the other hand, should be made available to meet more-temporal needs, such as cash-flow shortages of families with substantial assets. Packaging grant and loan aid along the lines of meeting lifetime and temporal needs would be in distinct contrast to the current system of packaging, in which the proportion of loans and grants is decided according to a much more subjective set of criteria having to do with the relative merits of the students rather than the type of need they might have.

McPherson's distinction between lifetime and temporal needs might also be helpful in resolving some of the financing barriers faced by older, nontraditional students. Picking up on Martin Kramer's point regarding the inappropriateness of the current needs-analysis system for older, nontraditional students, McPherson suggested that providing grants to meet the lifetime needs of nontraditional students and using loans to finance the cash-flow needs that arise from their temporary excursion from the work force would be one way to address the particular needs of this growing group of college students.

David Finifter, economics professor at The College of William and Mary, served as the commentator on the papers in this volume that discuss the various types of new financing plans. His focus was on how these plans should be evaluated. He suggested that one basis for evaluation is how well the alternative approaches fit into the existing system of student financial aid. For example, what need is being met by a new plan that is not being met by the more traditional programs? And how well does the new approach meet this need?

Finifter also suggested that each of the new approaches might be evaluated on the basis of the economic criteria of effectiveness, efficiency, and equity. Using these three economic criteria leads in turn to a set of questions that might be asked:

- Why is financing higher education different from financing a car, pensions, and health care needs? In this context, Sandra Baum's suggestion that higher education should be seen more as an investment than as consumption is very appropriate.

- What are the political, economic, and demographic factors that lead to these new approaches? The decline in the college-age population, the budgetary climate, and the pressures for cost containment are all part of this issue.

- What goals are we trying to achieve? One of the great difficulties in this arena is trying to identify the goals, such as greater access, relieving the middle class squeeze, and promoting service.

- How do we know if we have accomplished the goals? This requires answers to such questions as whether savings increased, whether participation rates improved, and whether middle-income people felt less squeezed.

Finifter acknowledged that getting answers to these questions would in many cases not be easy, but suggests that it is certainly worth the effort.

David Breneman, at the time President of Kalamazoo College and now a professor at Harvard, in his comments on what the roles and responsibilities should be, suggested that perhaps this is a macro issue that requires a macroeconomic solution. He described the current situation of policymakers "feeling like corks bobbing in a turbulent sea." To feel more settled, Breneman suggested that it may be necessary first to reexamine the basic, underlying student aid structure rather than introduce a new set of alternatives layered onto the existing system. For example, he indicated that the role of the proprietary sector has grown so fast and so large that it may require rethinking. He went on to suggest that proprietary school financing might be more appropriately addressed through training programs administered by the Department of Labor.

Similarly, Breneman said that it may be necessary to totally revamp the student loan system rather than introduce alternative programs on top of the basic Stafford (GSL) structure. He concluded his remarks by pointing out that the action in student aid is increasingly in the states and that wins and losses will both result from state experimentation.

Ernst Benjamin, of the American Association of University Professors, echoed some of Breneman's comments when he said that he believes the current system is broke. He pointed to the growing level of student loan defaults, the middle-class squeeze, and the decline in minority-student participation as indications of weakness in the current financing structure. His advice is to restore the federal role in student aid for needy students, although that would still leave the middle-class squeeze. For this, he recommends greater government subsidy for all of higher education, principally through the states' maintenance of low tuitions at public institutions. He further suggested that the role of philanthropy might best be to enhance choice. He concluded his remarks with a challenge by asking what can be done to improve elementary and secondary education to ensure that the students who enroll in college are of sufficient quality.

Looking to the Future: Coping with the Rapid Pace of Change

Since the conference occurred and the preparation of the chapters for this volume was completed, a number of developments have affected the landscape of alternative financing mechanisms for higher education. Additional states have taken action on tuition guarantee and savings plans, with most of these states opting for saving plans that do not involve a guarantee. As of fall 1990, roughly half the states reported having a program that allows parents to save for their children's education through the purchase of tax-exempt bonds. The provision has gone into effect that exempts from taxation the income on U.S. Savings Bonds that are used for college. A number of new private sector savings plans have also been introduced into the market.

Among plans that do not relate to savings, proposals to provide a greater linkage between student aid and service have been considered in both houses of Congress, and some form of legislation seems likely to be enacted. The number of philanthropists who have set aside funds to ensure access to college for economically disadvantaged youth continues to grow, and many states are contemplating following the lead of New York State in developing Liberty Scholarship programs of their own. It also seems certain that reform of the current structure of student loans will be a central focus of the upcoming reauthorization of the Higher Education Act.

This pace of change, while encouraging to those who believe the current system can and should be improved, makes it very difficult for a volume like this to remain current in its description and its analysis of new ways of paying for college. In recognition of this reality, the authors of the chapters in this volume were asked to pay less attention to the details of each plan than to the concepts and concerns raised in their development. What we have tried to do here is to provide a framework that will help policymakers as they work to develop alternative financing plans in the future.

The chapters in this volume are also intended to remind policymakers that they must be responsive to the needs of students and their families while also being responsible to taxpayers by not having government carry too large a share of the burden. They must balance the needs of the current generation of students with that of future generations in deciding which, if any, of these plans to adopt. And they must be flexible enough to recognize that the conditions that led to the current set of financing alternatives may well change in the future.

In this context, it is worth considering a number of possible issues and trends that could affect the future development of alternative financing plans. For example, if tuition increases in the 1990s begin to slow relative to the general rate of inflation, attention may be further shifted from tuition guarantee plans to other forms of savings incentives or to plans that help parents pay for college out of their current resources. On the other hand, a continuation of rapid tuition increases well in excess of inflation in the early

1990s could fuel a renewal of interest in tuition guarantee approaches. Increases in interest rates or in the amount of student loan defaults—each of which having the effect of raising the federal costs of student loans—could further accelerate the momentum for student loan reform. Experimentation through demonstration projects with programs of service and student aid could lead to new proposals for a broader linkage. Similarly, evaluations of the further experience with private and public programs that seek to ensure access to disadvantaged youth should lead to further refinement of this promising approach. Policymakers should be prepared to deal with these and other eventualities as they debate the merits of various approaches.

A discussion of new ways of paying for college that would take place five or ten years from now might be very different from what is laid out in this volume. What we have tried to do here is to provide a reasonable compass for current policymakers to help guide them through the changing thicket of higher education finance and the many alternative approaches that have sprouted up in recent years. The authors of the various chapters have done a good job in laying out the pitfalls and some of the rewards of pursuing the various approaches. The next several years should provide a good reading of the popularity and viability of these new ways of paying for college.

PART I

The Environment for New Financing Plans

1

Stresses in the Student Financial Aid System

MARTIN KRAMER

Thirty-five years ago the leading colleges and universities of the United States reached a consensus that student aid should be awarded ordinarily on the basis of measured financial need alone. That consensus has displayed remarkable staying qualities. Its neutrality toward the sources of aid funds has made it highly flexible as the sources of those funds have changed over time. In addition, the consensus has been able to deal—or appear to deal—with changing student budgets. Because of the apparent adaptability of the need-based financial aid system, it has been easy to assume that the aid system remains unchanged in all essentials, even though its role in financing college attendance has become much larger and more complicated.

This assumption is valid to a very important extent. Affluent parents usually do pay most of the educational bills of their dependent offspring. Students from low-income families usually do have most of their bills paid with aid funds. This income-relatedness of aid holds for most types of colleges and for most students, regardless of their differing talents, academic preparation, gender, and ethnicity.

Yet, of course, times do change. Some of the implicit premises of the need-based aid model would seem much less self-evident if the task of creating such a model from scratch had fallen to a group of knowledgeable people in the 1980s rather than to those who took on the task in the 1950s.

The Context of the 1950s

A pressing problem for many colleges in the 1950s was to suppress the practice of bidding for desirable students with competing aid offers. This was largely a problem for the private colleges, which then had most of the very limited aid funds available. Enrollments at these institutions were threatened by the rapid decline in the number of veterans with unused GI Bill entitlements. The private institutions also found themselves competing with each other for academic prestige. Then, as now, the issues of enrollments and prestige were related. More students want to enroll in institutions with "elite" reputations. Using aid to recruit the most desirable students thus could attract other students as well.

Although the motivation for the bidding wars was rational, it introduced chaos. Before the bidding wars colleges had awarded most of their aid on the basis of academic or other special promise—often, but not necessarily, with a preference for students who could not otherwise afford to attend college. A scholarship awarded to a student who did not need the money made egalitarians uneasy, but an institution that made such awards usually could say with a clear conscience that its methods for judging merit were fair at any rate. But the bidding wars could have the result that one student would get less money than another of equal merit merely because more colleges were eager to recruit the second student. This seemed unfair by any standard, academic or egalitarian.

The heart of the new consensus that emerged from the bidding wars was to limit aid awards to the difference between what the student's family could afford and what attending the college cost. If all colleges used the same method of measuring family ability to pay, then there could be no bidding wars. Colleges that cost more were allowed to make larger offers of aid, but the assessed family contribution would be the same at any college, so the student's choice among colleges would be financially neutral. This approach also required and enforced intramural fairness: the less a student needed aid to attend, the less the student could get, and students with the same need would get the same amounts.

One measure of the sense of urgency, financial and moral, that brought this need-based consensus into being is that the colleges were willing to impair a long-standing tradition of honoring the intent of philanthropic donors. When a nineteenth-century millionaire left a bequest to a college to provide scholarships to graduates of a particular high school, there was usually an intent that these graduates would be better off than others because of the benefaction. To honor bequests legally and still make the new consensus work, a college first would have to distribute earmarked aid to its designated beneficiaries and then use its unrestricted aid funds to bring the awards of equally needy but undesignated students up to something approaching parity. The tradition of special preferences for designated beneficiaries of trust funds was thus effectively overridden by the new consensus.

The procedure of evening-up, or packaging, as it came to be known, had an important consequence for policy: aid from public sources could be distributed according to the federal or state rules, and then any preference given by those rules could be offset by the distribution of the institution's own unrestricted funds. The continuity of the need-based aid system over thirty-five years of great change in the sources of aid funding owes much to this adaptability of packaging procedures, as well as to the strength of its ideas of equity across families and across institutions.

Sources of Strain in the Need-Based System

For all its adaptability, the need-based financial aid system is under increasing strain, and the lines of stress are exactly where one would expect to find them—in the areas where the consensus of the 1950s took for granted assumptions that are now considerably less valid. The discussion below focuses on four of these assumptions:

1. that the source of most aid funding would be philanthropy—either restricted or unrestricted and in the control of colleges and universities;

2. that the number of students eligible for need-based aid would be small relative to total enrollments;

3. that the bulk of aid would take the form of grants or scholarships, not loans; and

4. that the recipients of aid would be young full-time students dependent on supportive families.

THE CHANGING SOURCES OF AID FUNDS

The packaging concepts of the need-based aid systems readily allowed the incorporation of aid from nonphilanthropic sources. However, they were not designed to accommodate a predominant reliance on such sources. For example, in most states almost all aid to community-college students comes from public programs. There was virtually no aid of any kind at these institutions before the growth of the public programs. This growth unquestionably represented an increase in financial support for educational opportunities. But the result has also been that the amount of financial aid received by community-college students has rarely been determined by a calculation of need and a packaging procedure of the sort prescribed by the consensus. There has simply not been enough discretionary aid to even up the distribution. At high-tuition private institutions the award of aid according to the consensus model has not been similarly constrained. Federal and state aid awards do not constitute the entire aid package, leaving room for other sources of aid.

However, the consensus did not anticipate that much of the discretionary aid used to even up aid packages often now comes not from philanthropy in the ordinary sense but from the tuition revenues of the institution—that is, from tuitions and fees paid by other students, aided and unaided. The consensus model did not anticipate the growing importance of aid from this source and has nothing to say about it. Yet it is clear that this Robin Hood aid potentially endangers the financial well-being of the institution. Some colleges can be sure of enrolling enough students no matter how much they charge. But others must try to calculate the effects of their decisions about tuition levels, admissions policies, and aid awards simultaneously. Tuition must not be so high that the college loses too many affluent students who do not receive offsetting aid. Colleges must admit enough students from higher-income families, who will pay most of the tuition they are nominally charged, to raise enough aid money to support the lower-income students they also want to enroll.

The consensus model is compatible with many different solutions to the problems posed by trying to make tuition, admissions, and aid decisions simultaneously. Some of these solutions, however, can reintroduce the bidding wars of the 1950s through the back door: what is now called "merit" aid is often no more than a way of sanctioning grants to relatively affluent students to make sure that enough of them enroll to make the combined tuition, admissions, and aid policies of the institution work out as planned.

Another source of confusion and strain arising from the changing sources of aid funds is in the set of rules for estimating the ability of families to pay for a college education. The initial formulas of the need-based system expressed what private colleges would expect from middle-class parents who were willing to make substantial sacrifices of the family's standard of living to make a "good" college possible for their children. There was not, and could not be, a demonstrable basis for the validity of such expectations and formulas. They necessarily depended on the experience and judgment of college administrators. It was therefore difficult for colleges to resist growing pressures from state and federal governments to have a say in, and ultimately control over, the measurement of need once these public funding sources had come to provide a preponderant share of the aid available. Much of the empiricism, discretion, and self-governance of the original consensus has thereby been lost. Now, with the 1986 amendments to the Higher Education Act, Congress has prescribed in detail how financial need will be measured for all generally available federal aid programs.

THE GROWING PROPORTION OF AIDED STUDENTS

In the 1950s students receiving aid from all sources were seldom more than one-third of an institution's enrollment, and this only at private colleges with strongly egalitarian admissions policies. Now, at such institutions, the fraction is commonly more than one-half and quite often more than two-thirds. At public institutions the aided fraction usually was, and is, smaller, except for the community colleges, where the fraction aided was negligible in the 1950s and now can be as high as for expensive private colleges, although these students are almost entirely dependent on public resources.

Increases over time in the proportion of students who receive aid mean that student financial aid is no longer a marginal charitable activity of colleges and universities. This also means that aid administration has become a much more mechanical task. The consensus of the 1950s envisioned aid administration as a job depending on administrators' judgments about individual student situations in the application of rules, consisting as much in counseling as in calculation. That is not, and cannot be, the case now. Computers make it much easier to calculate eligibility for aid in large numbers of cases and to estimate the aggregate consequences of changes in the rules. But they also lead to much more inflexible application of the rules, because even the best-staffed aid offices cannot deal individually with large numbers of exceptional cases. In community colleges, where the aid function is often grossly understaffed, almost none of the hand-tailoring of aid packages envisioned by the original consensus is possible.

GRANTS VERSUS LOANS

The consensus of the 1950s assumed that most aid would be in the form of grants and scholarships. It has been an abiding assumption in the ideology of aid that grants equalize educational opportunity by taking the place of the financial support a low-income student's parents cannot provide.

Growing reliance on student loans—now about half of all aid—is undermining the validity of this assumption. Grant programs reduce inequality of resources, but loan programs perpetuate it when low-income graduates owe more than do their affluent contemporaries. Although educational opportunities and students' future incomes are equalized no less by loans than by grants, making low-income students dependent on loans undermines the rationale of leveling-up that was central to the consensus of the 1950s. With the growth in loans, student financial aid becomes more financial and less aid. In addition, because the sources of aid are less likely to be philanthropic, and the colleges now are less likely to act financially in loco parentis toward students, a sense of reciprocal obligation is undermined.

The foregoing perhaps suggests that the shift to reliance on credit only affects the "atmosphere" of the aid system. Far from it. Credit, unlike grant aid, does not have to depend on a legislature, college, or foundation appropriating a given amount of money for student aid, with the needs of students competing among other priorities. In a financial system such as that of the United States, the rationing of credit is by the market, and market forces are easily overwhelmed by the kinds of interest subsidies that are available under the federal student loan programs. As a result, credit has expanded into all the gaps, old and new, in the student aid system. Indeed, this is why more than half of a much larger total amount of aid is now in the form of loans. And, until recently, at least a portion of the credit under the Guaranteed Student Loan (GSL) program was outside the need-based system altogether. Federal legislation has traditionally exempted expected parental contributions from consideration in determining the amount of GSL eligibility, on the ground that these loans should be available to serve as loans of convenience for families that could, but would rather not, pay for education out of current resources.

Rationed neither by an appropriation process nor by a system of need-based awards, student loans have been made both to middle-income students who needed no aid and to low-income students for whom grants would have been the aid of choice. It has become easy to find "abuses" in the GSL program—students who are using GSL funds to subsidize consumer purchases or who later contrive reasons to default. Indeed, the loan program often has given all student aid a bad name. It has become hard to remember that in the early days of the need-based system the relatively small loan programs run by individual colleges with philanthropic funding were regarded as a character-building alternative to grants—a way for students to commit themselves to paying their own way, at least in part, on a par with "working your way through college."

The failure of the need-based system to come to terms with student loans has left a loophole that allows a college to comply with the letter of the system but to evade its spirit. The spirit is that like cases should be treated alike financially. But the consensus spoke to the total amount of permissible aid in individual packages, not to the kinds of aid making up the total. It is thus consistent with the consensus (although, many would say, not with "good practice") to include more grant aid and less loan aid in the package offered to a more meritorious or otherwise desirable student than in the package of a less meritorious or desirable student. To do so is not treating like cases alike, because loans represent a less valuable kind of aid. Even when subsidies and inflation make student loans a bargain, they are plainly less valuable than grants. It is hard to believe that the consensus of the 1950s would have taken hold as it did without addressing this possibility of evasion, if loans had been as important then as they are now.

THE INCREASE IN "NONTRADITIONAL" STUDENTS

The aspect of the need-based system that has shown the greatest degree of strain is the assumption that the task of the aid system is to make college financially possible for dependent, young, and full-time students. At many colleges and universities most students do not now match this description in one or more respects.

The reasons why students arrive at college not dependent, not young, or not full-time are infinitely varied. Students may be independent because they have a successful small business or because their divorced parents simply refuse to provide help. In addition, they may or may not have a spouse with financial resources, who may or may not be willing to pay for education. Students may be older because they are returning to an educational career after several or many years in full-time jobs. They may be part-time because they want to hold on to their jobs and to the living standards that their employment has made possible. Other students, although young, prefer a higher standard of living than the meager one an aid administrator would allow and also make the same choice of part-time enrollment.

The educational goals of nontraditional students vary as widely as their background circumstances. The education sought may lead to a credential of immediate cash value and therefore may be self-financing over the short term. Or the education may be recreational for someone living on social security and little else. Even people of the same age may have vastly different financial situations—for example, a successful teacher who is married to a physician and wants an Ed.D. and a welfare mother who wants a first postsecondary technical qualification. Their situations are as different from each other as either is from that of the young dependent student at a liberal arts college.

The concepts of the need-based aid system have been elaborated to try to take all this variety into account. But the problems of bending so many and such extreme variations in circumstances to fit the consensus model are probably insuperable as a practical matter. The need-based system contemplates a neat marshaling of student expenses on one side and student resources on the other. The difference between the two is "financial need," and the role of aid is to bring up the resources to equal (and only equal) the expenses. But for nontraditional students, there are tremendous problems in defining both expenses and resources. On the expense side, there are great differences in the standard of living that is reasonably regarded as "subsistence." The costs of this standard of living are commonly so inextricably mixed with the costs of the habitual and appropriate standard of living of the student's family— parents, siblings, spouse, and children—that just isolating the student's expenses can be impossible. There are too many joint products.

On the resource side, there can be large differences in what students earn in the year before they enroll and large differences in what they may be expected to earn during the academic year. There are also great differences in how much they will earn immediately after they leave school and therefore in their debt-service capacities. There are also great differences in what relatives and spouses, if any, can be expected to contribute.

Of course, standard amounts of expenses and resources can be imputed to impose some degree of uniformity on this variety. Such amounts will be highly arbitrary, however. Further, to the extent that these standard amounts provide generously for real hardship cases of students with large expenses and small resources, they will tend to bleed off aid funds at a rapid rate. Generous treatment of a welfare mother can cost as much as supporting a dozen average aid-eligible traditional students attending the same institution.

Almost from the beginning the need-based system recognized a category of independent students consisting of those whose parents were not expected to make a financial contribution. The problem was—and is—to define the characteristics of such students that make it reasonable to accord them this status. The enormous variability in the situations of nontraditional students in itself would assure the difficulty of the task. Moreover, the changes in family relationships that lead to real independence are usually subtle, private, and gradual, making the task harder still. Add further the difficulty in differentiating intentions from verifiable conditions, and the process of conferring independent status is bound to become more contentious. Finally, the fact that independent status can be enormously advantageous financially— making aid available to relieve parents of educational expenses—creates much room for bad faith, concealment, and contrived compliance with whatever criteria are adopted.

Even when independent status has been accorded, only one set of complications has been confronted. It does not follow from any of the general criteria of independence tried over the years that such a student can be expected to provide a given contribution from his or her own earnings. Even if previously attached to the labor force, students going back to school, especially full-time, will find their earnings shrinking or vanishing. It is for this reason that full-time versus part-time enrollment can be critical, with part-time allowing a greater contribution from earnings. Yet, when the reason for part-time enrollment is the responsibility to care for young children, part-time enrollment still may permit no earnings.

This case brings us to another difficulty: Should the subsistence costs of the children of a student be part of the student's budget, just as much as are the room and board of a younger student with no family responsibilities? The need-based system traditionally has allowed the inclusion of such costs in student budgets, but even if student aid funding were ample enough to cover them, the issue remains of whether a low-income family should be better off than others simply because one member is a student.

A Second System of Support

The maze of issues raised by the variety in the situations of nontraditional students makes it seem as though no human agency could ever resolve them. That may well be true if we approach the problem of aid for nontraditional students by starting from the concepts and procedures of the need-based system. There are simply too many permutations. But if we look instead at how postsecondary education is financed in fact, the problem is simplified.

Actually, there are two distinct patterns for financing educational participation beyond high school. One is the pattern for students who fit the assumptions of the need-based system with only minor and plausible elaborations. For these students, aid does indeed take the place—and only the place—of the parental support received by students from affluent families. The other pattern is that of most nontraditional students. Enormously different as their situations are from each other, they tend to finance their educations by one or another combination of the following resources: earnings from full- or part-time jobs; room and board provided in kind by parents, spouses, or friends; Guaranteed Student Loans; and grants, subject to the rules of the need-based aid consensus.

The reason for placing conventional student aid at the end of this list is that the forms of support higher on the list tend to eliminate or greatly reduce aid eligibility when quantified under the applicable need-analysis formulas. Living at home and part-time enrollment also often have the effect of reducing eligible costs of attendance.

To many, this result seems unfair—especially to representatives of institutions (such as community colleges) that enroll a high proportion of nontraditional students. It is difficult to attend a meeting on student aid policy of any size where there will not be at least one person who decries the neglect of nontraditional students by the need-based system. There is seldom a reply, for everyone present knows that these students often make heroic sacrifices to complete their educations. They also often lack the parental support and future prospects of students who receive substantial support from the need-based system.

Before we are overwhelmed by such comparisons, however, we should recognize that nontraditional students tend to lead considerably more complicated lives than do young full-time undergraduates. Many of the complications are the result of choice—for example, a decision to postpone college until after forming a family or to go to college part-time because of an immediate employment opportunity that holds out the prospect of a higher standard of living. It is not a reproach to the student aid system that it makes one path easier, but not all paths.

Moreover, we may ask whether the student aid system should be responsible when a student's path, chosen or not, turns out to be rockier than one would hope. The need-based aid system tends, by its own ideology and rhetoric, to suggest that the answer is yes. It is commonplace for student aid to be spoken of as removing "obstacles" to college attendance. The evening-up procedures of the need-based system emphasize compensation for disadvantage, and this makes it seem that *every* disadvantage may be grist for the student aid mill. But perhaps this tendency should be resisted. Think about the puzzles to which it leads: if student aid should be available to deal with the difficulties of someone who postponed college in favor of taking a job or starting a family, isn't it unfair to do something about the problem only if, and because, the person becomes a student? What about others in exactly the same situation who have decided not to go to college? And it surely does not make sense to do something for all nontraditional students who have made similar choices *whether or not* they have encountered difficulties along the way.

We can avoid some of these confusions and still maintain reasonable sympathy by thinking of how nontraditional students finance educational participation as a second, alternative system, alongside the need-based system. The main categories of support for nontraditional students were noted above, in an order that represented a set of guesses about the amount of financial support each provides. But another way of ordering them makes it possible to speak of a system—an order of preference. For example, with good reason, most nontraditional students probably would like to be able to depend more on student grants and in-kind support provided by relations and friends and less on earnings and GSL loans. What nontraditional students actually are doing, on their own or with advice, is working out their own packaging process. They see what need-based aid they can get, if any, and how much they can count on relations and friends, and then they figure out how much they must earn and borrow to pay fees and maintain themselves and their families. Some prospective students are able to add in support from employer-sponsored education programs or public income-maintenance programs. Then they decide whether to go ahead with postsecondary education, depending in part on whether they feel they can live with the results of their own packaging.

What the growth of student aid has done over the past two decades for nontraditional students is to add more sources of support to the list—Pell Grants and GSL loans most conspicuously. Student aid *has* made the situation of these students better, although not exactly in the way articulated by the need-based system and although there is a catch: the more they depend on increasing their earnings and reducing their educational expenses (by commuting from home especially), the less need-based aid they will qualify for. The resources they least prefer tend to disqualify them from precisely the aid they most prefer.

There are other ironies when we look at things from the point of view of the "second system." The continuing popularity and political appeal of the College Work-Study program depends on the high regard for the tradition of "working your way through college." Yet the students who best exemplify that tradition, the "nontraditional" students, tend to be excluded from the program if they have jobs in the unsubsidized private sector. Moreover, if they are awarded work-study jobs, they face a 100 percent tax rate on their earnings, because work-study is counted as a resource in the need-based system.

When the GSL program was made part of the need-based system in the 1986 amendments to the Higher Education Act, this was widely regarded as reform unalloyed. In the context of the need-based consensus, it certainly was a reform, because the subsidies provided by the program often were not used to meet measured need. But in the second system the fact that GSL loans previously had escaped need analysis gave them much of their value. They represented resources available for educational participation even if a student's costs were low and earnings high. Now the need-based catch applies to GSL loans as well as to grants and work-study.

Conclusion

Several observations are in order on how policies may be altered to relieve the stresses and bolster the effectiveness of the student aid system. When innovative financing mechanisms are considered, it is important to think about how they would fit in with the mechanisms of the existing system as it is, and not only as it is supposed to be or as one would wish it to be.

First, it should be recognized that at institutions (such as community colleges) whose aided students are almost entirely dependent on public programs, the packaging process can do very little to smooth out anomalies created by new programs. Although coordination between new and old programs is desirable in principle for all students, it is critical for these students.

Second, institutional interests need to be seen clearly. Private institutions have an enormous stake in programs that increase the availability of aid funds coming from outside the institution. They also have an enormous stake in any program that will tend to reduce measured financial need among their students, such as some of the proposed savings plans.

Third, the new dependence on student loans is proving very troublesome, and it is disquieting that many of the proposals for new loan programs are aimed at, or are consistent with, persuading students to depend on credit even more. This is usually to be done by lengthening repayment periods, making installments proportionate to income, or both. Attention should be paid to alternatives that would relate the amount of borrowing to student characteristics, such as cost of attendance, measured financial need, or year in college—formulas that might restrain dependence on loans rather than increase it.

Because of the continuing influence of the need-based model, it is easy to focus exclusively on the role new programs would play in the need-analysis and packaging process. Yet attention also should be given to how they might make the second system stronger or weaker. For example, some proposals for aid in compensation for public service would cut back on other aid in order to drive students into a service program. But for many students who rely on the second system, the public service approach would be a cruel absurdity. For example, what about a teacher's aide and mother of four who wants to go to college to get a bachelor's degree and a teaching credential and who is going to earn all the money she can in part-time jobs? Is this someone whose grant and loan entitlements, such as they are, should be constrained to force her participation in designated "public service"?

The extraordinary achievements of the need-based system should be recognized, and the system should not be interfered with lightly where it is working well. However, the strains that are disguised by these achievements also should be recognized and taken into account as innovations in college financing are developed.

2

The Evolution and Prospects of Financing Alternatives for Higher Education

TERRY W. HARTLE

Higher education is part of the American dream. In a 1985 *Wall Street Journal* poll, 77 percent of the respondents agreed that a college degree for one's children was an important part of the American dream—just one percentage point less than those who identified owning a home. But some families believe that rapidly rising college prices will make it impossible for them to achieve this goal. And the talk about cutbacks in federal student aid programs only adds to the uncertainty.

Not surprisingly, the financing of higher education has become a topic of widespread discussion and debate. For a long time, the issues related to paying for college were the province of a small band of economists and policy analysts. But in recent years, the topic has become much more visible as colleges, state governments, and financial institutions have rushed to develop new mechanisms to help families meet tuition bills.

The plans that have been developed or are being planned vary considerably. So does the reaction to them. A plan that one writer calls "the most promising innovation since the GI Bill" another dismisses as a "fad" whose "risks . . . far outweigh the limited benefits."[1] Determining whether the new college payment plans are the products of gimmickry or genius is a difficult task. This essay reviews forces that have led to the development of these new financing schemes, summarizes the types of plans that have emerged, and discusses the advantages and disadvantages of the new initiatives. Because no analysis of the rapidly developing new financing initiatives can remain valid for long, this analysis is offered explicitly from the perspective of September 1988.

Financing Higher Education: How It Evolved

The financing of American colleges and universities has always been an uncertain operation. Students usually have been asked to pay part of the cost of their education, but they have never been expected to pay the full cost. In the phrase of historian Frederick Rudolph, from the beginning, colleges and universities in the American system have been "cloaked with a public purpose." That is, they were intended to give more than they received from the particular individuals they were educating at the time, with the difference in cost made up by public and private subsidies.[2]

All colonial colleges were private institutions, but many received public funds. Harvard, Columbia, Yale, Princeton, Dartmouth, Bowdoin, Williams, and Union colleges all were supported by state governments. Public subsidies sometimes took the form of outright legislative grants, but they also included funds raised from toll fees, land grants, or lotteries. In fact, Princeton was given permission to operate lotteries in Connecticut and Pennsylvania as well as New Jersey.

Colleges also relied on subscriptions and gifts from private benefactors, because public subsidies were never adequate to pay for all the bills facing the colleges. During the colonial period, the largest gifts came from England. After the Revolution, such contributions plummeted, and domestic gifts, though steady, did not compensate fully for the loss.[3]

Tuition paid by students was an important, though modest, source of revenue for early American higher education. Yale charged about £20 in 1737; Dartmouth, $14 in 1779; and Harvard, only $20 in 1807. Tuition payments could be made in cash or in kind, and some colleges even accepted promissory notes. Thirty-three of Dartmouth's thirty-nine graduates in the class of 1806 owed money to their new alma mater, suggesting that institutional student aid is hardly a recent innovation.[4]

Around the mid-nineteenth century and into the twentieth, some American schools began to resort to a flawed financing scheme known as perpetual scholarships. Here, in return for a subvention, usually of about $500, a college or university would promise a donor guaranteed tuition-free enrollment "in perpetuity" for one or more descendants. This idea seldom worked as intended, however, because financially pressed colleges too often expended monies intended for the scholarships to meet current costs and failed to build the endowments necessary to support the descendants when they appeared to claim their educations.[5]

After the Civil War, the number of public colleges and universities began to increase significantly, stimulated in part by the Morrill Act of 1862, which provided for land grants to state governments to create or sustain universities that emphasized "agriculture and the mechanic arts." Increased state aid for public colleges often meant a decline in state subsidies for private institutions. In response, existing private colleges intensified their efforts to raise funds from wealthy donors and alumni, and new schools such as Cornell (1865), Vanderbilt (1872), and Johns Hopkins (1876) were even named for munificent benefactors.

Higher education continued to expand in the second half of the nineteenth century and into the twentieth, requiring ever-larger sums of money. As always, tuition and fees were central. Average tuition was $31 in 1860 and $238 in 1933. By 1964, tuition averaged $243 in public institutions and $1,088 in private colleges. Variation was considerable, however. Some public institutions, such as the City College of New York, were tuition free. At the other end of the spectrum, Bennington College tried to make tuition cover the full cost of instruction. Many colleges instituted scholarship programs to help academically promising but financially strapped students.[6]

Colleges frequently tried to balance their books by minimizing their largest expense—faculty salaries. As one historian put it, early higher education was "financed in part by the exploitation of the professor." Another writer argued that in effect, the college teaching profession was excluded from the "material pleasures and living standards that elsewhere defined American goals." Not surprisingly, it became difficult for many colleges to recruit capable teachers.[7]

Institutional student aid was born in the second half of the nineteenth century, when colleges realized that a scholarship could be awarded without handing over any money. By setting tuition levels a little higher than absolutely necessary, colleges could use some of the additional revenue to help disadvantaged students. The practice started slowly, but it became, and remains, an important source of financial aid.[8]

Federal and state support for higher education grew slowly but steadily in the early years of the twentieth century. New York created the first state student aid program in 1919, but only four states had developed similar programs by 1936. The federal government experimented with a small student aid program during the Great Depression as a way of keeping students in college and off the relief rolls, but this program ended during World War II. Despite these modest initiatives, students who attended college before the end of World War II had to rely primarily on themselves or their families to meet the costs.[9]

World War II marked a turning point in financial aid. The Serviceman's Readjustment Act of 1944, better known as the GI Bill, enabled millions of veterans to enroll in institutions of higher education. A slightly modified program was made available later to veterans of the Korean and Vietnam wars.[10] The GI Bill's most important effect was to help popularize higher education and to raise the educational expectations of veterans and their progeny. Whereas in 1940 only 4.6 percent of American adults had college degrees, in 1985 about 19.4 percent had them. Total expenditures on higher education grew over the same period from $758 million to $105 billion, and the percentage of the gross national product devoted to higher education rose from 0.7 to 2.6. The number of students enrolled went from 1.5 million to 12.2 million.[11]

The federal government facilitated the growth of higher education by creating a number of student aid programs. In 1958 the federal government enacted the National Defense Education Act. This law authorized several major student aid initiatives, including loans to undergraduates. The loans gave preference to those majoring in mathematics, science, and foreign languages and had a forgiveness provision for borrowers who became schoolteachers. There was also a fellowship program for graduate students.

Enactment of the Higher Education Act of 1965 shifted the focus of federal student aid. This omnibus bill authorized a grant program for financially disadvantaged students (Equal-Opportunity Grants), a loan program aimed at middle-income families (Guaranteed Student Loans), and a work-study program to encourage college students to earn money by working in on-campus jobs. The intent of these three new programs was to remove the financial barriers that restricted access to college.

Another student aid program was launched later in 1965, when Congress amended the Social Security Act and extended benefits to college-age dependents who were enrolled in higher education. By 1975, there were 700,000 students being helped under this program, at an annual cost of $1.2 billion.[12] The Higher Education Act of 1972 strengthened the federal emphasis on helping the financially disadvantaged. During the debate over this bill, the higher-education community sought direct, unrestricted federal grants to the colleges. But Congress chose to put the money in the students' hands and to let them decide where to spend it. The 1972 amendments further targeted federal aid on the disadvantaged by modifying the National Defense Student Loans and renaming them the National Direct Student Loans (now the Perkins Loan program), as they did the Educational Opportunity Grants (now Supplemental Educational Opportunity Grants).[13]

Later in the 1970s, however, the federal government began to consider proposals designed to funnel more student aid money to students from middle-income families. The proposals usually called for either federal income tax credits equal to a portion of the college costs paid by the taxpayer or expanded eligibility in the existing student aid programs. Eventually, Congress adopted the latter approach and, at President Jimmy Carter's request, enacted the Middle Income Student Assistance Act of 1978 (MISAA). This law modified the need-analysis calculations in the Pell Grant program and made more middle-income families eligible for assistance. The MISAA also removed any consideration of family income when calculating eligibility for Guaranteed Student Loans (or Stafford Student Loans). Two years later, the Higher Education Act amendments of 1980 made even more families eligible for need-based student aid.

The expansion of student aid programs proved very expensive. In 1981, as part of the Omnibus Budget Reconciliation Act, Congress made a number of changes to restrain the growth in student aid spending. The modifications limited GSLs to the amount needed to cover educational costs and required a needs test for students with family incomes above $30,000. Limits were also imposed on expansion of the Pell Grant program. Finally, Congress voted to eliminate the social security survivor benefits paid to college students, a modification that reduced federal spending by nearly $2 billion a year.[14] As a result of these changes and other eligibility restrictions added in 1986, federal student aid spending has increased at a slower pace in the 1980s. All borrowers in the GSL program are now required to prove financial need. Nonetheless, loan volume has continued to grow. In the Pell Grant program, federal appropriations have jumped from $1.8 billion in 1980 to $4.5 billion in fiscal year 1989, an increase of 84 percent in current dollars and of 29 percent in constant dollars. Most of this increase comes from an increase in the pool of eligible students. The maximum Pell Grant, which helps the most-disadvantaged students, has grown much more slowly.

Growth in the other three need-based student aid programs has been uneven. Perkins Loans, a repeated target of executive branch budget cutters, have fallen from $300 million in 1980 to $205 million in 1989. The number of Perkins borrowers fell during most of the 1980s, but it has increased recently to the point where the estimated number of recipients in 1987-1988 was almost identical to the number in 1980 (814,000). For Supplemental Grants, federal appropriations have grown from $370 million in 1980 to $438 million in 1989, but the number of recipients has decreased by approximately 50,000 students. In the work-study program, federal funding has increased from $550 million to $611 million, whereas the number of recipients has fallen by 80,000.[15] The expansion of federal student aid in the last three decades has encouraged the growth of state student aid programs. Today, every state has at least one student grant program, and some states have more than one. In 1987-1988, state grant programs awarded $1.5 billion to college students—an increase of 88 percent above the amount made available in 1980 in current dollars and of 47 percent in constant dollars.[16]

At the same time that the resources spent on higher education increased, the sources of the revenue shifted. Revenue from tuition and fees climbed from 20.6 percent of the total in 1975-1976 to 23.0 in 1984-1985. This 2.4 percent increase in the share of revenue coming from tuition is larger than the increase in any other category. At the same time that tuition revenue increased, the revenue from federal, state, and local governments dropped from 51.3 percent of the total to 44.9 percent. Federal support alone dropped from 16.3 percent of total revenue to 12.6 percent. This is the largest change in any of these categories. State revenue, perhaps surprisingly, declined slightly. The percentage of revenue coming from private gifts, grants, contracts, endowment income, and other sources increased from 28.1 percent to 32.1 percent. Within the sales and services category, the percentage of revenue coming from hospitals increased almost 2 percent, from 6.3 percent to 8.1 percent. The decline in public-sector support does not mean that governmental revenue is now insignificant: it still accounts for roughly half of the total. But it does mean that the revenue from students and auxiliary enterprises now constitutes a larger share of higher-education revenues than ever before.

The Emergence of New Financing Schemes: Reasons

Students and their families are providing a larger percentage of higher education's operating revenues than they have at any time in the recent past. They are doing so in a period when the cost of college is rising rapidly. And they are doing so at the same time that steps have been taken to restrict middle-class eligibility for subsidized federal student aid. To help meet rising college costs, loans have become an increasingly important way to finance a college education. But, as students borrow ever larger sums to finance their educations, there is growing concern that high debt levels will overwhelm student borrowers and distort personal and occupational choices.

THE RISING COST OF COLLEGE

There is no dispute that the price of higher education has increased sharply in the last fifteen years. The most rapid increases have taken place in the last seven years. Indeed, in the 1980s, tuition and fees grew by 83 percent at public colleges and by 90 percent at private institutions. In comparison, median family income increased by just 45 percent. Disposable personal income per capita (up 77 percent) grew faster than median family income, but still less than the growth in college prices. In the 1980s, college tuition apparently increased at a faster rate than food, medical care, energy, new cars, houses, and the "all services" component of the consumer price index (CPI).[17]

Sharply higher prices have created fears that a college education will soon be out of the reach of all except those from wealthy families. In a December 1986 survey, the Opinion Research Corporation (ORC) found that 82 percent of the adults polled agreed that college costs were rising at a rate that will make a college degree too expensive for most people. A similar finding emerged from a 1986 Field Institute poll in California, in which only 29 percent believed that most people can afford a college education today and 76 percent thought that college costs are rising at a rate that will put college costs out of reach for most people. Only about half of the respondents were satisfied with the way financial aid is apportioned among various target groups.[18]

Students appear to share these views. In a survey of college freshmen conducted by Cooperative Institution Research Program at the University of California, Los Angeles, 64 percent said that financing their education was a subject of concern. More recently, a fall 1988 Gallup poll found that most young Americans believe a college education costs three times as much as it actually does. The poll also found that many students do not understand that student financial aid is widely available. Among the misconceptions, 25 percent did not know that financial aid could be obtained from sources other than the federal government; 40 percent believed that aid was only for poor families; and nearly 50 percent believed that they could not receive financial aid to attend a private college if their parents could afford a state institution. The California Field Institute poll also found students poorly informed about financial aid and concluded that college freshmen are often "so unsophisticated" about student aid "that they do not understand why guaranteed student loans are considered aid." The poll continued by noting that students, often under pressure to complete college, may assume loans without reading beyond the second paragraph of the agreement and with only the most basic understanding of the loan's terms.[19]

Taken together, the examples of opinion polls show that there is a widespread belief that college costs are out of control, that financial aid is available only from the federal government and for low-income or minority students, and that the price of a college education will be even more prohibitive in the future.

CUTBACKS IN STUDENT AID

Coupled with the rising price of higher education is a fear that federal student aid programs will be curtailed. Nearly 70 percent of the respondents in the 1986 ORC poll said they could afford higher education only with the help of grants or subsidized loans. For most of the 1980s, federal student aid programs have repeatedly been on the fiscal chopping block. With only one exception, however—changes enacted as part of the Omnibus Budget Control and Reconciliation Act of 1981—Congress has consistently refused to approve major budget cuts in these programs.

In short, the publicity given to reduced funding for student aid is misleading. Student aid appropriations and outlays for the need-based programs have grown steadily during the Reagan administration. It may be that the widely publicized budget proposals—together with federal budget deficits—have generated fears that reductions in student aid are inevitable. And these fears, especially when coupled with slightly distorted views about the price of higher education and the operation of financial aid programs, have undoubtedly convinced some families that higher education will soon be unaffordable.

THE GROWING INDEBTEDNESS OF COLLEGE STUDENTS

Student borrowing to pay for higher education has increased rapidly in the last decade. Many analysts believe that the growing dependence on student loans is creating, or will create, serious problems for borrowers when they leave school.

There is no dispute that student borrowing has increased dramatically. In 1975-1976, a total of 922,000 students borrowed $2.5 billion under the Guaranteed Student Loan program. By 1987, 3.6 million students were borrowing $8.3 billion from the program (now Stafford Student Loan program). Over the same period, the number of borrowers in the National Direct Student Loans (now Perkins Loan program) climbed from 690,000 to 814,000.[20] Despite the concern about student borrowing, reliable and nationally representative data on student indebtedness are hard to find.[21]

A 1983 study of student borrowing concluded that roughly 35 percent of recent college graduates had borrowed to finance their education, with a median indebtedness of $3,200. Students in the social sciences, business, and biological sciences had somewhat higher debt levels, whereas those in the physical sciences had lower levels. Among graduate and professional students, the analysis concluded, the median cumulative debt among those who borrowed was $14,700 in law, $24,500 in medicine, $9,900 in business, and $6,800 in the arts and sciences.[22]

A recent study by the College Scholarship Service and the National Association of Student Financial Aid Administrators provides additional data on undergraduate borrowing. The report noted that among undergraduate borrowers in 1985-1986, graduates of two-year schools have an average debt of $3,033 in public schools and $4,461 in private. At four-year schools, borrowers at public colleges have average debts of $6,685, whereas their private-college counterparts owe $8,950.[23] Because the evidence on student indebtedness is sketchy, it is hardly surprising that the impact of educational borrowing on decisions about graduate or professional school, occupational choice, family formation, and major purchases such as housing is inconclusive. Nonetheless, available data suggest that student borrowing to finance higher education is widespread and growing. Many policymakers and analysts intuitively believe that educational debts do influence a borrower's life choices. As a result, there is considerable interest in financing mechanisms that reduce reliance on student loans or that minimize the repayment burden facing borrowers.

New Financing Schemes and Their Aims

Debates about financing higher education are set in a context of rapidly rising prices, increasing use of loans, and changes—both real and imagined—in federal student aid programs. Not surprisingly, such concerns have led to searches for new and less painful ways for families to meet college bills. This interest is probably motivated primarily by a desire to help middle-income families who are trapped between rising costs and reduced eligibility for student aid. Although the interest in helping middle-income families is not new and in the past has been laden with some important budgetary consequences, it has become salient in many recent initiatives.[24]

Recent proposals and plans intended to help pay for higher education vary considerably. One major difference is whether the plan is targeted at students currently attending college or at those who will enroll some years in the future. Programs intended to help today's students have short-run benefits and costs.

TABLE 2.1   New Initiatives to Help Students and Their Families Meet College Costs

| | TARGET GROUP | |
LEVEL OF SPONSORSHIP	TODAY'S STUDENTS	FUTURE STUDENTS
Federal	SLS/PLUS Loan consolidation Income-contingent loans (ICLs) National service	Education savings accounts Savings bonds National trust
State	State loan plans	Tuition guarantees Savings bonds Tax-favored savings Guaranteed-access plans
Institutional	Tuition prepayment Tuition stabilization Installment plans Student/family loans	Tuition guarantees
Other	Consortia loan plans Private-sector loan plans	Tuition guarantees Philanthropic initiatives (e.g., assured-access plans)

NOTE: There is a great deal of overlap among the categories. For example, guaranteed-access plans may be developed at the state or private levels; income-contingent loans, usually regarded as a federal option, are being implemented at the state and institutional levels as well.

Programs aimed at future students push benefits into the future and often delay the costs as well. A second difference between programs concerns who develops or offers the initiative. Some plans are most appropriate for federal or state governments; others are designed for single institutions or consortia. Breaking down the program types according to these two criteria—present or future students as targets, and level of sponsorship—gives us a structure for a brief discussion of the alternatives (see Table 2.1).

HELPING TODAY'S STUDENTS

A multiplicity of new plans and revisions to existing programs under federal, state, institutional, and other types of sponsorship are aimed at making college financing easier for the current generation of students.

FEDERAL INITIATIVES. Among the most basic changes in plans at the federal level are expansions of two federal student aid programs. One is the Parental Loans for Undergraduate Students (PLUS) program. The other is the Supplemental Loans for Students (SLS) program, which targets financially independent undergraduates and graduate and professional students. Both programs are for non-need-based, unsubsidized loans of as much as $4,000 a year, to a cumulative total of $20,000. The interest rate on the loans is variable and set annually, based on the average rate of one-year Treasury bills. There is only a sixty-day grace period after disbursement, although payments can be deferred while the borrower is in school. Borrowing criteria and eligibility are less strict in these programs, and with rising costs, borrowing has increased significantly. For example, borrowing under SLS has risen from about $300 million in 1986 to about $2 billion in 1988.

Other important changes in federal programs to help current or recent borrowers are the provisions for consolidating loans, which allow borrowers who owe more than $5,000 in Stafford, Perkins, SLS, or Health Profession Student Loans (HPSLs) to consolidate the loans, with the interest rate becoming a weighted average of the loans. These consolidation provisions also allow borrowers with high debt levels to extend payments up to twenty-five years.

Income-contingent loans (ICLs) have received a good deal of attention as proposals for federal action. Under this approach, the amount of money a student repays is contingent on the borrower's income. The concept is not new: University of Chicago economist Milton Friedman proposed it, for example, more than thirty years ago, and President Johnson's Science Advisory Committee actually developed a proposal for an "Educational Opportunity Bank" with income-contingent repayment features. Private institutions, such as Boston University and Yale University, have also argued for, or tried, this idea on a small scale.

Attention was focused on the ICL idea during the 1988 presidential election campaign by candidate Michael Dukakis in his Student Tuition and Repayment System (STARS) proposal. The proposal was that student loan repayment rates should be based on the borrower's income and deducted through increased withholding of social security taxes over a long period. Although the Dukakis version of the plan may have died with his defeat, similar ICL proposals have been made by Brookings economist Robert D. Reischauer (now head of the Congressional Budget Office) and by Representative Thomas Petri of Wisconsin. These proposals have a redistributional aspect: borrowers who become well-to-do after graduation could repay more than they borrowed (up to some ceiling amount), and borrowers who worked in less remunerative jobs could ultimately pay less. Although Representative Petri has lobbied strenuously for his proposal (Income Dependent Education Assistance or IDEA), the broad-scale ICL notion has not attracted widespread attention on Capitol Hill or within the higher-education community.

The Reagan administration also initiated a loan program with an income-sensitive repayment mechanism. Dubbed the Income-Contingent Loan Demonstration Program, this pilot program allows students at ten participating schools to borrow up to $17,500 over five years, with interest keyed to the ninety-one-day T-bill rate, accumulating from the time the loan is made, and repayments contingent on the total amount borrowed and the borrower's income during the preceding year. There is a repayment cap of 15 percent of the borrower's income, and there is no redistributional aspect to the plan: borrowers must repay the entire amount of the loan plus interest, and repayments will not exceed this amount. The 100th Congress refused to expand this program beyond its original scope of ten schools and about $5 million in loans to 2,500 students.

Still another way to help today's students is included in some of the recent proposals to establish community or national service programs. The best-known (and most extreme) version of this proposal was the initiative of Senator Sam Nunn of Georgia and Congressman Dave McCurdy of Oklahoma, which made receipt of federal student aid conditional on service in a "Civilian Corps." The mandatory linkage between national service and student aid created a storm of controversy, and the plan was soon abandoned. But the earned-benefits idea—that students who perform substantial community service should get a benefit—is at the heart of the Nunn-McCurdy plan and was also a centerpiece of service plans advanced by Senators Claiborne Pell of Rhode Island and Barbara Mikulski of Maryland. In July 1989, Senate Democrats introduced S. 1430, the National and Community Service Act of 1989. This compromise bill blended the best features of a dozen smaller bills into a single proposal. The Pell-Mikulski-Nunn earned-benefit proposals are a central feature of this new bill.

STATE INITIATIVES. At the state level, present-day students can be assisted through loan programs that often are made possible by the sale of tax-exempt bonds by a state agency. Connecticut, Maryland, Massachusetts, New Hampshire, and New York all have such programs, and families at most income levels qualify for state loans after passing a credit test and paying an origination fee. Repayments, which begin when the loan is disbursed, can be stretched to fifteen years.

In addition, some states have taken a page from the federal income-contingent book by developing such plans themselves. For example, Minnesota now has the Graduated Repayment Income Protection (GRIP) program, which allows students in the health sciences whose payments exceed 10 percent of the average income of their professions to consolidate their loans and make repayments that will increase proportionally with the average income of their professions over a period as long as twenty years.

INSTITUTIONAL AND OTHER INITIATIVES. At the institutional level, a common form of student financing alternative is the tuition prepayment plan. In this scheme, the college receives tuition payments up front, before the student registers, in exchange for a guarantee of no tuition payments (or increases) during the covered period. In other words, a family might pay for four years of tuition at the outset of their child's education and then pay nothing more. If tuition is $10,000 a year—common among high-priced independent colleges—a family using a prepayment plan might pay $40,000 for the four-year guarantee. If tuition during those four years increased at an annual rate of 8 percent (which is typical), the family would save $3,600 by prepaying. Families can sometimes borrow on favorable terms to make such payments, though of course this cuts down the amount of saving.

Other payment arrangements are tuition stabilization and installment payment plans. In a stabilization plan, a family might pay a 4 percent premium in the first year in exchange for a guarantee that tuition would not rise in subsequent years. Installment plans allow payment of tuition at regular intervals, with the delays in payment representing in essence short-term loans, often interest- or premium-free. Sometimes institutions can arrange to lend money directly to students at below-market interest rates and with favorable repayment terms. Or they may work creatively with local financial institutions to develop advantageous aid packages for students, consisting of consortium loans, commercial loans, governmental aid, and state aid.

HELPING TOMORROW'S STUDENTS

The picture of initiatives for the next generation of students is changing rapidly, so any account may be dated. Nonetheless, a brief account of the current alternatives may give some idea of the direction of development of financing arrangements.

FEDERAL INITIATIVES. Federal efforts to help students are concentrated in the need-based student aid programs administered by the Department of Education. More than twenty bills were introduced in the 100th Congress alone. Most recent proposals have been for federal financing mechanisms to facilitate long-term savings for education. One approach, modeled after successful (and costly) Individual Retirement Accounts (IRAs), would allow interest to accumulate tax-free in so-called education savings accounts, accounts designated as savings for postsecondary education. Up to $1,000 per year could be invested in such accounts, under a Reagan administration proposal. The deposits, however, would not be tax-free, and the tax break would be phased out for families with incomes above $40,000 a year. Congress took no action on this proposal.

A more elaborate federal initiative was proposed as H.R. 2509, the Parental Assistance for Tuition Investment Act, by Congressman Pat Williams of Montana in the House and, in slightly different form, by Claiborne Pell of Rhode Island, Edward Kennedy of Massachusetts, and Robert Stafford of Vermont in the Senate. This bill would create a quasi-independent national postsecondary education trust to encourage savings for college by enabling parents to invest in a tax-exempt program. The trust would receive and manage the investment of payments, forwarding money to the institution of higher education when the student matriculated. The legislation provides for favorable tax treatment of the money invested in the trust. Payments of up to $2,000 per year per beneficiary could be treated as a deduction from income, with the tax treatment eliminated for high-income families.

Education savings bonds are another popular proposal for the federal government. In a July 1987 speech, George Bush, then vice-president, suggested creating a "college savings bond" program with interest accumulating tax-free if ultimately used to finance postsecondary study. A savings bond approach was also embodied in a bill introduced by Senators Kennedy, Pell, Stafford, and Lloyd Bentsen of Texas. Under this plan, interest earned on existing U.S. savings bonds (the Series EE savings bonds) would be exempted from interest if the holder used the bond to pay for tuition and fees at a college or university.

Introduced as S. 1817 in September 1987, the bill was offered as an amendment to the Technical Corrections Act of 1988, passed in the closing hours of the 100th Congress and signed into law in November 1988. As passed, the savings bond provision applies only to bonds purchased after January 1, 1990, and the tax break is phased out at higher income levels. To receive the tax break, purchasers of such bonds must be at least twenty-four years of age, to prevent wealthy taxpayers from gaining a tax break by buying bonds in their children's names. The Joint Tax Committee has estimated that the program would cost $281 million in lost tax revenue over the first five years but would result in the sale of an additional $17.5 billion in savings bonds.

STATE INITIATIVES. States have discussed and adopted a wide array of programs to facilitate the ability of tomorrow's students to pay for higher education. Perhaps the most innovative are tuition-guarantee programs of the type pioneered in the Michigan Education Trust (MET). The MET allows parents to ensure that their child's tuition expenses will be covered at any of the state's public colleges or universities when the child comes of college age. This is done by having parents begin to make regular contributions to a special state fund when the child is young. The fund will pool and invest the money in securities to keep abreast of rising tuition costs. In addition, the amount families need to invest to guarantee that their contributions will cover the tuition will be adjusted according to projections made by the state.

The initial sales price of a Michigan tuition guarantee for families whose children will start college in the year 2006 is $6,800. The plan and Michigan's future taxpayers are thus taking the risk that the MET's investments will pay off at a rate sufficient to cover tuition increases and administrative expenses.

State-sponsored savings plans, pioneered by Illinois, generally involve selling state zero-coupon college savings bonds. Here, parents may purchase a bond that will be worth, say, $5,000 at some time in the future, with interest on the bond exempted from federal and state tax. Although nothing guarantees that a particular level of investment will match tuition costs exactly, investors are assured of the tax-exempt status, and the state and future taxpayers are insulated from the cost of administering a new program and the financial risk of guaranteeing tuitions a generation ahead of time. One drawback that such plans share with tuition guarantees is that they require substantial investments by families at an early time, and so generally wealthy families are best able to take best advantage of such opportunities.

New York, Massachusetts, and Missouri have discussed complex variations or amalgams of guarantee and savings plans. In Massachusetts, for example, a proposal was made to issue bonds that would be indexed as a percentage of tuition at particular colleges. For example, if a $1,200 bond represented 10 percent of tuition at a given college when purchased, it would be held by the college to represent the same proportion when redeemed. Such programs would place the inflationary risk primarily on the colleges, and it is unclear whether they will participate if the plan is approved.

ASSURED ACCESS PLANS. Still another group of initiatives are the guaranteed-access, or assured-access, plans that have been launched by individual philanthropists. Under these plans, a wealthy benefactor agrees to guarantee the college tuition of a group of students if the students stay in school and graduate. The best-known of these ventures is Eugene Lang's I Have a Dream project in New York City. This program started in 1981, when Lang, in a graduation speech, promised to finance the college education of a whole class of sixth-graders at Public School 121 in East Harlem, New York.

On learning—from the school principal—that few, if any, of the intended beneficiaries of Lang's largesse were likely to attend college, Lang hired a full-time assistant to run a tutoring program and began to meet regularly with the students and their parents. There were sixty-one sixth-graders in the audience when Lang made his promise, and of the fifty-two still live in New York City, fifty have graduated from high school, including the seven who became pregnant. As of August 1988, thirty-six were attending college. Lang's idea has been widely publicized, and other philanthropists have emulated his approach.

At least one state has enacted a plan modeled after assured-access plans. In August 1988, New York launched the Liberty Scholarship program. This initiative promises New York high school students who have family incomes of less than $18,000 that they will receive a grant equal to the difference between the institution's tuition and the amount of aid they receive under the federal Pell Grant program and New York's Tuition Assistance Program. Students also may use their Liberty Scholarships to attend a private college or university in New York. If the Liberty Scholarship program can even begin to approach the success of Lang's small venture, the implications for the financing of higher education will be enormous.

INSTITUTIONAL AND OTHER INITIATIVES. One of the most highly publicized campus initiatives was Duquesne's Alumni Tuition Plan, which inspired Michigan's MET. Launched in 1985 and hailed as a model program, the plan was suspended in 1988. The plan offered parents the opportunity to purchase tuition for a future student at a steep discount. For example, in 1985, for a child who would enroll in the year 2004, an alumnus could guarantee four years of prepaid tuition (estimated to cost over $92,000) for an investment of only $4,450. The assumptions behind such an arrangement were that Duquesne would invest the funds in U.S. Treasury zero-coupon bonds carrying an 11 percent interest but would gain closer to 14 percent through the administration of certain restrictions on use of the benefits. For example, if a student failed to gain entry to the school, did not want to attend, or died, the school would refund only the initial payment. If a student flunked out, the school would keep the money. If a student wanted to transfer, the student had to attend Duquesne successfully for a year before the school would pay an equivalent to its own tuition to another school.

The Duquesne plan was crippled by two main assumptions. First, the restrictiveness of the conditions was a problem. Students were restricted to Duquesne for at least a year, whether or not the school suited them. Second, the bond market yields were lower than anticipated, whereas tuition increases were higher than anticipated, forcing the school to raise the cost to prepay for four years sharply, by nearly 100 percent. At that price, enrollments dropped off sharply, and the plan was discontinued. Similar concerns have limited enrollments in a number of other colleges that followed Duquesne's lead.

The private sector and consortia of educational institutions have entered the financing market with a number of initiatives. Among consortium-based plans are CONSERN, run by a Washington, D.C., area group that allows borrowing of up to $15,000 a year, with twelve-year repayment terms, and SHARE, run as a private-sector venture by the Consortium on Financing Higher Education, the New England Marketing Corporation, and the Education Resources Institute. Other private sector plans include the CollegeSure CD, offered by the College Savings Bank and guaranteeing a rate of return pegged to increases in college tuition. This return, however, does not take into account an "issue premium" that may make the effective return of the investment substantially lower.

Conclusions

There is both good news and bad in the rapid emergence of new schemes for financing higher education. The good news is that institutions of higher education now see clearly that they cannot rely solely on increases in financial aid from the federal government to help students finance their educations. Although education has substantial national and social value, ultimately it represents a transaction between institutions and individuals that the federal government cannot and will not underwrite fully. Fortunately, there are a large number of third parties that have an interest in facilitating the efforts of students and their families in meeting the increasing costs of higher education. It is too early to tell which among the many initiatives and alternatives will come to represent major forms of assistance. It is probably safe to say, however, that the multiplicity of programs inject options and a healthy competition into the financing of higher education.

Another piece of good news is that many proposals are taking a longer-range view of financing, a tactic that takes higher education out of the realm of current-consumption purchases and puts it more appropriately into the realm of investments in human capital that pay dividends over a long period—the life of the recipient.

The bad news is that the initiatives now before us are complex and problematic. Students and families will be challenged by financing tasks, as will institutional financial offices already overburdened by administering a bewildering variety of programs, options, and revisions.

Another concern is the distributional aspect of the new plans. Most require investments, and thus, institutions with financial clout may get richer and those without it may get poorer. Public-support initiatives need to be framed with the dangers to the less-wealthy but still-vital institutions—for example, the community colleges, historically black colleges, and other institutions—clearly in mind.

A third issue concerns who will pay for education. The shift toward increased borrowing means a shift from parental responsibility to student responsibility for paying for higher education. From an actuarial perspective, this may be particularly problematic for the coming generation, which also faces mounting burdens of supporting the retirement and medical care of the large cohort before it.

A fourth concern is whether financing opportunities will be sufficient to broaden access to college. Research suggests that equally important to groups not firmly committed to receiving higher education may be early intervention, information, and counseling. With the exception of New York's Liberty Scholarships, most new financing schemes do not address this problem and thus may be tilting toward the middle class.

Because higher education is so vital to this nation's economic growth and progress, as well as to its social complexion, the debate over financing alternatives is laden with both opportunity and danger. How we settle these debates—and how well we settle them—will have a great impact on the nation's future.

The views expressed in the preceding chapter are those of the author and do not represent those of the members or staff of the U.S. Senate.

Notes

1. Arthur M. Hauptman, "The Tuition Futures Fad: The Risks Outweigh the Benefits for Families, Colleges, and States," *Chronicle of Higher Education*, December 3, 1986; and Lawrence Minard, "The CRIBs Age," *Forbes*, November 18, 1985, pp. 38-39.

2. Frederick Rudolph, *The American College and University* (New York: Vintage, 1962), pp. 177-78.

3. Rudolph, *The American College and University*, pp. 179-86; John S. Brubacher and Willis Rudy, *A History of American Colleges and Universities* (New York: Harper and Row, 1976), p. 36.

4. Brubacher and Rudy, *A History of American Colleges and Universities*, pp. 36-37.

5. Robert H. Fenske, "Student Aid: Past and Present," in Fenske et al., eds. *Handbook of Student Financial Aid* Fenske et al., eds. (San Francisco: Jossey-Bass, 1983), pp. 6-7; see also Rudolph, *The American College and University*, pp. 190-92.

6. Brubacher and Rudy, *A History of American Colleges and Universities*, pp. 36-37; National Center for Education Statistics, *Digest of Education Statistics, 1988* (Washington, D.C.: Government Printing Office, 1988), Table 218, p. 251.

7. Rudolph, *The American College and University*, p. 193; Brubacher and Rudy, *History of American Colleges and Universities*, p. 37.

8. Fenske, "Student Aid," pp. 7-8.

9. Fenske, "Student Aid," p. 9.

10. For a discussion of the GI Bill and its impact on higher education, see Alice Rivlin, *The Role of the Federal Government in Financing Higher Education* (Washington, D.C.: Brookings Institution, 1961).

11. Statistics taken from National Center for Education Statistics, *Digest of Education Statistics, 1988*.

12. Chester E. Finn, Jr., *Scholars, Dollars, and Bureaucrats* (Washington, D.C.: Brookings Institution, 1978), p. 73.

13. For an analysis of the development of the educational amendments of 1972, see Lawrence E. Gladieux and Thomas Wolanin, *Congress and the Colleges* (Lexington, Mass.: Heath, 1976).

14. For an overview of these changes in the student aid programs, see Terry W. Hartle and James B. Stedman, "Federal Programs: A View of the Higher Education Act," in Mary McKeown and Kern Alexander, eds., *Values in Conflict: Funding Priorities for Higher Education* (Cambridge, Mass.: Ballinger, 1986), pp. 137-56.

15. Paul M. Irwin et al., *U.S. Department of Education: Major Program Trends, Fiscal Years 1980-1989* (Washington, D.C.: Congressional Research Service, 1988); Gwendolyn Lewis, *Trends in Student Aid, 1980-1988* (New York: College Entrance Examination Board, 1988), p. 10.

16. Lewis, *Trends in Student Aid*, Tables 1 and 2, pp. 6-7.

17. Arthur M. Hauptman and Terry W. Hartle, "Tuition Increases Since 1970: A Perspective," *Higher Education and National Affairs*, February 23, 1987, pp. 5-8.

18. Eureka Project, Opinions and Attitudes, *How the Public, Students, and Parents View Student Financial Aid* (Sacramento: Eureka Project, March 1988); Terry W. Hartle, "Are College Costs a Problem?" *Public Opinion* 10 (May-June 1987), pp. 48-51.

19. Eureka Project, *How the Public, Students, and Parents View Financial Aid*, p. 19; Denise K. Magner, "Young People Widely Misinformed About Cost of College, *Chronicle of Higher Education*, October 12, 1988, p. 1.

20. Donald Gillespie and Nancy Carlson, *Trends in Student Aid, 1963-1983* (New York: College Entrance Examination Board, 1983); Lewis, *Trends in Student Aid, 1980-1988.*

21. One recent analysis concluded that "it is impossible to assemble precise and comparable nationwide statistics on student borrowing over the past two decades." See Janet S. Hansen, *Student Loans: Are They Overburdening a Generation?* (Washington, D.C.: College Entrance Examination Board, 1987), p. 4.

22. Terry W. Hartle and Richard Wabnick, *The Educational Indebtedness of Graduate and Professional Students* (Washington, D.C.: Educational Testing Service, 1983).

23. Cited in Hansen, *Student Loans*, pp. 6-12.

24. For example, Missouri governor John Ashcroft proposed an education savings initiative explicitly seeking to "directly benefit middle-income and other parents who may find their children ineligible for grants and subsidized loan programs."

3

An Inventory of Innovative Financing Plans to Help Pay for Higher Education

JAMIE P. MERISOTIS

In the last few years, the dominance of traditional programs of grants, work, and subsidized loans has been challenged by a host of innovative financing plans and programs, as policymakers and educators have sought to expand student and family assistance to help pay for higher education. New college savings plans have arisen at the federal, state, and institutional levels. Pioneered by colleges, innovative tuition-guarantee and prepayment plans have gained a high profile, as state-level plans in Michigan and Florida have been followed by proposals at the federal level. Alternative loan programs are multiplying at the federal, state, and institutional levels, the latter including plans by consortia. Finally, guaranteed-access plans and community and public service proposals are expanding as means to assure access to higher education through philanthropy and work.

In 1982 the search for alternative financing had barely begun.[1] Now, less than a decade later, the original alternative programs are maturing, and new ones are cropping up rapidly around the country. Not surprisingly, the proliferating programs and proposals have overrun most efforts at centralized record keeping, hampering analysts' efforts to assess the extent and effect of financing alternatives.[2] Hence, this essay seeks to provide an up-to-date inventory of alternative financing, categorizing plans by type and level of sponsorship. Naturally, even the most current taxonomy of programs must be provisional because of the rapid pace of change. Nevertheless, the present "who, what, and when" of programs gives us a snapshot of the structure and evolution of innovation at the federal, state, and private levels and may help us in assessing the extent to which novel plans—especially those of the last three years—are reaching their intended beneficiaries.

Savings Plans

College savings plans are of several types, including two major savings bond bills at the federal level, current savings proposals and plans in at least fifteen states, and a host of private-investment or certificate-of-deposit (CD) alternatives.

FEDERAL LEVEL

In 1987 and 1988, two bond-based proposals vied for eminence as the "best" federal savings plan. One plan, proposed by Vice-President George Bush and included in the fiscal year 1989 Reagan administration budget, called for the issue of special federal college savings bonds. Interest earned on these bonds would be exempt from federal tax if the proceeds were used for "tuition and related expenses" at any two- or four-year U.S. institution of higher education. The bonds could pay for college expenses for the bondholder, his or her spouse, or a dependent. Taxpayers with adjusted gross incomes of over $60,000 would have reduced tax benefits, and families or individuals with incomes of more than $80,000 would receive no tax break.

Another plan, sponsored by Senator Edward Kennedy of Massachusetts, received far more attention and support than the Bush proposal. Appended to the technical amendments bill for the 1986 Tax Reform Act in the waning moments of the 1988 legislative session, the Kennedy plan excludes from gross taxable income the amount earned through the redemption of U.S. savings bonds if the funds are used to pay for qualified higher-education expenses. Single filers with incomes under $40,000 are eligible for the full income exclusion, whereas those in the $40,000 to $60,000 range would receive prorated benefits. The lower and upper limits for joint filers are $60,000 and $90,000. These amounts will be adjusted for inflation on an annual basis.

"Qualified higher-education expenses" are defined under the Kennedy plan as the tuition and fees of the taxpayer or his or her spouse or dependent. The amount of these expenses is reduced by the amount of any nontaxable scholarship, veterans educational benefits, or any nontaxable payment for educational expenses. This new federal savings plan does not apply to students attending proprietary institutions. The law becomes effective for bonds issued after December 31, 1989.

STATE LEVEL

Much of the innovation in the tuition savings area has taken place in the states. Some states have already enacted laws that use a variety of mechanisms to encourage saving for college, and others have plans in the design stages.[3]

As of November 1988, fifteen states had passed bills encouraging college savings: Colorado, Connecticut, Delaware, Illinois, Iowa, Kentucky, North Carolina, North Dakota, Minnesota, Missouri, Oregon, Rhode Island, Virginia, Washington, and West Virginia. Of these, six have operational programs: Connecticut, Illinois, North Carolina, North Dakota, Oregon, and Washington. The others have later implementation dates, are studying the fiscal impact of the legislation, or are working on the development and marketing of the proposals.

In most of the state plans, college saving is encouraged through the use of some form of state-tax-exempt bonds, such as general obligation bonds or zero-coupon bonds. Typical of a straight savings bond approach is the program in Illinois, where the Baccalaureate Savings Act, signed into law in December 1987, allows for national marketing of general obligation bonds as college savings bonds. Denominations of these bonds currently range from $1,120 to $3,695. Maturities are from five to twenty years. The state also offers incentives to bond buyers: state-income-tax exemption, a 0.5 percent interest rate bonus if the bond is used to pay for tuition at an in-state institution, and an exemption of up to $25,000 (bond principal plus interest) from state student aid need-analysis calculations.

Kentucky, Virginia, and Rhode Island have developed variations on the straight savings bond approach. Kentucky will establish a savings fund as a public trust. One component of this trust is a "program fund" for parental investment and savings. The other is an "endowment fund" for public funds, gifts, and bequests, which will be used to enhance investment in the program fund if the proceeds are used for attendance at a state institution. Virginia will establish a "unit investment trust" made up of federal, state, and local bonds. This plan would operate in a manner similar to a mutual fund, with the added benefit of a guaranteed return and possible tax exemption. Rhode Island will provide both tax-free bonds and state-tax-exempt educational savings accounts.

A crucial but complex question remains about the state-level savings plans: Will they enhance families' net saving behavior? Here, we can offer suggestive, but not conclusive, summary data on bond sales in states with operational programs. Illinois, the first state to elicit major interest in bonds earmarked for college savings, sold out its initial bond issue of $90 million in three days, January 11-13, 1988. A second such sale, September 12-16, 1988, was for $175 million. North Carolina has sold approximately $30 million in bonds since its educational savings bond program was implemented in late 1987. North Dakota took orders for $15 million in savings bonds on June 20-24, 1988. Oregon sold $20 million in bonds in the summer of 1988 as part of a "pilot program" for state-sponsored college saving. Washington sold out its first bond issue of $50 million in September 1988. Exact figures are not yet available on Connecticut's December 1988 sale of general obligation bonds. Thus, in the six issuing states, at least $380 million worth of college savings bonds have been sold so far. Further bond sales in states currently issuing bonds and in other states that will implement bond programs in 1989 will push the total higher.

OTHER SAVINGS PLANS

Growing support for government-sponsored savings plans has been matched by an increase in private plans. A broad range of organizations— from financial services companies and banks to nonprofit corporations—are actively involved in college saving and investment programs, which represent the main focus of private-sector interest in financing higher education.

Most private plans involve calculating estimated tuition and other costs for some future year or years and developing a targeted investment strategy using existing financial instruments. A typical example is the Merrill Lynch CollegeBuilder program. This program offers a free "proposal" to parents that estimates costs at any institution in a selected year and then determines what annual level of savings or investment would meet the anticipated payment. A company financial consultant then works with parents to structure an investment program that combines government securities, stocks, bonds, and other instruments.

Even more well known among private plans is the CollegeSure CD program, operated by the College Savings Bank in Princeton, New Jersey. The CD pays a return that is linked to increases in total college costs, as measured by an index of five hundred independent institutions. CollegeSure offers maturities ranging from one to twenty-five years. The cost of each CD equals the total current costs at a selected college of the purchaser's choice (prospective CD purchasers receive an individualized plan based on a single institution), plus a surcharge. This surcharge is calculated as a percentage of total costs and increases with the length of maturity of the CD. For example, if a family purchases four CDs—one maturing CD per year of attendance—the CD with the latest maturity would have the highest price. CollegeSure CDs pay annual interest, guaranteed at a minimum of 4 percent, regardless of college cost increases.

It is worth noting that most private-sector programs are targeted at fairly wealthy and sophisticated investors. Advertisements for many plans, generally placed in financial periodicals or newspaper business sections, assume that parents will be sending their children to high-priced private colleges. Because families in such circumstances are relatively few, the potential impact of these programs may be limited. Yet savvy investors, even at more-modest financial levels, might benefit from programs that encouraged early financial planning for college, if the programs were targeted and marketed appropriately.

Unfortunately, we cannot know precisely the number and impact of the multitude of private savings plans until we have a fuller survey of who is saving, how much saving is involved, and whether these savings actually are being used to pay for college costs. The breadth of the range of organizations actively involved in college savings programs does suggest, however, that private saving for college has stimulated considerable interest.

Tuition-Guarantee and Prepayment Plans

Tuition guarantees and prepayments are of relatively recent vintage, having appeared first in private higher education, and then in highly visible form at the state level in Michigan and Florida and, most recently, as proposals at the national level.

FEDERAL LEVEL

Interest in tuition guarantees at the federal level heightened in 1987, perhaps in response to interest in plans such as Michigan's. Legislative proposals included two by House Postsecondary Education Subcommittee chairman Pat Williams of Montana and one by influential Senator Claiborne Pell of Rhode Island. As of late 1988, however, enthusiasm for a federal tuition guarantee appeared to have declined, perhaps in part because of the success of the Kennedy savings bond plan.

The Williams and Pell models would establish a national trust, governed by a board that might include the secretaries of education and the Treasury and a small number of presidential appointees. Families would contribute a specified sum to the federal trust fund in the name of one or more children. The trust would attempt to gain returns on investments in government securities sufficient to cover some projection of average tuition and fees charged at public and private institutions.

Contributions to the federal fund would be tax-deductible at the federal (and presumably the state) level, up to a maximum dollar amount per child per year. The rate of deductibility would depend on the family's adjusted gross income. Perhaps one of a federal plan's most attractive features is that it would be completely "portable"; that is, unlike institution- and state-based guarantees, a federal guarantee could be used to pay for tuition and fees at any approved postsecondary institution nationwide. The governing board would make benefit payments directly to postsecondary institutions on behalf of beneficiaries. Income earned from these federal tuition guarantees would be excluded from need-analysis calculations for federal student assistance.

STATE LEVEL

State tuition-guarantee or prepayment plans were, in a sense, precursors of savings plans. That is, interest in tuition financing plans really accelerated with the founding of the Michigan Education Trust (MET), a tuition-guarantee plan, in late 1986. Soon after, states began to discuss and adopt both tuition-guarantee and savings plans.

Currently, nine states have enacted tuition-guarantee plans: Florida, Indiana, Maine, Michigan, Missouri, Oklahoma, Tennessee, West Virginia, and Wyoming. Of these, only Florida, Michigan, and Wyoming have operational plans. Many of the state tuition-guarantee plans—and the federal plans—are modeled after Michigan's plan, the MET. Signed into law in December 1986, the MET did not begin selling contracts until August 1988, a delay caused by a provision in the MET statute that prohibited operation until rulings on the plan's tax status were received from the IRS.[4]

Michigan now offers two basic plans to purchasers. The main difference between them is the policy on refunds. With Plan A, a purchaser is entitled to a refund of the original investment minus the state's administrative costs. With the slightly more costly Plan B, a purchaser is entitled to a refund of the original investment, administrative costs, and interest earned. In both cases, the tuition guarantee is good for attendance at any state institution of higher education that offers a baccalaureate degree. Beneficiaries may attend a community or junior college first or may request a prorated refund after graduating from a two-year school.

The price of a state tuition-guarantee contract, as of August 1988, ranges from $1,689 for a full year of tuition for a newborn beneficiary to $2,055 for a ten-year-old. Contracts may be applied only for tuition expenses at state institutions and may not be used for room, board, fees, or other expenses. As of September 1988, the state had approved approximately 82,000 contracts, though only 27,000 families had actually purchased guarantees.

Trends as of late 1988 show a slowdown of legislative interest for state tuition guarantees but continuing support for state savings plans. Several states have delayed implementation of guarantees pending internal study, IRS tax ruling, or legal determination. In Maine, for example, the state attorney general has advised that the state's assumption of all financial risks in the event of the plan's failure violates Maine's constitution, leaving the future of that tuition guarantee in doubt. In all, twenty-two states enacted tuition savings or guarantee plans between December 1986 and November 1988. Another fifteen states had legislation pending or were actively studying savings and guarantee programs.

OTHER TUITION-GUARANTEE PLANS

In addition to the federal and state plans and proposals for tuition guarantees, postsecondary institutions and the private sector have developed and offered programs. Institutional programs—where the idea for guaranteed tuition actually began—seem to have fallen out of favor. Private tuition-guarantee programs appear to have become moderately successful, however, at least from a marketing standpoint.

Duquesne University developed the prototype for tuition-guarantee plans. Its plan, initiated in 1985, allowed parents to buy four guaranteed future years of tuition at a highly discounted price. For example, in 1985-1986, a four-year tuition guarantee for a child entering Duquesne in the year 2000 could be bought for $9,182. That is, the college guaranteed that such a payment would cover the full four years of tuition beginning in the year 2000, if the child was accepted for admission at Duquesne at that time.

Criticism of the Duquesne plan from finance experts, college officials, and parents appeared in numerous forums. Citing poor investment returns and higher-than-expected tuition increases, Duquesne suspended its guarantee program in March 1988. In all, the program attracted 622 participants. About a dozen other private institutions also have experimented with tuition guarantees. Most enrolled even fewer participants than did Duquesne, and at least three institutions—the University of Detroit, Nichols College, and Canisius College—now have suspended their programs as well.

A private organization that offers a tuition-guarantee plan is the National Tuition Maintenance Organization (TMO) of Plymouth, Michigan. The TMO concept is a simpler form of tuition guarantee that directly links current prices to future attendance. If a purchaser pays an amount exactly equal to tuition at a given institution in 1988, the beneficiary would be entitled to a year of tuition at that institution in some future year. Beneficiaries may use this tuition guarantee only at an institution that is a member of National TMO, which is a nonprofit corporation.

Payments into the TMO plan are invested exclusively in government securities, with maturity in the year that the beneficiary reaches age eighteen. Beneficiaries must use the benefits within six years of their eighteenth birthday, though extensions for military and other service are permitted. Member institutions receive a small percentage of actual prepayments, in addition to the full benefits from the government securities investments for each beneficiary that enrolls.

Alternative Loan Programs

Alternative loan programs are thriving at the federal, state, and nongovernmental levels. Because they generally have no grant components and lack interest subsidies typical of the Stafford loans, such programs have required tests of creditworthiness and have appealed more widely to families and independent students whose income or income expectations are in the moderate-to-upper ranges. An exception to this may be the recent federal Income Contingent Loan (ICL) pilot project.

FEDERAL LEVEL

The federal government has taken steps in recent years to broaden the availability of federally guaranteed loans and experiment with innovative repayment schemes. Over the past decade Congress has authorized two alternative loan programs, Parent Loans for Undergraduate Students (PLUS) and Supplemental Loans for Students (SLS), and one pilot project, the Income Contingent Loan (ICL)program. The PLUS program became operational in 1981; the SLS program, in 1982; and the ICL pilot project, in 1987.

TABLE 3.1   Annual Loan Volumes (in Dollars) and Numbers of Recipients of Parent Loans for Undergraduate Students (PLUS) and Supplemental Loans for Students (SLS) Programs, 1980-81 to 1987-88

	PLUS		SLS	
YEAR	LOAN VOLUME ($ MILLIONS)	RECIPIENTS (THOUSANDS)	LOAN VOLUME ($ MILLIONS)	RECIPIENTS (THOUSANDS)
1980–81	3	1	0	0
1981–82	57	22	16	7
1982–83	122	49	78	31
1983–84	171	66	145	56
1984–85	244	93	221	84
1985–86	246	93	265	100
1986–87	307	112	462	169

PLUS loans are available to the parents of dependent students, whereas SLS loans are available to independent undergraduate, graduate, and professional students. Since 1987, both programs have variable interest rates that are tied to changes in one-year Treasury bills. There is no in-school interest subsidy for these programs, unlike regular Stafford loans, and repayment begins sixty days after the loan is made. Annual loan limits for the PLUS and SLS programs are $4,000, with an aggregate maximum of $20,000.

Both programs grew modestly in their first several years. In 1987-1988, however, PLUS registered a 68 percent increase in loan volume, and SLS, a rise of more than 280 percent. Table 3.1 presents figures on annual loan volume and recipients for PLUS and SLS. Cumulatively, the PLUS and SLS programs have lent approximately $4.6 billion to parents and students over the last eight years, though nearly half of this was in the most recent year.

The other alternative federal loan program, the ICL pilot project, is a product of the 1986 reauthorization of the Higher Education Act. Ten institutions participate in this project, with approximately $5 million in loans made during the first year, 1987. The ICL pilot allows borrowers to repay on a scale that shifts according to outstanding debt and annual income. A cap of 12 percent of annual income applies to all borrowers, and low-income students pay as little as 5 percent. Students who participate in the program must submit income information annually to the institution. No interest rate subsidy is provided by the federal government.

STATE LEVEL

State-supported loan programs disburse, undoubtedly, a fairly small amount of funds, compared with the federal programs' annual outlays of more than $10 billion. For analysts, it has been difficult to quantify precisely the gross amounts of state-level loans, however, because so many different state agencies, governing boards, and other official organizations sponsor student loan programs. Yet state loan programs can be vital resources for many students, particularly those from middle-class families. Moreover, because state-supported student aid has grown in the last few years, in part because of the slowdown in growth of federal student assistance, it would be helpful to have even a good estimate of the dollar amounts of state aid that students receive. In the thirty-five states known to make loans for students in postsecondary education, the total amount of loans awarded for 1986, the most recent year for which comprehensive data were available, was $440 million.[5]

OTHER ALTERNATIVE LOAN PROGRAMS

Alternative loan programs have generated considerable interest at the nongovernmental level. These programs can be divided into private initiatives and programs run by institutions or consortia.

On the private level, there are two basic types of programs. One is programs supported by nonprofit organizations. For example, The Education Resources Institute (TERI) in Boston sponsors several alternative loan schemes, including a Supplemental Loan Program for undergraduate and graduate students and a Professional Education Plan for graduate and professional students. TERI loans have high annual limits (up to $20,000, according to recent literature from the organization), repayment terms of up to twenty years, and interest-only payment while the borrower is enrolled. A guarantee fee is charged on all loans (up to 5 percent of the loan amount), and interest is variable. Borrowers must meet a credit test to qualify for loans, and in many instances a cosigner is required.

Another private nonprofit program is CONSERN: Loans for Education, located in Washington, D.C. The Consern organization uses private capital to make loans to borrowers at any educational level, from elementary and secondary through graduate and professional. Annual and cumulative limits for Consern loans are $25,000 and $100,000, respectively, with the repayment term fixed at fifteen years. Borrowers may defer payment of principal while enrolled in school, paying only interest for up to four years. A discount fee of 3.5 percent is charged on all loans, and interest is variable. Like TERI loans, Consern loans require a credit test for all borrowers.

Many private for-profit student loan programs also exist. These plans are usually sponsored by banks or other financial organizations. One example is the Educational Credit Corporation (ECC) Loan Program, a subsidiary venture of TSO Financial Corporation. ECC uses funds supplied by Colonial National Bank, another TSO Financial subsidiary, to make loans. ECC then contracts with an independent organization for loan servicing. ECC offers loans of up to $15,000 a year and $60,000 cumulatively to creditworthy students and parents. Principal and interest payments begin sixty days after loan disbursement, with no fixed repayment period. A fee of 3 percent is charged on all loans, which carry a variable interest rate capped at 18 percent. As an inducement to encourage students to participate, ECC pays a portion of the origination fee to colleges, providing defaults are sufficiently low. Institutions assume no financial liability, however.

We do not know precisely how many private-sector loan programs are in existence; the examples cited above represent only well-established ventures. In general, however, private programs are geared toward middle- and upper-income parents and students who probably do not qualify for need-based student assistance. Most plans extend repayment terms up to twenty years or longer but require some form of repayment while the borrower is still enrolled. They also usually have interest rates that are tied to the prime rate or to the T-bill rate, thus ensuring a favorable rate of return to the lender.

Institutional or consortium-based loan programs are another type of innovative plan developed and expanded in recent years. These plans are sometimes offered as supplements to existing financial aid, or they may be extended to students and families that do not qualify for need-based assistance. At least sixty institutions are known to have loan programs, although the exact figure probably is considerably higher.[6]

A good example of an individual institutional loan program is the University of Pennsylvania's Penn Plan, which offers perhaps the broadest possible range of educational financing alternatives to families and students. The extensive menu of financing alternatives includes a guaranteed-tuition option, a monthly budgeting plan, and a series of loan programs that attempt to address specific financing needs. The Penn Plan's loan alternatives allow both aided and nonaided families to extend financing several years beyond the student's graduation. Included is a loan plan for aided families that may be repaid at a variable interest rate, a revolving line of credit for nonaided families to help cover the costs of nontuition expenses (with a variable interest rate somewhat higher than that charged to aided families), and a extended-repayment guaranteed-tuition plan repayable at a fixed rate of interest. The Penn Plan offers second-mortgage options, life insurance coverage for larger loan amounts, and other alternatives.

Programs operated by consortia are another type of alternative loan plan. Probably the best known is the SHARE program, which is offered to students attending one of the thirty institutions affiliated with the Consortium on Financing Higher Education (COFHE). SHARE loans allow students (or their families) attending a COFHE member school to borrow up to $20,000 annually to pay for their undergraduate educations.

SHARE loans are an intricately designed product of several entities. First, the COFHE institutions themselves may provide application information to potential borrowers and must verify general information regarding a borrower's enrollment and eligibility for a loan. Next, the New England Education Loan Marketing Corporation ("Nellie Mae"), a nonprofit secondary market agency, processes loans, holds notes, and arranges for capitalization through its network of participating lenders. TERI serves as the guarantor on all loans and also acts as the primary loan servicer.

The terms and conditions of SHARE loans are similar to those of other alternative loan programs. No needs test is required, a credit check is mandatory, interest is variable, and repayment of interest begins while the borrower is still enrolled. Repayment may be extended up to twenty years, depending on the amount borrowed. A guarantee fee equal to 4 percent of the loan amount is charged to all borrowers. Families may also secure their SHARE loan with a second mortgage.

The Consortium of Universities of the Washington (D.C.) Metropolitan Area has also established a loan program, dubbed DC CONSERN (different from the CONSERN: Loans for Education noted earlier). Loans are available to students attending any of a dozen Washington-area institutions or to District of Columbia residents attending any accredited four-year U.S. institution. Financing for the program was established by a $50 million tax-exempt bond issue in 1987.

Like SHARE loans, DC CONSERN loans are designed mostly for students and parents who are ineligible for subsidized federal aid programs. Borrowers may receive up to an aggregate of $48,000, with repayment made over a twelve-year period. Interest rates are variable and are tied to changes in the interest rates of the tax-exempt bonds. Repayment of interest begins immediately, and repayment of principal and interest must begin no later than four years from the date a loan is made. A discount fee equivalent to 5 percent of the face value of the loan is charged to cover default and administrative costs. DC Consern loans are subject to a prepayment penalty of 5 percent of the amount prepaid.

Consortium-based programs also play an important role at the graduate and professional-school level. For example, the Law School Admissions

Council offers a supplemental loan program called Law Access. Students may borrow up to $10,000 per year through this privately funded program. Similar programs are offered by the Association of American Medical Colleges and by a consortium of osteopathic medicine schools, among others.

Guaranteed-Access Plans

Perhaps the innovative financing plans with the most promise for low-income and minority students are the "guaranteed-access plans." Simply stated, such efforts guarantee that students will have access to a postsecondary education regardless of financial or other circumstances.

The idea for guaranteed access in its current form is credited to New York industrialist Eugene Lang, who, in a well-chronicled 1981 speech, promised a class of sixty inner-city sixth graders that he would pay for their college tuition if they finished high school. Lang's promise allowed these students and their families the security of knowing that he would pay the difference between the government grant aid they received and the cost of attendance at the institution at which they had been accepted. In addition, Lang established a community center in the neighborhood that served as a counseling and tutoring locus for these students.

Lang's success with this original class has been lauded. Some thirty-six of the original sixty students apparently have gone on to college. Of the remainder, nearly all have graduated from high school or received equivalency degrees. No doubt, educators and the media will follow the progress of these students for several more years.[7]

Not content to rest on his laurels, Lang established the I Have a Dream Foundation in New York, which encourages the establishment of guaranteed-access programs nationwide. With major centers now established in Dallas, Boston, Philadelphia, Washington, D.C., and other cities, the I Have a Dream Foundation has encouraged the "adoption" of some 125 sixth-grade classes. Sponsors are typically philanthropists, and not corporations, because of Lang's emphasis on mentoring and personal contact between benefactor and students. Churches and synagogues are also being encouraged to participate. According to Lang, an investment of approximately $3,000 per student when the child is in the sixth grade sufficiently covers the cost of support services and college tuitions.

Lang's successful experiment has also fostered other guaranteed-access efforts. New York governor Mario Cuomo proposed a program called Liberty Scholarships as part of his budget for fiscal year 1989. Cuomo's proposal sought to guarantee a college education to disadvantaged students while they were in, or entering, the seventh grade. Eligibility for the federal School Lunch Program, or an income of no greater than approximately 130 percent of the poverty level, would qualify students for a Liberty Scholarship. If the student successfully completed high school and was accepted to a state school, the scholarship would have guaranteed eligibility for an award equal to the difference between costs of attendance at that school and any federal or state grant assistance that the student received. Students entering private colleges would receive the same amount.

In July 1988, the New York legislature did create something called a Liberty Scholarship, but it was considerably different from Cuomo's original proposal. The new grant covers only nontuition expenses—including room, board, transportation, books, and supplies—for students from families with incomes up to $18,000. Although grant levels for New York's Tuition Assistance Program were increased to help cover tuition expenses, the early-intervention aspect of Cuomo's proposal and Lang's program is gone. State officials have estimated that the program will cost $70 million a year to operate. The program is scheduled to go into full operation in 1994, when an expected 94,000 scholarships will be awarded.

Other guaranteed access efforts have also been implemented. A few educational institutions have guaranteed full scholarships for students from local high schools with below-average graduation rates. Efforts involving local businesses and school systems are also under way. For example, the Action Center for Educational Services and Scholarships (ACCESS) in Boston provides counseling and financial assistance to hundreds of Boston public school graduates annually.

Although guaranteed access is really still in its infancy, its "human interest" aspects have generated considerable excitement, especially in urban areas. The extent to which access is actually "guaranteed" varies widely by program, however, and more research is needed on the extent and likely impact of these programs.

Community and Public Service Plans

Community and public service plans may be the most difficult to inventory accurately, because such programs are proliferating at a very rapid pace. Moreover, many of these programs, while important, do not apply directly to the issue of immediate concern here—namely, innovative financing. Nevertheless, it will be useful to clarify and review some of the better-known plans to give some sense of their relevance and levels of participation.

Campus-based community service programs appear to have gained considerable momentum in the past few years. One reason for this growth was the establishment in 1985 of Campus Compact, an alliance of college presidents that encourages the funding and support of student volunteer activities and community service projects. As of August 1988, there were 142 college presidents in Campus Compact, which is headquartered at Brown University.[8] Membership is split about 60-40 between private and public institutions. Annual dues are paid by member institutions, based on the size of the undergraduate student population.

Campus Compact appears to have made significant advances at some schools. Apparently, more than 40 percent of Yale undergraduates do some community service work, and upward of 60 percent of Harvard students now participate, nearly double the level of five years ago. Several Compact member schools, including the University of Southern California, Grinnell, and Dartmouth, offer fellowships that help to pay for living costs to students who do community service. And at least three institutions—Alverno College in Milwaukee, Berea College in Kentucky, and Mount St. Mary in Los Angeles—mandate public service as a requirement for graduation.

Students themselves have also taken steps to organize community service programs. An organization called Campus Outreach Opportunity League (COOL) is the largest and most successful of the student-based efforts. The group offers advice on establishing community service programs to students at more than 450 U.S. institutions and has seven full-time staff members, who act as recruiters for COOL and serve as consultants to schools seeking to establish or expand community service programs. Financed by philanthropic grants and assisted by participating institutions, COOL has regional offices in several states and a national headquarters at the University of Minnesota. So far, however, COOL has made no estimate of the number of students involved in community service.

Proposals from policymakers and others interested in national sponsorship of community service have become commonplace in the 1980s, but most operating plans focus on high school students, and not the postsecondary sector. For example, there are now more than forty state-based programs that encourage volunteer activity at the secondary level. In the last decade ten states—California, Connecticut, Delaware, Maryland, Minnesota, Montana, New Hampshire, New Jersey, North Carolina, and Vermont—have passed laws that require or encourage community service endeavors at the high school level.

Community service proposals at the postsecondary level have grown in number in the last few years. In the 1988 legislative session of Congress, at least nine bills supporting voluntary national service were introduced, including prominent plans from Representative John Porter of Illinois and Senators Barbara Mikulski of Maryland and Claiborne Pell of Rhode Island. Many of these proposed programs offer tuition benefits or other financial incentives to encourage participation, but such proposals have raised fears in some quarters that a national service plan might become a replacement for, rather than a supplement to, existing student aid programs.

Fears that service would replace aid were stimulated when the Democratic Leadership Council, a coalition of moderate Democratic politicians, released a report in 1988 proposing the creation of a Citizens Corps. The DLC proposal is one of the few that explicitly ties national service to student aid. Participants would receive vouchers that could be used to pay for college expenses or vocational training in exchange for one or two years of service at minimum wages. Over time, the vouchers would replace existing federal student aid programs by making service a requirement for educational assistance. Critics have noted that this would force students from low-income families to participate in the Citizens Corps, whereas those from middle- and upper-income backgrounds could avoid service.

Most programs that link financial assistance for education with public service usually put the requirements up front; that is, participants would perform their service before they enter school or while they are enrolled. Other programs, however, encourage service beyond graduation. For example, Harvard University Law School's Low Income Protection Plan pays off a graduate's loan obligations if he or she takes a low-paying public service job. According to the National Association for Public Interest Law, at least twelve other law schools offer comparable programs. Similar plans have been adopted at professional schools of medicine, dentistry, and business.

Conclusion

Innovative financing to help pay for higher education clearly has taken center stage in the last few years, as governments, institutions, philanthropic groups, and the private sector seek new ways to ease the burdens of rising college costs and other perceived deficiencies in higher-education financing. Innovation has taken on a variety of dimensions, from tuition savings and guarantees to alternative loan programs, guaranteed-access plans, and community and public service proposals.

Although tuition guarantees have seen diminishing support, particularly in light of the excitement they generated when first introduced, most innovative plans and proposals continue to command considerable public interest and support, especially savings programs and alternative loan schemes. Still, as the present inventory suggests, much of the detail of alternative programs remains obscure. State-level loan programs, a potentially important source of assistance, have not been accurately accounted for over time, nor have the multitudinous private-sector programs that offer savings options, tuition guarantees, loans, and other alternatives. Plans that encourage community or public service or that guarantee access—many of them still in their formative stages—have been studied only randomly. Particularly troubling is that in many cases the number of students or families that take advantage of these alternatives is unknown. Thus, developing a more complete picture of who takes advantage of financing alternatives, and analyzing what effects they may have on access, choice, persistence, and postgraduation decision making should be a high priority for further research.

Notes

1. Arthur M. Hauptman, *Financing Student Loans: The Search for Alternatives* (Washington, D.C.: College Entrance Examination Board, 1982).
2. Even when a person or organization exerts considerable energy on collecting

information, as the Education Commission of the States (ECS) has done in trying to keep up with the state-level savings, tuition prepayment, and guarantee plans, it sometimes takes a scorecard to keep track of the rapid pace of developments. See, for example, Aims McGuinness, Jr., and Jennifer Afton, *Survey of College Savings and Tuition Futures Plans* (Denver: ECS, July 1988).

3. Information on state plans was obtained from McGuinness and Afton, *Survey of Savings and Tuition Plans*; from conversations with ECS staff; and from Courtney Leatherman, "States Interest in Tuition Plans Grows: Focus Shifts Toward Savings Programs," *Chronicle of Higher Education*, September 14, 1988, p. 1.

4. The IRS made several points in its private letter ruling to Michigan on the tax status of its MET program. First, the investment by the purchaser is fully tax-exempt at the federal and state levels. Second, beneficiaries may have a minimal federal tax liability when the contract is redeemed, though state officials project that the total amount for an average beneficiary will fall below the minimum-tax threshold. However, the trust itself is taxable at the corporate rate, though again the state estimates a fairly low net liability because of corporate deductions. MET has applied for full tax exemption, based on its not-for-profit corporation status.

5. This estimate, made by the author, includes loans made to both undergraduate and graduate students. In some cases these loans are based on merit, such as loans made to outstanding math or science students. In other cases loans are used as an incentive for students to enter public-service-oriented jobs, such as teaching or health services. Tax-exempt bonds, state agency funds, and other sources are used to provide the loan capital.

6. This estimate is based on information provided by the National Association of College and University Business Officers and on other sources.

7. *Washington Post*, August 3, 1988, p. A18.

8. Kathryn Theus, "Campus-Based Community Service," *Change*, September-October 1988, pp. 27-38.

PART II

Choosing Among the New Financing Mechanisms

4

Developing a National College Savings Agenda

THEODORE L. BRACKEN

In its final hours, the 100th Congress passed the U.S. college savings bond legislation, giving the higher-education community and its supporters an unexpected opportunity to accelerate the development of a national agenda for precollege financing. To do this, educators and policymakers should build on the new legislation by creating a private nonprofit national education trust corporation that will serve as a central mechanism for supporting and advancing a national precollege saving system.

The new legislation is a landmark in itself. The college savings bonds it creates can become fully effective as part of a system of paying for higher education if the program is implemented with as much publicity and fanfare as higher education and the marketing arm of the U.S. Savings Bond Program Office can commit to the task. Public participation in the Michigan Education Trust and the Illinois bond programs has demonstrated that tax-favored savings vehicles for college are extremely appealing, and this aspect of the bond program should be sufficient to attract broad interest if the public is made more aware of the new legislation.

The new federal college saving program will face obstacles in marketing. The college saving program, like the existing Series EE savings bonds, will suffer from lack of public understanding about its variable rate of return and minimum guarantee provisions. Few know that since November 1982, U.S. savings bonds have paid a market-sensitive interest rate. Thus, a fresh

advertising campaign highlighting the value of tax-exempt saving for education should stress that savings bonds now compare favorably with other
investment alternatives.[1] It also would be desirable to differentiate college
savings bonds from other types by issuing distinctive certificates that highlight
their educational purpose. This would add to the administrative burden of the
program, however, and should be studied further.

Perhaps as important as the passage of the legislation itself is the possibility
of using it as a mandate for broader accomplishments. That is, in addition to
becoming an easily understood, trusted, and accessible college savings vehicle
for the general public, the new bond program could serve as a base on which
other state, institutional, and private options for educational finance could be
built, much as the Pell and Guaranteed Student Loan (GSL, or Stafford)
programs have provided a federal base in the grant and loan areas.

The first focus of this essay is a discussion of options that would facilitate
the operation of the new program. Next, the essay addresses, and attempts
to dispel, certain criticisms and misconceptions that may be holding back
development of a federal education savings agenda. Finally, the essay outlines
a more ambitious formulation of the savings idea, a national educational
savings trust.

Building on the U.S. Savings Bond Program

Options to enhance the operation of the federal savings bond program could
include savings stamp programs, shared partnerships, savings bonds as
awards for academic merit in the lower schools, and using bonds as compensation for education-related public service.

SAVING STAMP PROGRAMS

Included with the passage of the U.S. college savings bond program was
language in the conference report calling for a Treasury Department study of
the feasibility of implementing a savings stamp program that would become
another retailing option for the sale of college savings bonds. For many years,
the federal government sold savings stamps in small denominations (10, 25,
and 50 cents, and $1.00) to make it easier for individuals of modest means to
purchase U.S. savings bonds. During the patriotic period after World War II
this program was especially popular with elementary school children, who
would exchange their extra dimes and quarters for defense bond saving
stamps. Students could trade a full book of stamps for the appropriate
denomination of bond.

If the federal saving stamp program could be renewed, it not only would
make the U.S. college savings bond program more accessible to young people
but would provide private industry with the option of marketing the stamps

in low-cost ways to encourage college saving by consumers. The major infant- and child-care corporations are perhaps the most likely vendors or promoters of savings stamps, but commercial enterprises of all kinds could become involved.[2]

SHARED PARTNERSHIPS

For the new bond program to gain broad acceptance and use, it must convince prospective participants that they are not alone, that the program adheres to the tradition in the United States of shared partnerships among government, institutions, families, and the private sector. The federal government has done its part in sharing the burden of saving for college by providing a tax break in the savings bond legislation. Other parties must be challenged to do their part as well. State and local governments can become more directly involved by awarding college bonds to students who display exceptional academic promise or achievement, by aiding in the distribution of savings stamps, and by publicizing the availability of college savings bonds. Private industry can become involved by making use of payroll deduction programs, by offering matching-benefits programs, and by awarding savings bonds to academically promising students, particularly in economically and culturally depressed areas.[3]

Institutions of higher education must also accept the challenge of supporting college savings bonds by developing their own programmatic responses. For example, they could agree to exempt college savings bonds from the tax on assets for determining eligibility for financial aid.

SAVINGS BONDS AS AWARDS FOR MERIT IN THE LOWER SCHOOLS

A great deal of publicity has surrounded businessman-philanthropist Eugene Lang's astonishing commitment several years ago to an elementary school graduating class in his native Manhattan neighborhood and the subsequent I Have a Dream programs that his example has spawned in inner-city schools across the country. As Lang's experience has shown, putting lower-income students and their otherwise financially powerless parents in a position where their academic aspirations are raised during the years before high school years can have a dramatic effect on the likelihood that these students will go on to college or that they will be able to attend a more expensive alternative than they might otherwise have considered. The U.S. college savings bond program provides yet another vehicle for public-spirited private citizens and groups to become involved in these important new initiatives. For example, philanthropists could provide college savings bonds to students who passed certain mileposts, such as completing a grade or making certain kinds of academic progress.

In a related vein, on October 19, 1988, the Federal National Mortgage Association , better known as Fannie Mae, the federally chartered mortgage insurance corporation located in Washington, D.C., announced a new program that will set aside $500 per semester in a special account for each student at Washington's Woodson High School who receives all A's and B's. The money, which will be invested on behalf of the students to ensure a higher net reward, can be used only for college or vocational school tuition. Students with an all-A-and-B record in all eight semesters could earn up to $4,000 plus interest (about $4,500). College savings bonds could also be used in this way, particularly by smaller businesses that lack the financial resources of a Fannie Mae.

At the municipal level, the city of Washington, D.C., has been conducting a program for the past two years to award $1,000 to each of the District of Columbia's high school seniors who graduate in the top 10 percent of their class. The annual cost of this program is currently $550,000. A high school principal applauded the program, but observed that the awards should be given to high-achievers during the elementary and secondary school years, when such awards are likely to have a greater impact on students' future academic achievements than at the end of the academic cycle.[4] The U.S. college savings bond program would be ideally suited to provide such awards to young achievers, and local governments should be challenged to make such awards for academic and personal excellence.

These programs represent the kind of participation by private citizens, local governments, and corporations that can provide low-income families with access to precollege savings. Other options might include encouraging low-income families to participate in precollege financial planning via employers' matching payroll deductions or collective bargaining agreements that allot contributions to a college bond fund as a fringe benefit.

SAVINGS BONDS AND PUBLIC SERVICE

The concept of a national volunteer service has been discussed for many years, and during the 1988 elections the idea of tying college financial aid to national service surfaced in several different ways. Often mentioned in the context of service is the concept of developing tutoring and mentoring programs for academically underprivileged students, particularly in the inner cities. This kind of service, a critical element in the success of the I Have a Dream programs, could be further encouraged and supported via college savings bonds; that is, college-level students who tutored secondary school students in various settings could be compensated with college bonds. The cost of the bonds (generally one-half of the face value) could be met by a targeted federal program, by states and municipalities, or by institutions and private corporations. As an additional incentive for the recipients, bonds would not be treated as income for tax purposes unless they were redeemed for noneducational purposes. Tutors could use the bonds to help pay for their graduate education without either reporting them as income or paying a tax on any interest accrued as long as they fell under the established income limits.

An interesting twist in a bonds-as-payment scheme might be to allow recipients to hold the bonds for eventual use by their own children, at which time their taxability would be determined by the income-limit criterion. In this way, the reward to college students for tutoring underprivileged students from one generation could be passed on in the form of more educational opportunity for their own children in the next generation.

Precollege Saving: Misconceptions and Criticisms

As various models of savings plans have been debated by policy analysts and higher-education leaders, a number of misconceptions and criticisms have arisen about the feasibility of precollege savings. Many of these unnecessarily injure the idea of broadening the context of college savings and deserve some response.

One of the chronic and potentially dangerous misconceptions in the precollege savings debate is that savings plans are merely another form of financial aid. This is far from accurate. Traditional aid programs assist families when students are actually enrolling in college—when the relationship of financial assistance to the education being provided is immediate, the parents' earning power is well known, and the financial trade-offs a family will be expected to make are relatively easy to anticipate. Precollege saving, in contrast, poses a fundamentally different set of trade-offs for the family and requires a new set of techniques to get families involved.

So far, the various proposals that have been put forward for promoting precollege saving seem not to have considered that the traditional mechanisms for disseminating information about college financing are ill suited for savings plans—that is, for reaching the parents of younger children. This does not mean that precollege saving is impractical, but it does suggest that a fresh marketing approach must be found that recognizes how precollege saving differs from traditional aid if the idea is to be sold to the American public.

Another criticism of precollege savings programs is that they slight low-income families, because the poor are not in a position to save. Such arguments may be valid in a narrow sense, but they fail to consider the potential of a national precollege savings system to attract resources from beyond the primary family unit. College savings programs will always be more attractive to middle- and high-income families, who have the means and motivation to save for college. But many low-income families will be able to participate actively in saving for college and will reap benefits if corporations, foundations, and state and local governments can be encouraged to make precollege contributions and award bonds to promising students from families with limited financial means. The real issue, then, is not that the poor cannot save, but how a national savings bond program can be modified so that lower-income families will be able to gain access to funds that otherwise might be unavailable to them.

Can a college savings bond program allow people to save adequate sums to finance a college education? Both critics and proponents of such programs have made the assumption that it should, but this expectation is unrealistic.[5] Only a few affluent families could use a savings bond program to finance an entire college education in advance, and most of those families do not need a federal savings program in the first place. Yet if college savings plans cannot enable most families to put away enough funds, are they then of no consequence? The answer is no. Any precollege saving is important, not only for its economic utility in lessening a student's loan burden or lightening the burden of a family's current income but for its value in making children's academic aspirations a focus of the family's attention and planning. Moreover, properly understood, saving for college through bonds should be seen as a supplementary resource—as only one of many potential resources available to a family over the years.

All the misconceptions and criticisms of the college savings bond idea point to the need for the government and educators to effectively and clearly publicize and market the program and to establish systematic guidelines to inform and counsel families on what a realistic saving component in an educational finance plan should be. The success of the bond program will also require that traditional financial aid programs for financing higher education, including loans, remain available.

Beyond College Savings Bonds: A National Nonprofit Educational Savings Trust

With a federal college bond program in place that will encourage moderate-income families to save, and in anticipation that the program will be expanded to include other third-party participants, the next step would be to broaden and deepen the options available to families by creating a national educational savings trust corporation.[6] This trust would provide an additional flexibility that will be critical to the success of developing a national precollege saving mentality because the U.S. college savings bond program cannot be equally attractive to everyone. Many potential savers will anticipate being ineligible for the program's interest-forgiveness provisions because they anticipate that their incomes will eventually exceed the eligibility cap. Others may prefer a higher-risk investment return than the bond program is designed to accommodate, and some may be seeking an investment strategy not related directly to the rise and fall of five-year Treasury bills. There will also be families who, because they failed to begin saving early on in the child's preschool or elementary years, will find the savings bond plan inappropriate.

PURPOSES AND FUNCTIONS OF THE TRUST

The primary purpose of an educational savings trust corporation would be to focus public attention on the importance of early planning and preparation—both academic and financial—for college and to promote the development of a wide range of mechanisms (including those suggested above) that will attract financial resources from across the spectrum of American life.

This private nonprofit trust, in addition to serving as a retail sales outlet for U.S. college savings bonds and as a repository for the accumulation of bond assets, would also offer the public a variety of precollege investment products designed to supplement or serve as an alternative to college savings bonds. For example, the trust might offer a preferential self-collateralizing loan option tied to precollege savings that would minimize or eliminate the costs of insuring against default and qualify the borrower for a lower interest rate. It might also serve as a repository for private-sector academic achievement awards similar to the District of Columbia and Fannie Mae-Woodson High School programs. Another function might be to provide financial planning models to aid families in meeting their college financing goals, similar to what the Teachers Insurance and Annuity Association and College Retirement Equities Fund (TIAA/CREF) has recently embarked on to aid faculty members in retirement planning.

A nonprofit educational trust could serve a number of other functions as well. It could encourage and promote the development of private-sector and local government initiatives along the lines of the Lang, Fannie Mae, and D.C. government programs. It could provide a forum for colleges and universities, the need-analysis services, and the Congress to establish a rational system of precollege financing that works in concert with established aid programs. It could serve as a one-stop-shopping resource for precollege financial planning. And it could provide (with the necessary tax law changes) a tax-favored rollover option for families who have invested in U.S. college savings bonds and who anticipate that their earning will make them ineligible for part or all of the tax break when the bonds are to be used.

ORGANIZATION OF THE TRUST

In setting up the trust, the organizational model that would seem to make most sense is a hybrid that combines certain positive aspects of TIAA/CREF, the Common Fund, and the College Board—that is, a nonprofit quasi-independent corporation established and endorsed by colleges and universities that would serve as a central administrative system for the encouragement and enhancement of precollege financing. Like TIAA/CREF, which was organized by a group of education leaders and concerned citizens to provide a fair and universally available retirement program for college faculties, such an organization would be conceived in a benevolent spirit, funded initially by a foundation, and structured so that policy decisions could be controlled in large measure by the beneficiaries—the institutions and the participants.

Conclusion

The cost of sending children to college is, after the purchase of a home, the largest investment a family is likely to make in its lifetime. Should we not then have a college financing system that recognizes the magnitude of the cost by offering the American family an alternative to the current pay-as-you-go or borrow-as-you-must system?

We might begin to provide an answer to that question by developing a comprehensive national college financial planning system that seeks to make paying for college as familiar to the economic life of American families as retirement planning and home mortgage financing.

Central to the capacity of any national plan to assist families in preparing for college should be a recognition that its benefits will never become fully realized if it is seen as just another financial aid program. It is not a simple matter of offering more attractive economic incentives. To truly succeed, precollege savings plans must develop a mandate to raise the educational aspirations of young people, to enhance the family's early commitment to a student's course of study and academic performance, and to create partnerships among families, the private sector, and governments to reward academic achievement.

In brief, precollege saving, properly conceived and fully implemented, should be a process that has the power to encourage greater academic opportunity, intellectual achievement, community participation, and social responsibility.

Notes

1. The current return on U.S. savings bonds is 7.35 percent, which is equivalent to a marginal pretax return of 10.97 percent for a family in the 33 percent federal tax bracket and to 10.21 percent for those in the 28 percent bracket. Because U.S. savings bonds are already exempt from state and local taxes, the equivalent marginal pretax return can be as high as 13 percent for families where such state and local taxes will be levied on competing, fully taxable investment alternatives.

2. One of the more serious problems with the recently passed savings bond legislation is its failure to allow persons under the age of twenty-four to own bonds directly and benefit from the tax break. It is essential to the success of the program that young people be given the means (e.g., via savings stamps) to own college savings bonds outright and to remain eligible for the tax-forgiveness provision, as long as the parents continue to meet the income-limit standards. It is also

important that this provision be corrected if bonds are to be given directly to students by grandparents or other third parties.

3. There already exists under the auspices of the U.S. Savings Bond Program Office an organization of private sector chief executive officers called the U.S. Savings Bonds Volunteer Committee. This group should be challenged to accept the responsibility for the development of a nationwide corporate response to passage of the college bond legislation. Recently the nation's corporate and industrial leaders have been voicing their public concern with the academic preparedness of the American work force. The U.S. college savings bond program provides them with a new and unique opportunity to lend their support to the educational aspirations of the youth of this nation by committing corporate funds to college savings initiatives.

4. *Washington Post*, May 8, 1988, p. B1.

5. George Bush, then vice-president, made this mistake in 1988 when he announced his version of a U.S. college savings bond package. One of his examples included a case in which a family would have to set aside $140 a month ($1,680 per year) to enable their newborn child to attend a private college.

6. Such an enterprise should be entirely private, with no relationship to government. It would be particularly desirable if the organization could be established with the cooperation and endorsement of an umbrella organization such as the National Association of Student Financial Aid Administrators or the College Board, but this does not preclude a group of institutions from getting together, as some did in 1954 to form the College Scholarship Service (CSS), and agreeing to create such an enterprise in the public interest. The College Board and CSS have already begun to tackle the savings issue in their ongoing deliberations over the implications of the Sustained Annual Family Effort (SAFE) proposal. What seems missing from that debate is an appreciation of how fundamentally different precollege savings is from traditional aid and how important it is that a new structure be created to take on the challenge of "selling" American families on a new idea of how college should be financed.

5

Prepaying for Higher Education: Why It Works

RICHARD E. ANDERSON*

Parents, particularly those comfortably in the middle class, want to save for higher education. Yet few manage to save for all, or even most, of their children's college expenses.[1] The need for an effective college savings plan has triggered major political and commercial responses. Unfortunately, current college savings plans fall short of meeting family needs and making good public policy.

This essay addresses the current need for a good method of saving for college, by explaining why parents do not save for higher education and why a financial intermediary is necessary. Then, it proposes characteristics for a good higher-education savings plan and shows how existing and proposed savings plans do not meet them. Finally, it proposes forming a national nonprofit financial intermediary that would presell tuition.[2]

If implemented, the plan for preselling tuition would increase the rate of return to the average college saver, would be financially advantageous to colleges, would not cost public treasuries any money, and need not restrict college choice. The plan might even increase family savings rates—an

*The author is indebted to Peggy Heim and Teachers Insurance and Annuity Association and to Arthur Kalita and Morgan Guaranty Trust Company for providing access to their firms' libraries and data bases. Support for this analysis was provided by the Office of Educational Research and Improvement of the Department of Education (OERI/ED). The conclusions expressed herein are those of the author and not necessarily those of OERI/ED.

important change if America is going to have sufficient capital to replace public and private infrastructure.

Such promises sound like pipe dreams, but they are not. They can be achieved because a collective organization established by colleges and universities could invest with more financial savvy than parents. More important, if the organization assumes the financial risk that investment yield will keep pace with increasing tuitions, the investments can be structured in an advantageous manner that is essentially unavailable to the individual investor.

Institutional and state prepayment plans have been derided, often with good reason. College and university officials have favored instead some form of savings plan. Yet the investment vehicles that have been proposed generally offer parents a likely rate of return that would be unacceptable—indeed, too ridiculous to consider—for college and university endowments. If college officials really want to encourage families to prepare financially for higher education, they must create plans that raise the rates of return that families can expect, reduce the risk, or both. If they do not, most parents will continue to use their homes as their primary focus of savings.

Why Families Don't Save

It is fashionable to reprove Americans for their low savings rate.[3] But, as a nation, we are not very thrifty for two good reasons. First, many families do not need to save. Also, it is very difficult for retail savers (investors) to increase the value of savings after inflation and taxes. Those who would alter the patterns of family financial preparation for higher education must recognize the former and deal with the latter.

Why should families save?[4] Although some families save to pass wealth on to their children, most of us save to "smooth out" our standard of living. That is, we save so that in an emergency, such as loss of income or a major medical problem, we can generally maintain our life-style without selling our car or home. We also save for certain large planned needs. Retirement is the most significant of these, but higher education is also in this category.

Almost all traditional needs for saving have been assisted by government intervention, directly through legislation and indirectly through the tax system. For example, we and our employers must contribute to federally sponsored disability insurance and to the social security system. Almost all large employers have medical insurance and retirement plans that go well beyond social security. Most have life insurance plans. The benefits of these plans, except some retirement income, will never be taxed, and even the retirement plans have significant tax advantages. If we conclude that these plans are inadequate for our needs, we may supplement them with private insurance and supplemental retirement plans—both of which receive favorable tax treatment. In addition, many civil service employees and union workers are sheltered from loss of employment and thus have less need for a financial nest egg. With this array of subsidized income-smoothing plans, families are saving less, and their largest form of savings is in home equity.[5] Higher education, particularly the independent sector, is conspicuously alone in creating a need for savings for which there is an acknowledged public value yet no public inducement for private capital accumulation.[6]

Even under these circumstances, families will save for various needs, including higher education, but their savings rate will be linked to the prospective rate of return that the funds will earn and to the associated risk. That is, families will be more likely to put off the purchase of a car today and save for a later purchase if that thrift will allow them to purchase a better, or at least equivalent, car next year. But this is not easy to achieve. For many conservative savers the opposite occurs. Table 5.1 shows the historic rate of return to a variety of investments after inflation but before taxes. Although all of the rates of return are positive, it is clear that higher rates of return are generally achievable only by investing in riskier instruments. In relation to higher education, where the rise in costs generally has been about 2-3 percent above the rate of inflation, the table shows that only the returns on oil and gas, common stocks, and real estate are likely to exceed that rate of cost increases.

After taxes are paid, the historic return to all of the investments listed in Table 5.1—except tax-exempt bonds, of course—will be lower. For example, adjusting for the actual inflation rate of 3 percent of that period and assuming a marginal tax rate of 28 percent, the real rate of return to some of these investments is close to zero or even negative, as shown in Table 5.2. For taxpayers subject to a state income tax or to the federal 5 percent surtax, the yields will be even lower.[7] During periods of higher inflation, real after-tax returns may be lower still, as income taxes are assessed on nominal income.

Clearly, investment in debt instruments does not offer a very attractive return to a taxpaying saver. Moreover, the only savings vehicle in this table

TABLE 5.1   Annualized Return to Investments After Inflation, January 1926 to December 1987

Investment	Return (percent)
Oil and gas	8.0*
Common stocks	6.6
Real estate	4.0*
Long-term corporate bonds	1.9
Long-term government bonds	1.2
U.S. Treasury bills	0.4
Long-term tax-exempt debt	0.2**

Source: Ibbotson Associates except as noted.

*Estimate from Cambridge Associates.

**Estimate based on Standard & Poors data.

TABLE 5.2   Estimated Annualized Return to Investments After Inflation and Taxes, January 1926 to December 1987

INVESTMENT	RETURN (PERCENT)
Oil and gas	4.9*
Common stocks	3.9
Real estate	2.0*
Long-term corporate bonds	0.5
Long-term government bonds	0.0
U.S. Treasury bills	–0.6
Long-term tax-exempt debt	0.2**

NOTE: This table assumes a taxpayer in a 28 percent bracket and no tax advantages to any investment except tax-exempt bonds. This absence of tax advantage is obviously not the case for oil and gas, common stocks, and real estate. Consequently, the historic after-tax returns to those investments will be considerably higher. Finally, this table does not include transaction costs, which would lower all returns slightly.

Source: Ibbotson Associates except as noted.
*Estimate from Cambridge Associates.
**Estimate based on Standard & Poors data.

that carries no risk is Treasury bills, which have the lowest return.[8] A saver who paid 28 percent of investment income in taxes and who rolled over cash in T-bills would have lost 0.6 percent of general purchasing power every year and considerably more in relation to college costs. That does not seem like much, but—as money managers are fond of pointing out—with compounding, the return is quite significant.

With few reasons to invest in liquid assets and some considerable disincentive, it is not surprising that Americans save so little in standard financial assets and that their major capital investments are in their homes and in tax-sheltered pension and insurance plans. College officials can urge families to save until their throats are sore, but under such circumstances little is likely to change.

Or they can urge Congress to provide significant tax subsidies to college savers. In the current environment of large federal deficits, this is not likely to happen, and if it should happen, it would probably drain funds from needier students. Alternatively, college officials can acknowledge the real investment disadvantage that parents face and take positive steps toward meeting their needs.

Why a Financial Intermediary Would Help

Given the rates of return on easily accessible savings vehicles, why don't parents just invest their college savings in stocks and similar investments? This recommendation has some merit, particularly for families with significant savvy and a large amount of capital, but it is not reasonable guidance for middle-income families with limited funds and financial expertise. Most families who want to save for higher education have three hurdles to overcome: they cannot sufficiently diversify their investments, they cannot purchase the necessary expertise; and their investment horizon is too short.

It is important to understand each of these disadvantages as we ask families to save for higher education. First, small investors cannot sufficiently diversify their direct investments to protect against changing market conditions and "event" risks. Time limitations and transaction costs make it impossible. The apparent solution, investing in mutual funds, is not an adequate response. The saver must, of course, select a mutual fund. But last year's winners could be this year's losers. These investor-savers are inescapably buying a market philosophy and a management team. Yet managers can leave, and a philosophy that succeeded in one market period can fail in the next. Families could use more than one mutual fund, but, again, time and transaction costs generally make this impractical.

A second problem is that investors with $10,000 or even $100,000 are unlikely to have either the time or the expertise to monitor closely their own investments. They can buy advice, but as small investors, they must purchase it at "retail," whereas the market is moved, now more than ever, by "wholesalers." In essence, small investors simply cannot get investment clout.

Finally, there is the problem of the limited time horizon of college savers. Some diligent parents may labor to select good investments and to choose a well-managed mutual fund. Yet college savers will be systematically hobbled by their limited investment horizon. That is, even if they begin to save at the birth of a child, they must have the appreciated investment available when the child reaches college age. This is their most serious liability as investors. Table 5.1 shows that long-term returns to a variety of investments are positive. But these returns span a number of highly variable market cycles over sixty years, and college savers cannot count on evening out returns by spanning market cycles. Timing for them is critical.

A partial solution for families might be to shift investments as children approach college age. When children are young, the family might select a mutual fund that emphasizes capital appreciation. As the children grow older, the family could systematically shift investments to funds that emphasize capital preservation. Obviously this is a sophisticated strategy and not for the garden variety college saver. Moreover, the strategy necessarily will underperform a balanced portfolio that does not need to shift to capital preservation.

In sum, a typical family probably cannot save efficiently for higher education. That is why college savers need a financial intermediary that can diversify investments, tap the best investment advice available, and assume a long-term investment perspective. This is what life insurance companies and defined-benefit retirement plans do, and it is what a similarly effective intermediary for college savings could do.[9]

Characteristics of a Good College Savings Plan

A good college savings plan would offer families security for their funds, a reasonable rate of return, and unlimited college choice. From a policy perspective, the plan should operate with little or no subsidy. And, to the extent that there are risks, whoever assumes the risk should be appropriately rewarded.

Investment vehicles must be tailored to specific individuals and their needs. Spare money, for example, can be invested more aggressively than funds that are essential for some purpose. Families with a lot of resources will, and should, invest differently from those with limited funds. No college savings vehicle can be designed for all families. For purposes of discussion, it is assumed that a college savings plan should meet the needs of middle-income families with some extra cash (up to a few thousand dollars a year). It is further assumed that these funds, if they are saved, would constitute a large percentage of the families' investments outside of their home, pension contributions, and insurance. Finally, it is assumed that in the absence of these savings, the family income could not support broad college choice unless the family were willing to take on significant debt. In essence, preserving the purchasing power of these funds is essential.

We should not expect parents to save unless the rate of return is attractive. Generally, the prospective yield should be positive. But the greater the risk, the greater the return parents should expect. If these savings are earmarked for college, parents ought to consider the likely appreciation in relation to college costs. Fund growth should at least keep up with college costs. If there is risk that the funds may not keep pace with college cost increases, the prospective return should exceed that rate.

Of course, the funds should not be available for just one college or a small group of colleges. An investment vehicle that limits choice has considerably less value—educationally and financially—than one that does not.

Public officials considering the college savings issue face a policy dilemma. There is strong political support for higher-education savings, but a public policy that directs funds to those with the wherewithal to save will certainly be regressive: the ranks of college savers are likely to be heavily populated with upper-income families. Thus, officials should strive to create a plan that encourages saving but does not use tax dollars.

A year or two ago, a number of investment houses were proposing prepayment plans. What they all had in common was that colleges would assume the risks and the financial organization would earn a guaranteed profit. College officials resoundingly rejected these schemes. In general, colleges have opted for parents to assume both the risks and rewards of saving. Unfortunately, as suggested, the risk-reward equation is not an attractive one for parents. Colleges have an opportunity to assist parents in saving. Admittedly there are risks. To the extent that colleges assume those risks, they should benefit.

Present Proposals and Their Shortcomings

As substitutes for prepayment, two prominent plans are being developed to encourage college saving. One approach, using zero-coupon tax-exempt bonds, has been enacted in a dozen states. The other uses U.S. savings bonds, recently endowed with a tax advantage when used to pay college bills. Both plans have some strengths, primarily in their simplicity, but both have salient weaknesses that should be understood.

ZERO-COUPON TAX-EXEMPT BONDS

In response to parental concern about skyrocketing tuitions, state officials have been looking for a savings vehicle with a tax advantage for families. Of the state options, only tax-exempt debt clearly provides a federal tax advantage. Investment bankers, sensing a profit to be made, have pointed out that these bonds paid about 8 percent interest in 1988, when inflation was only at about 5 percent. Moreover, states can modify tax-exempt bonds for college savings by issuing them in zero-coupon form and by eliminating the call feature.[10] Illinois, which has taken the lead in this type of college savings, has also added a small extra interest subsidy if the bond proceeds are used to pay the costs of attending an in-state college.

Zero-coupon municipal bonds are simple and have an undeniable appeal. But they do not fit all the criteria for a good savings plan. Their most serious shortcoming is that families are assuming a significant risk, probably without realizing it. Although long-term tax-exempt bonds currently are paying a real return (interest less inflation) of 2-3 percent, this is a financial anomaly that reflects, among other things, concern in the financial markets that inflation will return.[11]

Tax-exempt money market funds, which invest in short-term tax-exempt notes, avoiding interest rate risk, pay only about 5 percent interest. The prospects for inflation are, of course, unclear. Future inflation may be in the 2-3 percent range. In that case, families who purchase the bonds today will have made a very profitable investment. On the other hand, if Congress and the next administration were to accept, if not embrace, policies that bring about protracted double-digit inflation, the college savings of these families could be significantly eroded.[12]

An additional problem is that for many families, the purchase of "college" tax-exempt bonds is not part of a balanced portfolio. It is, indeed, a gamble that this type of state-sponsored program will be appropriate for them. This shortcoming could be essentially eliminated by issuing the bonds in a variable-rate format, but this would significantly complicate the bond issue, and parents would be less likely to understand it. Moreover, the lower interest rate would undoubtedly reduce the attractiveness of, and participation in, the program.

Finally, although bonds like those sold in Illinois offer an 0.2 percent interest subsidy, it is only available if the beneficiary attends an in-state institution. In effect, for those who purchase these bonds, there will be an increased price differential for attending an out-of-state college.

U.S. SAVINGS BONDS

Series EE savings bonds pay holders a rate of return equal to the greater of 85 percent of the three-year moving average of five-year Treasury bonds or a floor percentage (currently 6 percent). Bondholders may defer taxes until the bonds are redeemed. The 1988 technical corrections to the Tax Reform Act of 1986 have liberalized the tax treatment by eliminating all tax liability for many families who use these bonds to finance college costs. (The availability of this benefit is being phased out for bondholders with incomes between $60,000 and $80,000.) Again, simplicity is a major strength of this plan. Moreover, unlike the state bonds, there would be no disincentive for attending an out-of-state college, and because interest paid on these bonds is variable, purchasers assume no interest rate risk.

CHART 5.1

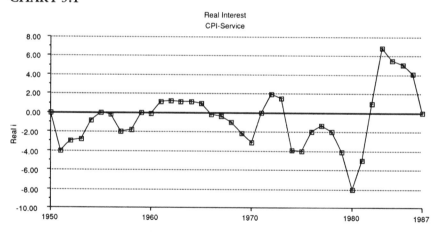

The primary shortcoming of these savings bonds is that the prospective rate of return is very modest. Chart 5.1 graphs a yield equivalent to 85 percent of the rate paid by five-year Treasury bonds and indexes this yield against the Consumer Price Index Services deflator from 1950 to 1987. Only for brief periods has 85 percent of the rate of return to five-year Treasury bonds exceeded this inflation index. This suggests that even with special tax allowances, funds invested in EE bonds are likely to lose significant ground to college costs.[13] And, of course, the tax advantage is never available to upper-income savers.

In the current financial environment, bonds seem to be a reasonably attractive college savings vehicle. But the current environment of high real interest rates is an anomaly. High real interest rates increase the expense of replacing plant and equipment, dragging down the economy. Moreover, when real interest rates exceed national growth, as they do now, the burden of U.S. foreign debt grows ever larger and further diminishes our living standards. A major policy initiative—indeed a mandate—for our national leadership should be to increase savings and reduce real interest costs. When that occurs, the apparent advantage of using debt for college savings will quickly evaporate.

A Proposal for a National Nonprofit Agency to Presell Tuitions

A satisfactory college savings plan, this essay argues, will have five characteristics. The saved funds will be secure. The funds will appreciate as fast as college costs. College choice will not be limited. There will be no, or very little, public subsidy for middle- and upper-middle-income savers. And, whoever bears the investment risk will stand to earn a commensurate return.

PROBLEMS OF DESIGN

College costs, like other service costs, are expected to increase at about 2-3 percentage points above inflation. If the return to college savings is to match this rate of escalation, the investment vehicles must be more robust than the general array of debt instruments. Table 5.1 shows that at least some of these funds will have to be invested in oil and gas, common stocks, real estate, or some other similarly risky vehicle.

As suggested, there are very real structural reasons why most families are not in a position to assume these risks. What is required is a collective financial intermediary that can presell college education for the benefit of both families and colleges. As soon as the term "tuition prepayment" is mentioned, higher-education officials begin to think about Duquesne University and the state plans and about the flaws inherent in both. Public college officials are undoubtedly worried about extravagant public financial promises.[14] Private college officials are concerned about interstate attendance barriers. But these flaws are not inherent in the concept of tuition prepayment, only in the execution. Just as retirement plans need not lock employees into a firm and need not be financially unsound (although many do and some are), a well-crafted prepaid tuition fund can be created for the mutual benefit of colleges and families.

A NATIONAL COLLEGE FUND

A higher-education consortium, investing for college savers, can overcome each of the inherent investment disadvantages that families face. A well-conceived college fund could be investing hundreds of millions, perhaps billions, of dollars. Such a pool of money could be diversified easily. Because the proposed fund would be run for and by colleges, it would gain immediate access to the very best investment advice available, and probably without charge.[15] Marketing costs for this organization would likely be modest because of its connection with colleges and universities. And without a need to provide profits, costs could be further trimmed.

How Would It Work? A nonprofit fund should be initiated by a group of institutions prestigious enough to be credible and few enough in number to be a manageable collective. These "core" institutions would set administrative and investment policies. The purpose of the fund would be to serve all of higher education and all college savers. The fund would enter into contracts with the core colleges and with any other college that wanted to presell its tuition to families.

Families would purchase tuition certificates denominated in dollars for sale (e.g., $1,000, $2,000, and so on) and in the tuition charges of all participating institutions for redemption. A $4,000 certificate, for example, might be worth ten semester credits at a high-priced independent college or fifty semester credits at a moderately priced public college. The certificates could also be denominated in graduate tuitions. The family need not choose a college when it purchases certificates.[16]

When a prospective student applies to college, the application process will be unaffected. If the student selects a participating college, the certificates will cover the same credits that they did when purchased—no more, no fewer. The college bursars will accept the certificates and redeem them for their appreciated value from the fund, just as if they were redeeming shares from a mutual fund. If the fund has earned a rate of return that most college endowments have historically achieved, the certificates will be worth somewhat more than prevailing tuition charges. If, either because of market conditions or a failure of management, the investments have not kept up with tuition charges, the college will receive less than current tuition charges. The college thus assumes the risk. But, if sixty years of market history are any guide, the fund will almost certainly produce a gain over the long term.

All the gain produced by the plan may not be "available" to colleges and universities, because some allowance for potential taxes needs to be made. In addition, many colleges probably will want to return some of this gain to the savers. Institutions, for example, might first set up a reserve account. When the reserve reaches a comfortable level, excess "tuition fund revenues" can be distributed proportionately to all savers, to savers with need, or to any needy students. If all participating institutions pledged to implement such a progressive policy for distributing gains, the Treasury and Congress would undoubtedly be more open to a favorable tax policy on these plans. Certainly families should find such a policy of sharing gain very appealing and would be more likely to participate.

If students choose to attend a nonparticipating college, the family will receive a refund that includes capital appreciation calculated in such a manner that the refund will neither drain the fund nor place participating institutions at a competitive disadvantage with nonparticipating institutions.[17] There should probably be some loss of appreciation if the family decides to use the funds for something other than higher education.

WHY SHOULD FAMILIES PARTICIPATE? Obviously, not all families should participate. Families with a large amount of capital, some investment sophistication, and a long-range investment horizon might be better off investing on their own. Families that believe there is a significant likelihood that their children will not seek higher education probably should not participate either. But parents with a modest amount of capital should find that the plan meets the characteristics presumed to be important to college savers. The funds are secure and, in contrast to other "safe" investments, appreciate as fast as college costs. Finally, there are no limitations on college attendance.

WHY SHOULD COLLEGES PARTICIPATE? The motivation for institutions to participate in the plan varies by institutional type. Because affordability is a more salient issue at private institutions, these colleges and universities will naturally have more interest than low-tuition public colleges. Institutions with a thin applicant pool should see more advantage in the plan than colleges where applicants greatly outnumber matriculants. The probability of success, however, increases dramatically if the fund is supported by the leading independent colleges and universities. This section reviews why these institutions should be willing to assume leadership or, at least, to explore the possibilities very carefully. The advantages to these institutions are both general public service and future benefits.

Most institutions engage in a variety of public service activities. These services range from agricultural extension to economic development, to cultural enrichment. Typically these services are synergistic activities that not only support the region, state, or nation but also provide institutional enrichment. Assisting families to save for higher education could be this type of effort. During a period when a growing proportion of the public seems to think that the most expensive colleges and universities are beyond their financial reach, an effective savings plan initiated by those in higher education could be an important part of a campaign to blunt criticisms of uncontrolled costs.[18]

Certainly there are limits to institutional ability to finance public service activities. In this case, the effort should be costless and might even produce modest excess revenue. Admittedly, this advantage is modest, and there is a financial risk. If the plan is structured as outlined here, the financial advantages should exceed the dangers by a modest but predictable margin. In the broadest terms, this can be understood by thinking about this fund as an extension of an institution's endowment. If the fund is managed in the way common to most college endowments, it will earn 5-6 percent above inflation after investment expenses—say, 5.5 percent. If college costs rise at 2.5 percent above inflation and families pay the sales costs, the net long-term annual gain to participating colleges and universities should be about 3 percent. The long-term benefit of this spread can be significant. Under these investment and cost assumptions, tuition prepaid for a newborn should be worth 70 percent more to the institution than tuition paid in cash eighteen years later.[19]

Even if these institutions currently have more than enough qualified applicants, this favorable ratio is not guaranteed. The U.S. economy faces very serious challenges with severely limited policy options. Upper-middle-class affluence could erode in the coming decades and, with it, the primary support of the expensive colleges and universities.[20] More-immediate threats to the applicant pool of these institutions are the state savings and prepayment plans, which tend to discourage out-of-state attendance. Of course, U.S. savings bonds, with their added tax advantage for college attendance, may undercut the political need for state plans. But, again, these bonds cannot promise to keep up with college costs and will be considerably less attractive to upper-income families because they will not receive any tax advantage from these bonds.

WHAT IS THE EFFECT OF TAXES? A financial intermediary should be created to presell tuition because it makes good financial sense. A tuition fund can invest these savings more efficiently than parents. There may or may not be tax advantages. Certainly the letter ruling on the Michigan Education Trust (MET) is not encouraging. But this determination by the Treasury Department does not have the weight of law and should not be taken as such. Treasury ruled that the student was liable to pay a tax on the increase in value of tuition. This does not disable the concept. Of more concern is the determination that the MET can be taxed on its earnings. This ruling almost certainly will be tested in court. Moreover, it is unclear whether this potential liability is based on gross earnings or on earnings after contingent liabilities are estimated.

In this era of behemoth deficits, the Treasury will part with revenue very reluctantly. A plan that accumulates capital for future college expenses cannot expect to shelter those funds entirely from taxes. But, unless the ultimate tax on this plan is confiscatory, families will be better off, because the underlying financial base is more sound.

The notion of prepaying college expenses is clearly radical, and the tax law is ambiguous. Consequently, it may be more instructive to consider a theoretical tax assessment. That is, if we apply a standard annual tax rate of 28 percent to all nominal income (real plus inflation), what do the numbers look like? Assuming that college costs increase at 7.5 percent per year and that the fund earns 10.5 percent per year, a 28 percent tax reduces the nominal return to 7.56 percent. That is, the plan just breaks even. But the spread of investment income over cost increases can be improved by raising sales charges, imposing cash-out provisions, or providing public or private subsidies.

The point is that the advantages of a college savings financial intermediary seem to be large enough that a plan that is close to revenue-neutral to the Treasury could be created. If such a plan were established, a political bargain could be struck that was satisfactory to savers, to colleges and universities, and to the Treasury. Recall that both U.S. savings bonds and Illinois tax-exempt bonds include subsidies. Despite these subsidies, both plans pose more risk for families *and* offer rates of return that are considerably lower—by about 2 percent per year—than prospective increases in college costs.

Conclusion

The future security and prosperity of the free world does *not* depend on the creation of a fair and efficient college savings plan for the middle class. Colleges and universities are involved in helping to solve any number of far more serious problems. Nevertheless, there are very few issues for which the solution creates advantages on all sides. Building a nonprofit financial intermediary to power family savings for higher education may be just that— a "win-win" opportunity.

Perhaps colleges should not act. We may assume that demand for our institutions will continue unabated. Even though a larger percentage of the population believes that attendance at the best private colleges is out of their reach, we may expect that politicians will not attempt to interfere in pricing decisions, as they have with medical services. Similarly, we may plan that others will have to subsidize family savings for college expenses. But these are dangerous suppositions. Alternatively, we can take the type of collective action proposed here to assist families in preparing to finance the education of their children and, at least partially, to demonstrate that increases in college costs are manageable.

Certainly there are many questions that will require study and analysis. The first step is to study the merits and prospective market acceptance of this type of plan relative to the newly proposed savings plans. In addition, we need to analyze thoroughly the possible administrative problems and potential extra advantages. One example of an extra advantage is that there may be an arbitrage opportunity to use funds that parents save to capitalize student or institutional debt.

This proposal is complicated. But imagine how complex the proposals for health insurance or retirement plans must have seemed when they were first introduced. The public knows that paying for higher education is a problem. Politicians understand the public's concern. Those of us concerned with the future of higher education should confront the issue and resolve it before it is taken out of our hands.

Notes

1. See *A National Study on Parental Savings for Their Children's Higher Education Expenses* (Washington, D.C.: National Institute of Independent Colleges and Universities, 1984).
2. For the sake of simplicity, this essay considers only the presale of tuition, both undergraduate and graduate. Colleges could also sell room-and-board contracts.
3. The answer to how much families save depends on how saving is defined. A few issues are clear, however: (1) Americans save considerably less than their counterparts in other developed nations; (2) they save relatively less than their parents saved; and (3) they save in different forms, putting more money into their homes and less into retail financial instruments. It is this last form of savings that most families consider "available" to pay the costs of higher education. See Patrick H. Hendershott, ed., *The Level and Composition of Household Savings* (Cambridge, Mass.: Ballinger, 1985).
4. This discussion was taken from an article by the author, "Tuition Prepurchase Plans," *Change* (March-April 1987).
5. Table 5.2 offers evidence that housing is one of the more efficient form of savings available to the middle class.
6. Families who send their children to public institutions of higher education receive significant public subsidy, which, of course, is not taxed. Part of this subsidy can be considered a return of the families' own tax payments—a forced savings program that, because the payments are deductible from federal taxes, brings some tax advantage.
7. After tax-reform transition rules, the marginal federal tax for married taxpayers filing jointly with net taxable incomes between approximately $30,000 and $72,000 will be 28 percent. For taxpayers with taxable incomes between $72,000 and $149,000, the rate will be 33 percent.
8. Investors in corporate debt run the risk that the firms will default as well as an interest rate risk. The risk to long-term government bonds is assumed to be primarily interest rate risk; that is, if savers purchase a long-term bond just before a protracted upward shift in inflation, their real return is likely to be negative. Of course, if they purchase before a drop in inflation, interest rates are likely to come down, and they could profit handsomely.
9. The intermediary could be a commercial organization, and several firms are trying to develop these plans. If this were a different era, they probably would succeed. In the current fiscal environment, however, these organizations face two very significant obstacles. First, this type of plan requires enormous capital. And, in a period when investors with a spare $100 million can initiate an unfriendly takeover and earn 30 percent on the investment from "greenmail," the margins

on a college savings enterprise probably are not great enough. Second, the tax issue is very problematic, and the Treasury, understandably, is being less than helpful. If, however, a nonprofit plan were capitalized with the "commitment" of colleges and universities, as is suggested in the argument below, the tax issue probably could be resolved amicably.

10. Bonds issued in zero-coupon form do not pay periodic interest. Instead, the purchaser pays considerably less than the face value of the bond. The price is set so that the amount of appreciation provides an equivalent return to a bond sold at face value with interest reinvested. A call option on bonds allows the issuer to call in the bonds and pay off the bondholders if interest rates fall.

11. Tax-exempt money market funds, which invest in short-term tax-exempt notes, avoiding interest rate risk, pay only about 5 percent interest.

12. A number of knowledgeable observers assert that high inflation is one of the few politically acceptable ways that the nation can crawl out from under its almost trillion-dollar debt. Benjamin M. Friedman, a Wall Street economist who is now a professor at Harvard, makes this argument in *Day of Reckoning* (New York: Random House, 1988), p. 106.

13. The floor interest rate increases the prospective rate of return, but it is difficult to calculate by how much. Moreover, the Treasury Department changes this floor from time to time to reflect changing market conditions. The restriction that the tax subsidy is lost if the proceeds are not used for college costs reduces the rate of return by some inestimable amount.

14. The original Michigan plan was premised on a rate of return that would have been difficult to achieve under current financial assumptions.

15. The fund, of course, would pay for investment management. But very talented trustees who serve without pay could undoubtedly be recruited to help set policy and oversee the management.

16. Although the family would not preselect a college for application, it might designate several colleges of interest and a tuition accumulation goal. The fund would periodically report to the family how much tuition has been purchased and progress toward the accumulation goal.

17. The redemption might be the lesser of (1) the actual appreciated value of the prepaid funds or (2) the amount the funds would have appreciated to if they had grown as fast as the average tuition of the participating colleges. In either case, a small administrative fee would be deducted.

18. Expensive private colleges and universities should not underestimate the political threat to their operation. Former Secretary of Education William Bennett voiced popular discontent with college costs, and the 1986 Tax Reform Act may have put teeth in it. The $150 million tax-exempt bond cap will cost the largest private universities millions of dollars in added interest costs. Of more concern is the fact that all bonds issued by private colleges are no longer considered "public purpose debt." At least for the time being, these bonds are excluded from state uniform volume caps, but there is no guarantee what the pressures of deficit reduction will bring.

19. Potential total gains and risks will be considerably smaller because not all families will prepay, and few will prepay the full amount when a child is very young.

20. Robert E. Litan, Robert Z. Lawrence, and Charles L. Schultze, eds., *American Living Standards* (Washington, D.C.: Brookings Institution, 1988).

6

Issues of Equity in College Savings

SANDY BAUM*

Saving for college is clearly a good thing. The recent trend toward encouraging parents and students to think of college as an investment that must be paid for over time, rather than as a pay-as-you-go experience that lasts for one or two or four years, is long overdue. It is apparent that the higher education system as we know it cannot survive for long if this view does not become widely shared. Furthermore, all public or private organizations interested in promoting higher-education opportunity—educational institutions, state legislatures, banks involved in the student loan industry, guarantee agencies, the federal government, and nonprofit educational organizations—can fruitfully become involved in the movement toward encouraging savings for college.

Although savings plans from many sources may have merit, not all plans deserve unconditional support. Some programs may expend public funds without encouraging significant savings. Some actually may limit the educational opportunities of the children of people who participate in them, either by generating profits for the institutions that sponsor them or by restricting the schools at which savings may be used. And some may divert public or institutional funds away from students who are most in need of them toward middle-class students whose families have been able to participate in savings plans.

*This essay is based on comments presented to the National Forum of the College Board, Washington, D.C., November 1988.

93

Achieving Vertical and Horizontal Equity

For policymakers trying to choose from among savings plans, an important objective should be to design or select plans that genuinely encourage savings and that embody a basic fairness in the way their benefits are distributed. It is easiest to look at the fairness of public policies through the categories of vertical and horizontal equity. Achieving vertical equity requires different treatment of people in different economic circumstances. For example, people with low incomes would be given greater subsidies to finance higher education than would people with higher incomes. Achieving horizontal equity requires equal treatment of people in similar circumstances. In other words, families with similar incomes should have access to similar subsidies, regardless of the choices they make about how to manage their personal finances.

A discussion of vertical equity in educational policy should begin with programs designed to increase educational opportunity. Such policies can be directed at different constituencies and will have different effects on each. At the bottom rung of the economic ladder are many young people who do not complete high school or who do not receive adequate elementary and secondary educations. Although it will take a lot more than dollars to solve their problems, significant funding from the federal education budget can have great benefits for such students in the vital early levels of education. In addition, these youth also need focused assistance when they are about to enter the labor market. Many prospective young workers need further education, either formally or through on-the-job training, and most need financial support to attain that education. Here, then, is a way in which education dollars can be spent fruitfully if the intention is to help the "truly needy."

Further up the ladder of economic and educational achievement, about 40 percent of undergraduates are enrolled in public or private institutions whose programs run two years or less. Most attend public community colleges, but some attend private for-profit schools, and a few attend private not-for-profit institutions. Almost half of these students finance their educations through some combination of financial aid and their own contributions—without any parental assistance.

It is well known that students in two-year and vocational institutions tend to come from families with significantly lower incomes and with weaker educational backgrounds than do students at four-year colleges and universities. Limited economic opportunities explain why most of these students have chosen brief programs: they may have limited resources to pay for college; they may need to contribute to the support of a family, or their lower socioeconomic backgrounds may have generated lower educational aspirations. Many two-year and vocational students would receive no postsecondary education if financial aid were not available. Such students typically are reluctant to borrow to finance their educations and frequently have the most difficulty repaying the loans they do take. They are, then, an important constituency in need of public funds to ensure and improve their educational opportunities. And they are not likely to benefit much from family participation in the type of long-term savings plans currently being proposed and implemented.

Finally, there is the population at whom savings plans are primarily targeted—young people from middle- and upper-middle-income families who attend four-year colleges and universities. Faced with declining real federal aid to college students, increasing diversion of federal aid dollars to students in two-year and vocational schools, and skyrocketing college costs, this subset of the college population now bears a much heavier burden. In the last decade, tuition at public four-year colleges has risen an average of 141 percent, and at private four-year colleges it has gone up 191 percent. Median family income has risen only about 70 percent in this same period.[1] Clearly, families are having greater difficulty in financing their children's educations. Presently, only a few of the wealthiest families can hope to do so out of current income. Thus, savings plans have become imperative.

Savings Plans and the Middle Class

Given the increasing relative and absolute burdens on middle-income families, the question is not whether we should encourage middle-income families to save but *how* we should encourage their saving and, in particular, whether we should use public funds to encourage their saving. Plans or proposals for savings have been developed already at the state and federal levels. For example, several states have implemented college savings plans that depend on tax-free bonds and that sometimes involve the payment of bonuses to families that use the bonds to finance higher education at an in-state institution. Tuition-guarantee plans such as the one developed in Michigan also are essentially efforts to encourage parents to save for college.[2]

At the federal level, recent legislation has exempted from taxation interest earned on government savings bonds by families with incomes of $60,000 or less if the proceeds are used to finance higher education.[3] Another proposal for a federal role in educational savings is for a plan resembling an Individual Retirement Account (IRA). This plan would allow families to save pretax income, thus deferring, diminishing, or eliminating tax obligations on the money saved and used to finance college education.

All of these proposed and legislated savings plans involve a public subsidy of savings. This means that they will increase the effective rate of return to savings for participants by increasing the government budget deficit.

A critical question concerns the effectiveness of such plans. Will they really increase the level of savings of the families involved or will they merely divert funds from other forms of saving? Economists disagree on how sensitive savings patterns are to changes in the rate of return. Until recently, the consensus was that small changes in the rate of return made virtually no difference in how much people saved. The belief was that although a higher rate of return makes saving a dollar more lucrative, it also makes it possible to accumulate a given amount of wealth by saving fewer dollars. Empirical evidence seemed to suggest that in practice these effects pretty much canceled each other out, leaving no measurable change in the savings rate. For example, economists found that the insertion of the IRA provision in the federal tax code led many people to change the form in which they saved, but not to save more.

Recently, new evidence has undermined the consensus that small changes in rates of return make no difference in savings rates.[4] A 1987 study by the National Bureau of Economic Research, for example, suggested that the vast majority of IRA saving does represent new saving and is not accompanied by a reduction in the growth of other financial assets.[5] The study indicated that as many as 14 percent of families with incomes between $20,000 and $30,000, and 20 percent of those with incomes between $30,000 and $40,000, contributed to IRAs in 1983.[6] The new evidence on IRAs clearly implies that middle-income families can be encouraged to increase their net saving for retirement through public subsidies. But the evidence also shows that half of the IRA contributors had incomes over $40,000 a year and that almost 30 percent had incomes over $50,000. In other words, at least half of the subsidy went to high-income families, who are likely to have other assets as well.

By analogy with the IRA studies, we can conclude that public subsidies for educational savings might well encourage net increases in middle- and upper-income saving for college. But we must recognize as well that much of the public subsidy in such a program probably would go to families that could hardly be defined as needy. Perhaps, however, a well-publicized but unsubsidized program—involving payroll deductions or other regular payments, for example—would boost saving for education just as much as a subsidized program. If subsidies were not disbursed to the middle and upper classes, public funds could be spent on closing the gap in educational opportunity for the truly needy (although we have no guarantee they will not be spent on tax cuts, Star Wars, or pork-barrel projects).

It is also important to recognize the regressive nature of subsidies accomplished through tax exemptions. Because of the progressive income tax structure, families in higher tax brackets receive a larger dollar subsidy for any given amount of tax-exempt income. That is, if a family with an income of $55,000 a year buys the same tax exempt-bond as a family with an income of $15,000 a year, the tax exemption will cut the higher-income family's tax bill by a larger amount than it will cut the lower-income family's bill.

This distributional aspect of subsidized savings plans is critical. Families that will be able to participate in these savings programs may well save more than they otherwise would. Of course, some savings plans have been carefully designed to encourage lower-income families to participate. A plan discussed in Massachusetts, for example, proposes the sale of college bonds in denominations as small as $50 to allow a wide variety of savers to participate. Still, the benefit clearly will go primarily to families who are not "truly needy."

It is certainly possible to argue that it is worth some public expenditure to encourage middle-income families to save, because these families will then be less dependent on financial aid, and financial aid dollars can be focused on less-privileged families. On the other hand, the amount of savings that would have to be generated (and the level of subsidy that would be required to generate that new savings) to make the middle class comfortable about their ability to finance high-cost educations without assistance is probably far above any reasonable expectations for the types of programs currently envisioned. Moreover, as long as college costs put a strain on middle- and upper-middle-class pocketbooks, these groups will continue to exert their considerable political pressure to gain relief.

Those for whom paying for college is most difficult are least likely to be aware of savings plans and least likely to participate. Their financial resources are so limited that even if they do participate in the proposed plans, they will be able to save only nominal amounts. These people are also significantly less politically vocal than the middle class. But they are the groups who should be the main focus of public programs for increasing educational opportunity and for whom paying for college seems most out of reach. Thus, if public subsidies for savers divert funds from aid for these people, then they are hard to justify.

In light of these considerations, it would seem logical that every effort should be made to encourage all families who can possibly save for college to do so, but that this encouragement must be provided with the lowest possible expenditure of public and institutional funds. Although the discussion here has focused on public money, institutional funds should be included in this statement because of concern about savings plans that would guarantee tuition costs at participating institutions. Although a plan that promises a family that if it saves a certain number of dollars a year, it will definitely have what it needs to pay for college has obvious appeal, it also has potentially serious side effects. If colleges are forced to accept lower tuition payments from students whose families have participated in savings plans, they may be forced to raise tuitions for those who do not have the privilege of such a guarantee. And although some students who have not participated in plans will be wealthy enough to have no need for the plans and no real vulnerability to increased tuitions, most nonparticipants will be those who lacked the foresight or the financial wherewithal to get involved. The problem is that someone has to pay. If participating parents are guaranteed that their burden will be limited, then the government and the taxpayers—or the schools and the other tuition-payers—must bear the burden.

Recommendations

Despite the problems with subsidized savings plans, developing programs to help families save for college should remain high on the policy agenda. Encouraging saving reinforces the important social values of planning ahead, of parental responsibility for children, and of the priority of education. But it also vital to the fairness of our financial aid system. The strongest arguments in this direction are based on considerations of horizontal equity.

Two major types of horizontal inequity exist in our current financial aid system. Both discourage families from saving for college. One horizontal inequity stems from the historical premise of the need-analysis system that families should be accepted as they are. In other words, if two families with equal incomes come to the need analysis with different asset levels, the family with lower assets is eligible for more financial aid. There is some logic to this system, because people who have inherited money or benefited from housing booms obviously have greater capacity to pay than do those who have not been so fortunate. The problem is that families that have limited their consumption to save for college are expected to make greater contributions than those that have had exactly the same opportunities but have chosen to live more extravagantly.

The College Scholarship Service (CSS), through its Committee on Standards of Ability to Pay, is currently attempting to revise its guidelines for need analysis to incorporate savings expectations and to minimize this horizontal inequity. The main idea of the Sustained Annual Family Effort (SAFE) program that CSS is devising is to convince families that they can, and should, save and that they have to expect to pay for college over, say, a twelve-year period rather than out of current income. Their family contribution will be based on *expected* savings rather than on actual savings. In other words, families with similar long-term incomes would have the same family contribution, whether they had lived extravagantly or frugally.

A second major horizontal inequity in the current aid system is the imbalance in the way it treats saving and borrowing. Families that choose to borrow to finance college educations are currently subsidized—but only if they transfer the burden to their children—through the Guaranteed Student Loan (GSL, now the Stafford Student Loan) program. If society is indifferent about whether families save or borrow, subsidies should be equal. If we prefer that families save, as seems implicit in the current rash of savings plans, then certainly the existing system is ill conceived, and either the subsidy for borrowing should be reduced or a national plan for subsidizing savings should be implemented.

This problem is considerably complicated by intergenerational considerations. We want to encourage parents to save, but we do not want to penalize the children of parents who fail to do so. We provide financial aid based on the economic circumstances of the family at the time just before college, but the subsidies involved in borrowing go largely to students after they finish college, when their incomes are not always closely related to their parents' incomes.

Another thing to guard against is exaggerating the benefits of saving over borrowing. We can get a clearer view of the choice between the two by understanding borrowing as postponed saving. Different family circumstances will result in different optimal choices about the timing of saving to pay for higher education. The current financial aid system is too heavily weighted toward borrowing. But we need not end up with a system that carries heavy penalties for postponing savings until after college, when many families may be at the peak of their earnings profiles, may have paid off their mortgages, and no longer have dependent children to support.

Efforts toward encouraging saving are in the right direction and should be increased. The ideas of trying to make contact with families several years before the children are ready to start college and of keeping them informed of how much they will need to save each year to pay for college (or to meet their family contribution levels) are vital. It is reasonable to believe that many families will be encouraged to save if they have these guidelines and incentives. A specific savings plan that involves payroll deductions or some other form of required monthly contribution could be an important component of a plan to encourage savings. It is not at all clear that adding a subsidy to the plan is necessary.

In sum, everyone involved in the college financing issue should work toward providing more information to families with young children about how they can save for college and about what will be expected of them in the coming years. Setting up savings plans is also very important. We should be wary, however, of plans that involve significant funding. The difficulties of middle-class families should not divert our attention from the plight of those less well off, those who cannot even think of saving for college. Every effort should be made to help middle- and upper-middle-income families without diminishing the funds available for the people who need them most. A variety of savings plans will be required to solve the growing problem of college financing for middle- and upper-middle-income families. Public and private educational and financial institutions all have a role to play. But that role should be a cautious one, limiting the losses of low-income families with children aspiring to college and protecting the savings and the educational opportunities of more-privileged families that participate in the plans and of those that choose to save through independent channels.

In one sense, the savings programs now being proposed and implemented are a step in the right direction, because the current policies for subsidizing postsecondary students are too heavily weighted toward subsidized borrowing. Focusing some of our attention on encouraging saving before college—and perhaps diminishing the subsidy associated with providing access to funds for those who need to borrow—has the potential to redress the horizontal inequity of subsidizing those who do not save.

But without minimizing the seriousness of existing horizontal inequities and of the financial squeeze on the middle class, it is important to understand that savings programs do have the potential for creating substantial vertical inequity. Federal policy toward higher education traditionally has been directed toward assuring access to postsecondary education for students from families with low incomes. Future efforts must continue in this direction at the same time that they ease the burden imposed on the middle class by rapidly rising college costs.

Notes

1. Based on a 1988 report of the College Board cited in Gary Putka, "Benefit of B.A. Is Greater than Ever," *Wall Street Journal*, August 17, 1988, p. 23.
2. A detailed discussion of state-sponsored college savings plans appears in Courtney Leatherman, "States' Interest in Tuition Plans Grows; Focus Shifts Towards Savings Programs," *Chronicle of Higher Education*, September 14, 1988. See also Chapter 13 of this volume.
3. This law was a provision of the 1988 technical changes to the 1986 Tax Code (H.R. 4333 and S. 2238).
4. See Lawrence H. Summers, "Issues in National Savings Policy," in Martin Feldstein,ed., *Savings and Capital Formation* (Chicago: University of Chicago Press, 1988), for an accessible discussion of economists' views on the subject of the interest sensitivity of savings rates.
5. Steven F. Venti and David A. Wise, *Have IRA's Increased U.S. Saving? Evidence from Consumer Expenditure Surveys*, NBER Working Paper no. 2217 (Cambridge, Mass.: National Bureau of Economic Research, 1987).
6. This can be compared with 7 percent of those with incomes between $10,000 and $20,000, and with 58 percent of those with incomes over $100,000.

7

New Varieties of Student Loans

MARTIN KRAMER

This essay argues that the case for a monolithic student loan program is far weaker than often is assumed and that the case for multiple loan programs is much stronger.

In this era of proliferating financial instruments, student loans have remained a remarkably standardized product. Guaranteed Student Loans (GSLs; now officially called Stafford Student Loans) compose almost 90 percent of all student loans made, and they differ very little from each other in terms, subsidization, or servicing. They do not differ at all by type of educational institution or kind of student, except that upperclassmen and graduate students may borrow more.

The main reason GSLs have dominated the market is that only these loans qualify for a unique package of guarantees and subsidies offered by the federal government. Loans that do not meet these specifications have a hard time competing with ones that do. Moreover, even where the GSL statute and regulations allow lenders to vary the terms of a loan, borrowers can refuse to accept these variations, and they cannot be denied a standard loan for doing so. Thus, the ingenuity that lenders might display in attaching special or innovative features to new kinds of student loans in exchange for nonstandard costs, limits, or risks is effectively frustrated.

Financial innovation does occur in lending in excess of the amounts allowed by statute for GSLs. Mainly, this has been an area for private colleges to exercise their ingenuity. Because their tuitions often are so high, many private colleges now provide loans in addition to the credit provided by the

GSL program. However, these supplemental and often exotic programs may not represent what families in general want in the way of credit for college.

Because the GSL program occupies such a dominant place in educational credit today, any discussion of innovations in educational lending must take that program and its features as a point of reference. Innovations, then, can be thought of as having any of three purposes:

1. improving the structure of the GSL program;

2. replacing the GSL program altogether; and

3. providing ancillary credit vehicles that would exist alongside the basic GSL program (with or without the guarantee and subsidy advantages of GSLs).

Improving the GSL Program

Possible improvements in the GSL program can be thought of as involving administrative reform or policy redirection. Administrative changes would seek to make the program less costly and more efficient. Redirection of policy would entail defining more precisely a set of purposes in the financing of postsecondary education and then modifying program mechanisms to do these jobs better.

Some might argue that an agenda of administrative reform could be carried out more easily than one of policy redirection. This is not the case. A list of desirable changes in program administration that could be accomplished without policy redirection is a short one. First, the government could reduce interest subsidies to a minimum that would allow students a constant and predictable interest rate while providing lenders with an acceptable yield that varies with market conditions. But if movement in this direction went much further than it has already, it would raise basic policy questions about using interest subsidies at all as a vehicle for subsidizing educational costs.

Second, the largely mechanical and often redundant roles of colleges, commercial lenders, state guarantee agencies, secondary market agencies, and the U.S. Department of Education could be consolidated to provide student borrowers with something like one-stop shopping. However, such reforms might be limited by the interest that students and taxpayers have in promoting competition among originating lenders, secondary market agencies, and loan service organizations as a way to get better rates and services.

Third, current regulations could be modified to address the worrisome default rate. Current rules demand that lenders and loan-servicing organizations work through checklists of steps in originating and servicing a loan to make a loan eligible for a claim under the federal-state guarantee against default. Lenders could be forced to tighten up origination reviews before the government guarantee was granted, or students could be given an incentive to make timely payments by, for example, a quarter percent increase in the interest rate if the borrower missed two payments. Student loan paper then might be regarded genuinely as a full-faith-and-credit obligation of the federal government. This, in turn, might allow the federal government to reduce the subsidies it now pays lenders to induce them to participate in the program.

No doubt other administrative reforms could be added to the three noted above, but the list would still remain a short one. That is because many of the troublesome administrative features of the program really are tied—as program apologists maintain—to its mission. That mission has not been clearly and explicitly redefined since 1965, when the program began as loans of convenience for mainly middle-income families. Subsequently, the program came to be used heavily by private college students at all but the highest income levels, by proprietary school students, and even by low-income students attending public institutions.

The students using GSLs thus are in financial situations that are very different not only from each other but from what the program planners originally anticipated. Accordingly, the implicit mission of the existing program can only be specified in terms that apply to all participants. These goals are (1) inducing commercial lenders to make loans to students without regard to the creditworthiness of individual students or their families, (2) assuring the availability of such loans without regard to the kind of institution attended or the stage in the student's postsecondary career, and (3) reducing the repayment burdens of student borrowers by subsidies that reduce or eliminate the compounding of interest until the student is available for full-time employment and ready to begin repayments.

If these three common denominators are the specifications for the kind of student loan program we want, there is simply not much room for administrative reforms that will hold down subsidy and default costs or improve the match between student needs and program features. It would not be consistent with these specifications to provide colleges, students, and lenders with powerful incentives to make the program work better, or to impose sweeping limitations on which colleges, students, and lenders may participate. Doing these things would jeopardize one or more of the objectives of the program, and important groups of lenders or borrowers would be squeezed out or would opt out.

But is this kind of monolithic program what anyone really wants? Apart from a rather abstract egalitarianism, there is not much to be said for a program that attempts to do all things for all students. It is not even clear that the common-denominator specifications noted above serve those students who would seem to have most to gain if all students were treated alike. Such individuals would presumably be first-year students from low-income families with little creditworthiness who also happen not to have very good academic or career prospects. Surely, these students would usually consider themselves better off if they could take their share of interest subsidies as grants that do not have to be paid back if their educational programs do not work out. Why should they care that the federal government has guaranteed their access to credit in exactly the same way as M.B.A. candidates at highly selective universities?

Actually, those who stand to gain from a monolithic loan program are not students at all. Some institutions stand to gain—chiefly proprietary schools that award little student financial aid of their own and are highly dependent on publicly financed aid to maintain paying enrollments. Commercial lenders also have a stake, to the extent that the GSL subsidies make student loans more profitable than alternative investments. Finally, the current program serves those who must cope with the problem of the federal budget and who find their task made easier by an off-budget source of funds for student aid.

But if there really is no student need for a uniform loan program meeting the listed mission specifications, then there is no reason not to think about very sweeping redirection and reform. Interest subsidies could be reduced or eliminated, even the "special allowance" subsidies that make more or less GSLs fixed-rate loans to students and variable-rate loans to lenders. The "cashed out" subsidies could be reallocated to grant programs, where they would be very useful. Eligibility to borrow could be limited to students in their second and subsequent years of postsecondary education. Students then would not be expected to borrow until they could see where education was likely to take them.

These two reforms alone—reducing subsidies and altering eligibility to borrow—could reduce federal subsidy and default costs substantially. They would probably also reduce greatly the number of GSL borrowers, a result that would require attention to increasing alternative forms and sources of student aid.

Replacing GSL

Targeted reforms within the GSL program have not received nearly as much attention as proposals to replace the program altogether. This is probably because of the practical constraints on changing the existing program very much if it is to remain an off-budget source of almost universally accessible loans to postsecondary students. Most economists and policy analysts have accepted—have shared—the goal of a universally accessible program. Indeed, they often seem to wish that loans would become so easy to get and to repay that loans could take the place of all other financing for higher education, whether by parent contributions, the public, student earnings, or grant programs. This view conflicts with a reform agenda that would get rid of the awkward and unattractive features of the GSL program—the costs and the perverse incentives—by shrinking the program and relying more on noncredit financing. To those who favor a universal program, it is also unattractive to make the use of credit a more precise reflection of different student circumstances by having a family of subprograms. They tend to find the multiple-program structure of the existing student aid system already much too cluttered, and thus they would argue against adding a variety of new loan programs.

Most proposals to replace the GSL program altogether usually encompass some set of the following objectives: (1) making student loans automatically available without tests of creditworthiness or limits on the amount of borrowing, (2) avoiding costly dependence on commercial lenders as originators of loans or providers of capital, (3) providing a highly reliable and relatively painless mechanism for collecting loan repayments, and (4) placing the ultimate burden of financing postsecondary education on the individuals (the students) who benefit from it.

There are difficulties for this replacement agenda that are technical and political, but it is perfectly consistent and feasible in principle. The GSL program already provides essentially universal access to educational credit, limited in amount only by politically imposed ceilings. A national student loan bank certainly could be created to obtain capital from the federal Treasury and to disburse it directly or indirectly to borrowers, thus bypassing commercial lenders. The Internal Revenue Service certainly could collect repayments as the agent of either a national student loan bank or the social security system, if a payroll tax were preferred to standard installment credit or an income tax. Payments could be spread over the borrower's working life, minimizing the repayment burden in any year. A tax calculated as the product of the amount borrowed and a proportion of income would assure that those who obtained education and its benefits would be those who would pay for it, rather than the public at large. In principle, subsidies to higher education could be ended altogether.

The technical problems of such a scheme are formidable but not insuperable. There would have to be ways of verifying the educational use of the credit provided. The experience of the GSL program shows that this can be exceedingly difficult. The disbursement of funds, whether directly by a national student loan bank or through intermediaries, could be tricky. So could the budget treatment of Treasury advances to the program. Finally, the formula for assessing a borrower's annual repayment installment would be difficult to devise. It would involve a choice about how heavily to weight cumulative borrowings and how heavily to weight income and what income measure to use. (For example, should the system count only "earned" income or all income?) There would have to be some way of dealing with cases of long-term withdrawal from the labor market.

There is no reason to despair of finding solutions to these technical problems if the public and its political representatives really want such a program. But do they? The idea of financing much or most of higher education through the Treasury is itself an almost insuperable obstacle at a time when the federal budget deficit has reached an unprecedented level and has become a political issue in its own right. Further, the people and the politicians are only too aware of how far things can go wrong in enormous systems of federal disbursement and assessment. And, most important, there seems very little desire to do away with all kinds of public subsidy of higher education, or even with all kinds of public subsidies in the form of grants.

Of course, the agenda for replacing the current GSL program need not be taken as monolithic. It would be possible, for example, to have a student loan bank and still have limits on borrowing or a family of subprograms. It still would be possible to use the IRS as a collection agent for a more modest program. But is any part of this agenda for replacing the GSL program altogether very attractive unless one believes that students can, and should, borrow a larger share of their costs of education than they do now? That is what the replacement agenda would gear up to make possible. If, instead, one believes that dependence on credit should shrink rather than expand, one is less likely to be enthusiastic about such sweeping changes. The kinds of mechanisms proposed would seem administrative overkill if, for example, relatively few students were allowed substantial borrowings.

GSL as an Umbrella Program

It is probably a mistake to use the license granted by setting aside the mission specifications of the present program *only* to think about how the program could be modified across the board and made less costly. It should also be a license to consider how an array of subprograms, differing considerably from one another, could be constructed under the GSL umbrella. We should think about loan programs that do not purport to deal with the needs of all students alike but that deal variously with different situations and leave some needs to be met by other forms of student financial aid altogether—by grants, for example.

At least four obviously useful subprograms are possible. First, a program of loans could be devised that were limited to a percentage of cost of attendance, so that such a loan could become a standard self-help component of student aid packages. Colleges and universities might require such a loan as a precondition of receiving other aid. If these loans were small individually, as they probably should be, it might be most appropriate for colleges to originate the loans, batch them, and sell batches to secondary market institutions without involving commercial lenders as originators. It would be appropriate to continue the GSL tradition of applying no tests of credit-worthiness to such loans, but it is hard to see why interest subsidies would be called for if the loans were small individually.

A second subprogram of loans under the GSL umbrella could comprise loans to students contemplating a large accumulation of debt to finance attendance at professional schools. In lieu of the usual tests of creditworthiness, certification that the student was progressing in a satisfactory way toward qualifications to practice the profession might be required of the school. A long grace period and a repayment period of twenty years or more might be standard, with or without making each year's repayment a percentage of adjusted gross income as reported to the IRS on 1040 forms.

Yet another subprogram of loans could be available to undergraduates facing high tuition charges, either at private colleges or at out-of-state public institutions. It might be appropriate to require parents to cosign these loans, except where the institution itself agreed to do so. A fifteen- or twenty-year repayment period probably would be appropriate, but an elaborate scheme tying repayment installments to income probably would not be necessary. A repayment schedule requiring installments in the first five years of half the amount of installments in subsequent years would deal adequately with problems of excessive loan service burdens for most of these students.

Finally, a program of hardship and emergency loans could offset parental contributions that failed to materialize, earnings not available as a resource because of disability, or other crises. The aim of the program would be to prevent unusual or unanticipated circumstances from frustrating the student's educational career. The institution attended could be called on to certify such circumstances in lieu of tests of creditworthiness.

It is not hard to imagine additions to this list. The point here is not to be exhaustive but to suggest that the GSL program might become a family of subprograms, each having a defined purpose and each representing a precise policy decision about appropriate uses and conditions of credit.

Unless the GSL program or a replacement is so subsidized as to give it an effective monopoly on providing credit for college expenses, there will be some room, small or large, for other credit programs to exist alongside it. It is one of the advantages of reducing the eligibility for subsidies that the amount of such room will be increased. It is in this "space" that we can expect innovation and sensitivity to the changing realities of student and family situations.

Something that is needed as an integral part of all of these possible programs—and of the GSL program for that matter—is an arrangement to deal with the possibility that very low income will make repayments excessively burdensome. Existing and commonly proposed arrangements fail to deal with exactly this problem. The GSL program cancels loans in cases of total disability, but there are some former students, even graduates, who do not earn normal incomes, even though they could not pass the usual kinds of test for total disability.

It is on the basis of this need that advocates of income-contingent loan schemes—using a national student loan bank or similar administrative structure—seem to be on their strongest ground. But these schemes are not exclusively and precisely focused on the problem of catastrophically low income. They have as their ideal a formula under which borrowers make repayments proportional to income at *all* income levels, except perhaps the very lowest and the very highest. This is because they share common ground with those who advocate loan-forgiveness programs for teachers and others in relatively less well paid professions. That is, they want to reduce differences in after-loan-service incomes generally. The idea, however, of other student borrowers (rather than all citizens or all taxpayers) shouldering a burden of "correcting" compensation patterns among the professions is not an idea that really stands up to much examination. It has the wrong people paying for social changes the labor market does not think much of. Besides, the members of the low-paid professions do not really need a full-fledged income-contingent loan plan to make their repayment burdens manageable. At typical present cumulative borrowing levels and incomes, almost all of them could manage repayment fairly comfortably if repayments in the first five years were scheduled at half of those for a further ten-year period (as suggested before for students attending high-priced private colleges). Or they could manage if repayments were proportional to income, but there was no mutualization of the risk of relatively low income and there was an extension of the repayment period (as advocated by the Reagan administration).

The real problem of catastrophically low income does not call for a full-fledged income-contingent loan or national student loan bank scheme, and the problem need not be attached to an agenda of changing compensation patterns for the professions. The problem really arises only for a narrow band of cases between the totally disabled and the struggling employed. Sometimes the problem in these cases results from labor market conditions, sometimes from family responsibilities, sometimes from geographic immobility. Other cases probably represent what is really disability, but could not pass the ordinary tests: the effects of drugs, delinquency, or a rejection of financial independence as a personal goal.

Whatever the problems in this band of cases, there will continue to be hardship and defaults in student loan programs until something is done about them. The most plausible solution is the most focused solution. That would be a program of insurance against the risk of income so low that it would rarely be wholly voluntary. (In the case of loans to students at professional schools, the risk should be of income very low for a person qualified in the profession in question.) If such an insurance program were instituted along with other measures to reduce hardship and defaults, valid claims would be few. Measures such as substituting grants for loans to high-risk first-year students and halving repayments in the first five years would probably hold claims to a level that would permit financing the scheme through a modest addition to the insurance premiums now charged borrowers. If the premium were low enough, it would not seem very unfair to require it as a condition of obtaining a loan, largely avoiding the risk of adverse selection that haunts the full-fledged income-contingent loan proposals.

The most undeveloped area of educational credit is loans to parents. The federal program guaranteeing loans to parents (Parental Loans for Undergraduate Students, or PLUS, loans) differs from that guaranteeing loans to students only in the ceilings on amounts borrowed (higher), interest rates (also higher), and the time until repayment must ordinarily begin (much sooner).

Otherwise, loans to parents are treated as an almost indistinguishable variety of loans to students.

There is considerable irony here. The original GSL program was clearly intended to benefit parents, allowing low-interest credit to substitute for expected parental contributions from current resources. Indeed, many parents have considered their children's loans as their own moral obligation, even if the legal obligation was the child's. Before interest rates on student loans became so very advantageous in the late 1970s, 10-15 percent of GSLs were paid off in full at the time students were expected to begin payments, indicating that someone—surely, most often the parents—took responsibility for the loans. If the GSL program, or an advantageous component of it, had been addressed directly to parents from the beginning, many of the problems now plaguing the program might have been much reduced—especially defaults and the difficulty of tracing defaulting borrowers. Now that new ways to tap parental resources to meet college expenses are being discussed widely—especially savings plans and prepaid tuition—loans to parents clearly deserve another look as well.

A long list of features could be grafted onto parent loans to make them fairer or more attractive. Among them are the following: (1) mixed parent-student loans (for example, loans for which the parents would be responsible during the first ten years of repayments, and the offspring, thereafter); (2) loans to parents tied to the prevailing need-analysis system so that, for example, the parents' annual repayment installment would equal one-tenth the expected parental contribution that would be assessed for a child still in college; (3) a choice from among repayment periods of various lengths so that parents could plan to amortize loans taken out for their offspring over the whole period until they, the parents, expect to retire; (4) subsidization of parent's home equity loans to make them equally advantageous with GSLs to students; and (5) life insurance and unemployment insurance.

Any of these suggestions would be controversial if seriously proposed. The second one, for example, would share many of the advantages and problems of income-contingent loans to students. All of them raise issues of equity, both among income groups and among generations. But such issues have not been avoided so much as ignored in the ten-year slide toward greater and greater dependence on GSLs to students for the financing of education. They should not be avoided or ignored in framing alternatives that would bring back parental responsibility by subsidizing savings or prepayment of tuition.

8

Philanthropy, the Public School, and the University: The "Albany Dreamers" Program as a Model for At-Risk Youth

ROBERT H. KOFF

As educators, we usually talk about programs or policies as they affect large numbers of students. We work to improve education for "children at risk" or "inner-city sixth-graders," and we see a composite picture when we evaluate success or failure.

But sometimes a program's potential is more easily grasped in terms of its effects on a single student. Consider, for example, Aristides Alvarado. In 1981, Aristides and some of his friends were sitting, half-asleep, in the back row at their sixth-grade graduation ceremonies at P.S. 121, an East Harlem elementary school in New York City. The guest speaker, a former student at the school, was praising education and the idea of "pulling yourself up by your bootstraps." They had heard it all before. In their school system barely twenty-five of every hundred sixth-graders graduate from high school, so Aristides and his friends were not impressed with Horatio Alger stories—even though the speaker, Eugene Lang, truly personified the self-made man.

But suddenly, through the buzz of background noise and his own drifting thoughts, Aristides caught some words that galvanized him. He sat up and poked his friends: "What did he say?"

Lang had thrown away his notes and was making a startling, spur-of-the-moment offer: "Stay in school, get your high school diploma, and I'll pay your college tuition."

The Evolution of a Dream

What was the fate of Eugene Lang's generous impulse? Lang was quick to realize that the inspiration of a guaranteed college education probably would not be sufficient to overcome the endemic poverty, one-parent homes, peer pressure, and behavioral and social problems that face the children of East Harlem. As a businessman, Lang perceived that making good on his investment would commit him not only to paying college costs for sixty-one children but to ensuring that they acquired the necessary skills and attitudes to make it through high school.

To supplement his own personal commitment of money and time, Lang hired a full-time coordinator to work with the children and their families. Through trial and error, Lang and his assistant learned the value of approaching each child as an individual and of coping with a gamut of difficulties that could affect gains in academic performance. They learned how to listen, how to assist children with problems, and how to help them learn inside and outside of school. They also sought to make sure the children connected with the network of social services available to them so that they would not fall between the cracks of various bureaucracies.[1]

Lang sought from the beginning to involve the students' families. Although the families of East Harlem did not respond strongly to his efforts, Lang was able to broaden the students' horizons by taking them to museums, to the theater, to the library, and even to his place of business so that they could see a world different from their own. He worked at creating a new ethos among the students—one that would help students learn from, and support, one another and that would strengthen their capacity to resist social, economic, and personal pressures to drop out of school.

Educators, journalists, and the world at large gradually became aware of Lang's New York City program, and their attention was riveted by the reduced dropout rate for Lang's class. Lang became possessed by his spur-of-the-moment offer. He established the I Have a Dream (IHAD) Foundation—drawing on the famous phrase and vision of Dr. Martin Luther King, Jr.—to encourage others to become sponsors. The spin-off programs also require sponsors to work closely with the students from the time a program begins until the students complete college. In fact, Lang conceives of the responsibility of a sponsor as a lifetime commitment.

The results of Lang's unique personal involvement were startling. As of 1988, of the original sixty-one students at P.S. 121, fifty-four were still in the program. Only one student had not graduated from high school, and thirty-six had enrolled in college, including one at Harvard, one at Swarthmore, and one at Renssalaer Polytechnic Institute (RPI). Lang expects that eventually two-thirds of his students will earn college degrees. But in addition to serving a single class of East Harlem students, Lang's impulsive gesture in 1981 has been a beginning for an estimated 1,000 other children who are now part of I Have a Dream programs around the country.

Individual sponsorships have not been the only products of Lang's initiative: Lang's example has helped launch and give substantive direction to the innovative Liberty Scholarship program in New York State, signed into law in 1988 by Governor Mario Cuomo. This legislation, which goes into effect in 1991-1992, gives all New York State students who meet financial qualifications and who graduate from high school an entitlement similar to the promise made by Eugene Lang. All basic college costs (tuition, room, board, and books) will be covered if students attend a public New York State institution of higher education. The equivalent amount of public tuition can go to a private in-state institution of higher education. Furthermore, the legislation establishes Liberty Partnerships, an out-of-school tutorial and mentoring program similar to the one that proved so instrumental to Lang's endeavor. The mentoring component, funded at up to $10 million, is scheduled to begin in spring 1989. The program as a whole ultimately will serve some thirty thousand students and will cost about $90 million.

As for Aristides Alvarado, he is now a sophomore at RPI, in Troy, New York—a college that accepts from the top 7 percent of high school graduates nationwide. Last winter Aristides spoke about his experience to a group of ninety-eight sixth-graders and their parents at the Arbor Hill Elementary School in Albany, New York. First, he bragged to them: "Me and Eugene," he said, holding up two tightly bonded fingers, "we're like that." Then he warned them: "Don't do drugs. Stay in school." In a sense, Eugene Lang's words had come full circle. The children listening to Aristides had heard a sponsor tell them just minutes before, "Stay in school, get your high school diploma, and I'll pay your college tuition."

The Albany Dreamers Program: A Collaborative Effort

The school in Albany whose class Aristides Alvarado addressed is part of an I Have a Dream program administered by the School of Education of the State University of New York at Albany. The School of Education plays a vital role in the program by offering administrative expertise and by planning enrichment activities for the children. It is the fiscal agent for the program, handling all financial matters, including fringe benefits for employees and liability insurance. Faculty and program staff, in cooperation with school district teachers, conduct diagnostic testing, arrange for tutoring, take students on field trips, and teach at computer camps.

Moreover, the School of Education is conducting a ten-year research study to document and publicize the program's impact. Its faculty, in cooperation with school district teachers, monitors student academic performance, maintains individual student performance records, and tracks all services the students and families receive from state agencies and the project.

This program is one of a number of initiatives—both public and private—that sends a strong message to schoolchildren that they are valued and that we value education. But with these initiatives come new challenges. It is vital, then, to examine these programs as they evolve from impulse to systematic policy, to help us refine this model for educating students at risk.

ORIGINS AND PRINCIPLES

The initiative for the Albany Dreamers program came from E. Richard and Janet Yulman, residents of the Albany area who wanted, in their words, "to return, in a sense, some of the opportunities we have enjoyed." They not only committed considerable time and resources to the project but also selected the State University of New York at Albany's School of Education as its administrator, thus beginning a unique partnership.

It was clear from the outset that the project required the university and the school district to forge a strong, working partnership that would build on their history of cooperation. A memorandum of agreement developed in meetings between both parties described the effort as "collaborative" and established three guiding principles: (1) The needs of each individual student would determine the types of activities and interventions to be employed. (2) Sensitivity to parents' needs and concerns would be of paramount importance; not only would parental activity be required for participation in project-sponsored activities but parents would be invited and encouraged to be involved as much as possible. (3) All aspects of the project would be conducted in accordance with the policies of nondiscrimination approved by both the university and the school district.[2]

It was the Yulmans' wish to sponsor the entire sixth-grade class of Arbor Hill Elementary School. Although many I Have a Dream programs begin in June, at sixth-grade graduation, the Yulmans wanted to give the Arbor Hill students a slight head start. Accordingly, the program was begun on January 14, 1988—the day before Martin Luther King, Jr.'s birthday.

COORDINATION OF EFFORT AND RESPONSIBILITY

Months of planning, negotiation, study, and consultation made it clear that money alone—important as it is—could not assure the success of a group of children at risk. Indeed, research shows that well-intentioned intervention often exacerbates the problems it seeks to erase.[3] Moreover, even when school districts have dealt with the problems of dropouts and underachievement through highly specialized programs, the effects have often been "recuperative" and have not addressed "the origins or conditions of academic failure, alienation or teen pregnancy."[4] The Albany partnership thus had a special responsibility to ensure that the project would be fortified by appropriate planning and a clear focus on the needs of each participating child.

To ensure that the goals of the program were met, it was structured to include professional administration by a director and case management by a program coordinator and assistant coordinator working with university faculty and administration.[5] An advisory board, with members from different state and county agencies, was formed, and a parents' steering committee was asked to help with communication matters and to provide input to teachers and staff. Outreach to parents also includes potluck dinners and programs to help parents strengthen their own literacy skills.

Much planning went into addressing potential ramifications before the program was in place. For example, which children would qualify to participate in the enrichment activities? How should transfer students be handled? What research should be undertaken? These and dozens of other questions were thrashed out in collaborative sessions, resulting in question-and-answer documents that spelled out the program in straightforward detail.[6]

In addition, the program depended on specific contributions from each of its partners.

THE UNIVERSITY. One of the university's primary contributions was to the principles and structure of the program. In general, the university sought to support out-of-school learning, to coordinate services offered by a variety of agencies to prevent children from "falling between the cracks" and to avoid duplication of services, to coordinate with parents, to monitor student performance and assist children and parents in planning, and to coordinate with the public school system.

School of Education faculty were particularly concerned to create a program that would wisely "invest" the resources being made available by addressing the totality of a child's experience. That is, it would not be sufficient to target specific subjects, such as reading, for remediation without dealing with the many other needs exhibited by children at risk. Hence, the university undertook a unique role as coordinator of services to the children.[7]

To facilitate the enrichment of the students, the university made available its own academic, recreational, and cultural resources (classrooms, gymnasiums, theaters, computer facilities, and so on) for supervised use by the Dreamers. It also provided university graduate and undergraduate students to serve as mentors and tutors. All tutors were supervised and were either enrolled in a class for academic credit or paid.

The university appointed the project director; recruited and selected, in consultation with the school district, the project coordinator and assistant coordinator; and provided them with office space on campus.

Additionally, in the belief that the schools cannot accomplish educational goals alone, the university agreed to make continuing education programs available for parents and teachers working with the Albany Dreamers. Moreover, the School of Education would provide ongoing teacher support and training and continuing-education programs in adult literacy.

Finally, the university decided to commit members of its faculty, who, in consultation and collaboration with the school district, would design and develop the project comparative study.

THE PROJECT SPONSORS. The Yulmans agreed to provide funds to support a six-and-a-half-year program of educational, cultural, and recreational activities designed to help the students complete high school. The activities would include counseling, tutoring, mentoring, workshops, and trips to plays, concerts, summer camps, and the like. All educational and cultural activities would be considered complements to—not replacements for—school- and family-initiated activities.

The Yulmans also agreed to pay college tuition for four years for each student at any accredited college or university, up to a maximum equivalent to the amount charged that year at the University at Albany. The Yulmans' total financial commitment was in excess of half a million dollars. Their personal commitment would include establishing relationships with the children and their parents and serving as mentors and friends to the Dreamers.

After the launching of the Albany I Have a Dream program the Yulmans visited every private college located in the Albany region to encourage their participation, and a large group of institutions pledged that for IHAD students admitted to their college under their normal admissions criteria they will "provide the full financial aid package . . . the student needs to attend."[8] In addition, the financial aid package does not preclude that these institutions may also be able to provide special remedial support and guidance to help Dreamers derive the full advantage of their higher-education opportunity, and each college has asked that students be provided with information about their programs and admissions procedures.

In addition, the Yulmans were involved in conversations with regional and local corporations that have led to their involvement in various aspects of the program. For example, the Golub Corporation, owners of a supermarket chain, has pledged to provide summer or after-school employment in their stores for all Dreamers who want or need additional income. Several other corporations are considering underwriting or becoming involved in initiatives that include a two-week summer computer camp, travel and tickets to the Saratoga Performing Arts Center, and numerous internship possibilities.

THE ALBANY CITY SCHOOL DISTRICT. The Albany City School District agreed to provide office space in school buildings for the coordinator and assistant coordinator. It also promised to make available student records— with appropriate parental release—to I Have a Dream coordinators and research staff on a need-to-know basis and in keeping with university and school district policies. It also promised to facilitate a case-management approach to working with individual students. This process would include regular meetings and discussion between IHAD staff and classroom teachers and school counselors for the purpose of developing ways to help students better meet expectations for their academic performance. The school district also would assist the university in facilitating the development of a close relationship between IHAD staff and district faculty and administration.

Finally, the district would provide information, resources, and other assistance as required in preparing for the public announcement of the program and in meeting the educational needs of the children.

A WINNING COLLABORATION

The Albany I Have a Dream program lost no time in start-up concerns, because it had a well-established structure in place at the school and at the university. All of the university-led administrative functions were coordinated with the principal, teachers, and program staff. Now in operation for almost a year, the Albany I Have a Dream program, still one of the few IHAD efforts administered by a university, has been fulfilling its promise as a collaborative approach that maximizes the strengths of all participants.[9]

For enrichment activities, the I Have a Dream program has tapped the expertise and experience of School of Education faculty and staff. For example, writing workshops, held on Saturday mornings for interested Dreamers, were designed through the combined efforts of program staff, faculty, and school district officials.

In addition, the school district takes advantage of the physical resources of the university in expanding horizons for the ninety-eight children. In the spring of 1988, for example, Dreamers spent a day on campus learning about college and what an education could mean to them.

SUNY at Albany undergraduate students, assisting as tutors and mentors, conducted a tutoring program that proved beneficial for both Dreamers and college students. Students enrolled in the teacher education program were also involved in tutoring. They were able to relate what they were learning in their classes to real students with real learning problems.

For its part, the university has found the opportunity to administer the Albany Dreamers program supportive of its mission of teaching and public service. Faculty are developing better links with the community, and undergraduates are gaining valuable experience as teachers and observers in a unique community project while they obtain academic credit. The current interest in educational reform makes this program as important to the university campus as a whole as it is to the School of Education.

Finally, the Dreamers program fulfills the university's mission of research in the public interest. As it helps the current Dreamers, the university is providing data that will guide the systematic enrichment of education in local schools and is pioneering techniques that may serve the state and nation. Because the quality of education is increasingly being viewed as vital to a nation's economic strength, research that can strengthen the delivery of effective education clearly has long-term value.

THE COMPARATIVE STUDY

The research component of the Albany Dreamers program enables the School of Education to monitor the Dreamers' progress through more than six years of enriched education and four years of college. The assessment process was designed not to intrude on, or diminish, the experience of the ninety-eight Dreamers. In fact, all participants specifically agreed that evaluations must be conducted unobtrusively and only with the full cooperation of parents and school officials. The ten-year inquiry will reveal not only the number of students that graduate from high school and go on to postsecondary education but also the effectiveness and costs of specific aspects of the intervention.

Evaluators will routinely collect, with parental approval, information such as teacher report cards, attendance records, and standardized test results. Records of students' participation in activities such as tutoring and field trips also will be made available. A cohort group of students (fifty who are a year younger than the Dreamers and fifty who are a year older) will be drawn from those students who attended and are presently attending Arbor Hill Elementary School. In addition, assessments include regular face-to-face interviews with children and their parents to collect information about their views and perceptions of the program.

Dr. Richard Clark, a professor of educational psychology in the School of Education, directs the research initiative, in cooperation with a faculty advisory board. Clark notes that some factors—such as the personal involvement of the Yulmans—are difficult to quantify. Moreover, the project's time frame necessitates patience and sustained effort if useful results are to be developed. Still, Dr. Clark and the advisory board members are optimistic that over time, the inquiry will yield valuable information on what works, why it works, and what it costs.

After a year's hard work, researchers have raised more questions than they have answered. For example, the Albany public schools administer the Iowa Tests of Basic Skills. Profiles have been established for the children in the Dreamers program based on their previous year's records, and their current test has been examined on an item-by-item basis. Researchers have looked at how many children responded correctly to each item and at which wrong answers they selected. The I Have a Dream children score as well as the national sample on many of the test items, but they fall behind on other items.[10] Why do they learn the meanings of some words but not others? We do not know yet.

Similar questions pervade other areas of the curriculum. The children seem to approximate national averages in their mastery of some arithmetic skills but lag behind in others.[11] Teachers are now examining test items that show the most notable differences in search of an explanation.

School attendance has long been a problem for inner-city children. Some of the Albany children have missed the equivalent of a year of school by the number of absences through the sixth grade. In this group, there are small but significant links between attendance and academic achievement. For example, fourth-grade attendance correlated 0.36 with fourth-grade mathematics problem solving and 0.34 with reading comprehension. Will the support staff for the program be able to improve school attendance? If they are successful, will youngsters who attend school more regularly achieve better?

Which children need the most help? We know that the Dreamers are very diverse, ranging, for example, on group IQ tests from below 70 to above 130. Some children are scoring at about the ninetieth percentile on standardized tests, whereas others are scoring below chance. Obviously, the low-performing children need help, but those at the top of the distribution also may need help to stay there. That is, even the top I Have a Dream children, like inner-city children studied in other research, show a tendency to slip in comparison with national norm groups as they progress through school. For example, in the fourth grade, a seventy-fifth-percentile Dreamer scored at the eighty-first percentile on national norms, but by the end of sixth grade, that child had dropped to the sixty-fourth percentile. Can the program affect this drift? The answer should become clearer in the next few years.

Collaboration: A Key for the Future

The model in place at SUNY at Albany, with its administrative and evaluative components, is simple in structure and could be replicated and modified according to the needs of an individual school system or institution of higher learning. Because it builds on a logical partnership between the public school, the university, and even the corporate sector, it can magnify the strengths each would bring to an intervention program. There is no doubt that individual philanthropic involvement in the public schools is increasing. In 1981, when Eugene Lang embarked on his I Have a Dream project, the idea was so unusual that it rated significant coverage from the national media. Today, more than a hundred such programs involving more than forty sponsors are in place in a score of American cities. The I Have a Dream Foundation, based in New York City, estimates that these numbers will continue to increase. Clearly, the movement to reform education and to strengthen the teaching profession has increased sharply the interest and attention paid to public schools by businesses. Yet, IHAD programs, as effective as they appear to be, cannot meet the needs of all students who require assistance.

Recent research on the achievement levels of minority and non-English-speaking youth reveals that at-risk children represent about one-third of all elementary and secondary students in the United States. Although the last two decades have witnessed efforts to provide government-subsidized programs for at-risk students, funding has been relatively modest. According to government studies of Chapter I of the Education Consolidation and Improvement Act, less than one-half the students who qualify for aid receive services.[12]

Clearly, federal and state government involvement is needed if more at-risk students are to complete high school. But what role should government have in providing services? How should "new" services be coordinated with existing programs?

Recent research reported by the High Scope Educational Research Foundation has shown that it is increasingly possible to document the nature, extent, and consequences of serious problems of children.[13] This has helped clarify the relations between risk factors, education, and later outcomes. It thus is possible to fashion clear guidelines for preventive action by putting together what we know about risks with intervention that is proven or plausible. Ongoing research, especially within innovative programs such as I Have a Dream, will help ensure that education dollars are invested wisely.

Critical to the success of intervention programs is the ability of government agencies, institutions of higher learning, and school districts to work collaboratively to help students succeed. Universities with resources, expertise, and research facilities have much to offer such a partnership. Moreover, school districts with experienced teachers, hands-on teaching, and student assessment mechanisms must be involved in an integral way in efforts to intervene and to assess outcomes. Federal, state, and county programs that provide services to at-risk youth must be better coordinated. Working in a synergistic cooperation with the public schools, they can make significant advances in the education of children most at risk.

We began by looking at the program through the eyes of Aristides Alvarado, one of Eugene Lang's original Dreamers. Today he is thriving at RPI. It is too soon, of course, to foresee how the nation's schoolchildren in general will be affected by this kind of intervention. It may be worth noting, however, what happened after the Albany Dreamers first heard the announcement from their sponsor. They listened to a number of speakers, including Aristides, Governor Cuomo, and various school officials. Much later, after pictures had been taken and things had calmed down, a long line of Albany Dreamers could be seen moving slowly past Aristides.

They were asking for his autograph.

Notes

1. Many of the students and their families received various kinds of help from as many as seven different state or city service agencies. Lang became expert in

dealing with the bureaucracy. Some of the girls became pregnant; he saw to it that they got the medical attention they needed and stayed in school. One boy, convicted of a crime, continued his studies in Attica Prison, thanks to Gene Lang.

2. The relationship between the university and the school district is formalized in "Memorandum of Understanding [Between the Albany Public Schools and the University at Albany, State University of New York]," School of Education, State University of New York at Albany (Photocopy). For a copy of the memorandum, write to the Office of the Dean, School of Education, SUNY at Albany, 1400 Washington Avenue, Albany, New York 12222.

3. Specifically, participants in many programs rarely, if ever, develop into readers who demonstrate adequate abilities to extract meaning from text efficiently and effectively. See Richard Allington, "Civic Literacy and At-Risk Learners," paper read at the Conference on Reading, Writing, and Civic Literacy, School of Education, State University of New York at Albany and the St. Louis Public Schools, December 1988.

4. Center for the Study of Social Policy, *New Futures Initiative: Strategy Planning Guide* (Washington, D.C.: Center for the Study of Social Policy, 1987), p. 14, prepared for the Anne B. Casey Foundation.

5. Dr. Nelson Armlin, university senior staff associate and associate director of the Capital Area School Development Association, was appointed director. Janice Mwapaga, a graduate in mathematics of SUNY at Albany, tutor in the Educational Opportunities Program, and resident of the Arbor Hill Elementary School service area, was named program coordinator. Neal Currie, whose degree from Siena College is in marketing and management, was employed as assistant coordinator.

6. "Questions and Answers on Albany Dreamers," press release (Albany: Albany Dreamers, 1988). Information is available from the Office of the Dean, School of Education, SUNY at Albany, 1400 Washington Avenue, Albany, New York 12222.

7. Many of the at-risk children were receiving services from as many as seven different agencies, and some "turf" issues needed to be resolved. For example, in one case, when one of the children needed medical care, two service agencies got involved, but each thought the other was processing the child's papers. University program staff brought the two different caseworkers together, and the problem was solved.

8. The institutions include Rensselaer Polytechnic Institute, Skidmore College, the College of St. Rose, Russell Sage College, Siena College, and Union College.

9. Other institutions of higher education that are administering programs are the Bank Street College, the City University of New York, Cleveland State University, and Springfield College.

10. For example, the word *pleasantly* was correctly defined by 90 percent of the national norm group and 90 percent of the Dreamers. It was an easy word for both groups. *Culprit* was defined correctly by only 35 percent of the national group and 37 percent of the Dreamers. It thus was a hard word for both groups. Yet *gradual* was defined correctly by 75 percent of the national sample but only 39 percent of the dreamers. Likewise, the difficult word *dilute* was defined correctly by 43 percent of the national group but only 25 percent of the Dreamers.

11. For example, in response to the question "How much would the value of 35,267 be increased by replacing the 3 with a 4?" only 74 percent of the national sample

got the correct answer, whereas 80 percent of the Dreamers got the question right. On another item, children were told, "Frank split an apple into four equal parts. Jane split a different apple of the same size into equal parts. Jane's pieces were larger than Frank's. How many pieces could she have?" Choices given were 8, 5, 4, or 3. Here, 49 percent of the national sample chose the correct response, but only 27 percent of the Dreamers got this question right.

12. Allington, "Civic Literacy and At-Risk Learners."
13. J. Berruta-Clement, L. Schweinhart, W. Epstein, and D. Weikert, *Changed Lives: The Effects of the Perry Preschool Project Youth Through Age 19*, High Scope Educational Research Foundation Monograph no. 8 (Ypsilanti, Mich.: High Scope Press, 1984).

9

New York State's Liberty Scholarships Program

PETER J. KEITEL

In his State of the State message for 1988, Governor Mario Cuomo committed New York to reducing its high school dropout rate by at least half in the next five years. "We are making that commitment to our children," the governor announced, "not just this year, not just until the next election. We are making the next ten years the Decade of the Child."

A major part of Governor Cuomo's Decade of the Child initiative is the Liberty Scholarship program. It provides incentives for low-income students to stay in school. It tells them, in no uncertain terms, that if they stay in school, graduate from high school, and gain admission to a college in New York State, lack of money will not prevent them from getting a college education.

In part, the scholarship program seeks to support the dignity and autonomy of our youth, to ensure that they have access to, and choice of, the highest level of education to which they aspire and are capable of attaining.

But the Liberty Scholarships were not created from moral obligation alone, although that would be reason enough. The other compelling reason is that it makes very good economic sense. A look at some socioeconomic and demographic data will underscore the importance to all of us of seeing to it that our youth stay in school and get a good education.

Dropouts' Cost to Society

The dropout problem has implications not only for those who leave school but for our entire society. That the problem is significant is confirmed by U.S. Census Bureau data showing that lower income is correlated with lower college attendance. Moreover, dropouts mean forgone national income and forgone tax revenues. Dropouts have reduced intergenerational mobility. They and their families experience poor health, with the associated costs, and they create an insufficient and underqualified work force. A brief examination of these points will illustrate the seriousness of the problem.

LOWER INCOME MEANS LOWER COLLEGE ATTENDANCE

Census data indicate a strong relation between family income and college attendance. In 1986, there were 11.5 million families in the United States with one or more members aged eighteen to twenty-four. Of these families, about 35 percent had one or more members attending college full time. But college attendance rates varied considerably, with lower-income families falling below the average and upper-income families having a greater participation rate.

For example, at the upper end of the spectrum, 56 percent of families with incomes of $50,000 or more had a family member aged eighteen to twenty-four in college. In contrast, only 14 percent of families with incomes below $10,000 had a member in college.

DROPOUTS PLACE OUR NATION AT RISK

The social and economic consequences of dropping out place our nation at risk. Consider that 52 percent of dropouts are unemployed or receiving welfare and that 87 percent of pregnant teenagers are dropouts.[1] The forgone income of dropouts from the high school class of 1981 was $228 billion. The forgone tax revenues from that group were $68 billion.[2]

DROPPING OUT AFFECTS INDIVIDUALS

Dropping out hurts individuals. Many find it difficult to secure steady employment and an adequate income, for example. The *Monthly Labor Review* reported in 1983 that in the fall of 1982, dropouts from the 1981-1982 school year had unemployment rates almost twice those of 1982 high school graduates—42 percent versus 23 percent.[3]

Even those dropouts who are able to secure year-round full-time employment still earn only 83 percent of the average earnings of workers who complete high school.[4] Census data also indicate that the difference in expected lifetime earnings from ages eighteen to sixty-four between a high school graduate and a dropout is more than $250,000.[5] The disparity in earnings is even greater between the high school dropout and the college graduate—$640,000.[6]

DROPOUTS ARE MORE LIKELY TO BECOME INVOLVED IN CRIME

Another social cost of dropping out involves increased use of our criminal justice system. Harold Hodgkinson of the Institute for Educational Leadership reported that 80 percent of those between sixteen and twenty-four in New York State correctional facilities are dropouts. Moreover, crime is expensive. Hodgkinson noted that one prisoner in New York costs as much as eight college students, in terms of public funding. On this basis alone, supporting students through college is a public policy that produces a net gain to society.[7]

DROPOUTS THREATEN THE SECURITY OF OUR RETIREMENT

In 1950, seventeen workers paid the social security benefits of each retiree. By 1992, only three workers will be available to provide these funds for each retiree. If they are unemployed or underemployed, our retirement will be at risk.[8]

DROPOUTS DEPRIVE OUR SOCIETY OF WORKERS IN THE MOST IMPORTANT AND FASTEST-GROWING OCCUPATIONS

The loss of an educated talent pool is a cost we can ill afford. Our ability to attract and keep business in our states depends on having a well-prepared work force. Moreover, our nation's competitive position in the world market hinges on our flexibility in adapting to changing technologies.

The New York State Labor Department projects that professional and technical occupations are expected to contribute forty thousand new jobs annually, or 30 percent of the state's employment growth. The projected growth would make professional and technical occupations the largest major category by 1991. This growth depends on the availability of a college-educated work force.[9]

Over the 1984-1995 period, the three major occupational groups having the largest proportion of workers with a college education or specialized postsecondary technical training are expected to increase faster than the 15 percent average for all occupations. Those three groups are as follows: executive, administrative, and managerial, 22 percent; professional specialties such as computer engineering and health, 22 percent; technicians, 29 percent.[10]

The Record on Dropouts and the Need for Intervention

We have not been able to provide the incentives to keep our students in the educational pipeline, to high school graduation, college entry, and degree attainment.

In 1984-1985, more than 49,000 students dropped out of New York's public schools. Among ninth-graders who attended New York State's public and private schools in 1983, only 71 percent made it to the twelfth grade in 1986. Retention of minority students is even lower. Of the black students who in 1983 entered the ninth grade, 53 percent were not in the twelfth grade in 1986. The comparable figure for Hispanic students was 57 percent.[11]

This dropout problem is not likely to change without intervention, given the demographic changes that are occurring in New York State. New York schools are now 36 percent minority, up from 25 percent in 1970.[12] Without intervention, minorities experience greater attrition. Students who come from one-parent households or whose parents are relatively uneducated (especially parents who were dropouts themselves) are three to five times more at risk of not completing high school. In 1980 half of all black children in New York State and 42 percent of Hispanic children lived with a single parent.[13]

Something had to be done. New York's response was the Liberty Scholarship program. The idea was simple. It had already been proven on a smaller scale when businessman-philanthropist Eugene Lang sponsored the college educations of a class of inner-city sixth-graders. The concept was to provide an incentive for students to stay in school. If you let them know, in simple terms and early enough, that lack of money will not prevent them from receiving a college education and that people are available to help them along the way, then they will persist and make plans. Students will be encouraged to complete high school and go on to college.

Liberty Scholarships Address the Dropout Problem

The design of the Liberty Scholarship program is such that it addresses needs of high-risk students at a critical point. By letting them know that the basic costs of attending college will be covered, this program underscores the importance our society places on education.

HOW LIBERTY SCHOLARSHIPS WORK

Liberty Scholarships are an entitlement grant program for New York State students who complete high school or receive a general equivalency diploma (GED) and pursue higher education in New York State. There is no qualifying examination. It is the first state grant program of its kind, designed, in combination with other programs, to meet all college costs for low-income students.

Applicants for Liberty Scholarships must complete high school in New York State or obtain a GED from New York; begin college within two years of completing high school or obtaining a GED; be less than twenty-two years old at the time of first award; receive a Pell Grant; receive a Tuition Assistance Program (TAP) award, if studying full-time; be an undergraduate student receiving TAP or state scholarship awards for the first time in the 1991-1992 academic year or thereafter; and meet the citizenship, residency, and other general eligibility requirements established for the TAP and other state scholarship and grant programs.

Awards are scaled to income levels. Although there is no income eligibility ceiling, awards will be reduced by $1 for every $3 of adjusted gross income beyond $18,000. As a result, eligibility is targeted at low-income students, with awards adjusted on a tapered basis as income rises.

The first Liberty Scholarships will be awarded during the 1991-1992 academic year. The awards will be used to offset the costs of such nontuition expenses as room and board, transportation to and from college, and books and supplies. In combination with other existing state and federal student aid programs, Liberty Scholarships will enable an eligible student from a low-income family to choose to attend a State University of New York (SUNY) or City University of New York (CUNY) campus and have his or her educational costs paid. If the student attends a private college, the award will be equal to the amount the student would have received at the state university.

The Liberty Scholarship program tells students that they are important to us, that we care about them and want them to succeed. The message it conveys is that if students persist, if they stay in high school and graduate, and if they are accepted for admission to a college in New York State, they will not be kept out because their family has difficulty paying for their education.

By enabling students to fulfill their dreams of attending the college of their choice, New York is taking positive action to meet its goal to reduce the state's high dropout rate. And by receiving the information early enough, at the junior high level or earlier, students and families have enough time to plan, both academically and financially, for college.

HOW LIBERTY PARTNERSHIPS PROVIDE SUPPORT

Although the provision of both financial resources and early information is essential, these things alone cannot turn around the dropout situation. All research to date has stressed the importance of improving the self-esteem of students at risk and of the value of mentors and role models.

This need is addressed through an important component of the Liberty Scholarships program, the Liberty Partnerships. Under the Liberty Partnerships, competitive grants will be provided to higher-education institutions and community-based organizations to implement mentoring and other counseling services for dropout-prevention programs in elementary and secondary schools.

The Liberty Scholarships program underscores the importance that New York State places on education. The Liberty Partnerships will provide the personal attention and counseling support needed to foster the self-worth that is so important to educational success. Liberty Partnerships begin operation in 1989-1990. They will ensure that students have the opportunity to get help on a one-to-one basis for any problems—personal, family, social, and academic.

No other state program has the scope or potential of the Liberty Scholarships and Partnerships. By 1991, more than thirty thousand students will be receiving assistance through the Liberty Scholarship program. By 1994, that number will be more than ninety thousand.

The legislative package that created Liberty Scholarships also provided the single largest increase in TAP since its inception. The TAP already provides grants to half of the students attending college full-time in New York. The revised program will provide higher maximum award levels and will make TAP awards available to more middle-income students. By 1990, students who are most in need of assistance will receive up to $4,125 in tuition assistance. At the other end of the spectrum, even students with family incomes up to $50,500 in net taxable income (about $60,000 in gross income) will be eligible for the TAP.

Through these initiatives, New York State continues to work to make things easier, to eliminate confusion, and to send a clear message to our young people that higher education is not only possible but their right and that we want to help. Liberty Scholarships and Partnerships and the generous increases in the TAP clearly support this position.

The Liberty Scholarships and Partnerships make good sense, not only in terms of educational opportunity and human rights but also of economics. The costs of dropping out are great, in terms of lost productivity, a shrinking tax base, greater reliance on welfare programs, and an overburdened criminal justice system. Dropping out, in sum, represents a tragic loss of human potential, one that affects our entire society. New York's investment in human capital today will pay huge dividends far into the future.

Notes

1. Byron N. Kunisawa, "A Nation in Crisis: The Dropout Dilemma," *NEA Today*, January 1988, p. 61.
2. J. S. Catterall, *On the Social Costs of Dropping Out of High School*, Report no. 86-SEPI-3 (Stanford, Calif.: Stanford Education Policy Institute, Stanford University), cited in Russell W. Rumberger, "High School Dropouts: A Review of Issues and Evidence," *Review of Educational Research* 57 (Summer 1987), p. 115.
3. A. M. Young, "Students, Graduates and Dropouts in the Labor Market," *Monthly Labor Review* 106 (August 1983), Table 4, cited in *Review of Educational Research* 57 (Summer 1987), p. 113.
4. U.S. Bureau of the Census, *Current Population Reports*, series P-60, no. 114 (July

1978), Table 48, and no. 142 (February 1984), Table 48, both cited in *Review of Educational Research* 57 (Summer 1987), p. 113.

5. U.S. Bureau of the Census, "Lifetime Earnings Estimates for Men and Women in the United States: 1979," in *Current Population Reports*, series P-60, no. 139 (1983), cited in *Review of Educational Research* 57 (Summer 1987), p. 113.

6. This estimate was calculated by the U.S. Department of Education and communicated to the author by William Madzlan of the Office of Education. It is based on data from the U.S. Bureau of the Census, *Current Population Reports*, 1984, and presumes year-round full-time employment beginning after completion of school. The total amount is in 1987 dollars, with no adjustment for cost of living.

7. Harold L. Hodgkinson, *New York: The State and Its Educational System* (Washington, D.C.: Institute for Educational Leadership, 1987), p. 3.

8. Harold L. Hodgkinson, *All One System* (Washington, D.C.: Institute for Educational Leadership, 1985), p. 3.

9. New York State Department of Labor, *New York State Occupational Needs, 1989-1991* (Albany: State of New York, 1988), pp. 11-25.

10. New York State Department of Labor, *Annual Labor Area Report, New York State Fiscal Year 1987*, BLMI Report no. 23 FY 1986 (Albany: State of New York, 1986), p. 64.

11. New York State Education Department, Information Center on Education, cited in *Learning in New York*, January 1987, p. 4.

12. Hodgkinson, *New York: The State and Its Educational System*, p. 7.

13. New York State Council on Families and Children, *The State of the Child in New York State*, Chapter 2, Table 4, cited in *No Time to Lose* (Albany: New York State Department of Social Services, 1988), p. 6.

10

Corporate Support for Scholarships: A Tale of Two Cities

JOSEPH M. CRONIN

How best can corporations and foundations help low-income students from the inner city plan for, and pay for, college? What are the advantages and shortcomings of various models of financial assistance to students?

During the 1980s, business leaders in Cleveland and Boston raised millions of dollars to support inner-city student scholarships. Their private-sector initiatives are perhaps less personalized than Eugene Lang's I Have a Dream foundation, which involves sponsorship of a single class of students. But the Cleveland and Boston efforts cast a much broader net for needy high school students and leveraged a much larger sum of money for more students over a longer span of time.

Cleveland has two programs. One, a long-standing effort, is the Cleveland Scholarship Programs (CSP, or "last-dollar" scholarships), which since 1967 has provided financial aid counseling and supplementary scholarship assistance to more than a thousand Cleveland-area students annually. A new Cleveland program is the Scholarship-in-Escrow (SIE) plan, begun in 1987. It sets aside sums of money for students working for good marks in the seventh to twelfth grades.

Boston also has a major initiative under way. In 1984, Boston business leaders built into the privately sponsored Plan for Excellence in the Public Schools a program called the Action Center for Educational Services and Scholarships (ACCESS). This program for Boston public school students was based on the Cleveland last-dollar scholarship and counseling model. Corporations and Boston-area foundations raised an endowment of $5.5 million, with interest earnings paying the costs of counselors and providing scholarships.

The Cleveland and Boston scholarship programs are important models for several reasons. All students are eligible for assistance. Moreover, these programs provide expert financial aid counselors who guide the students and their parents. The aid these scholarships offer is available year after year, not just to one class on graduation in a certain year. Finally, existing state, federal, and campus sources of aid are tapped to the fullest.

Thousands of students in each of these cities benefit. No one gets a scholarship unless he or she can demonstrate actual need, a cornerstone of most financial aid programs. Other cities and several states have launched similar activities, all for related purposes. Hence, it is worth examining the origins, functions, and effects of the efforts in both cities.

Pioneering Efforts

Cities in the 1960s faced such turbulence and discontent that both public officials and private-sector leaders reexamined the adequacy of educational opportunity programs. During the 1950s Cleveland's Markus Foundation created a foundation program of college scholarships and loans that, surprisingly, were rarely applied for by inner-city youth. Cleveland attorney Robert C. Coplan, manager of the Markus Foundation Funds for College, discovered that many eligible youngsters never thought college was attainable and had no idea of how to apply for assistance. Cleveland Board of Education officials reported that only 12 percent of Cleveland public school students applied for, and actually entered, college. What was missing? There were too few well-informed college guidance experts who could help the students negotiate the paper maze of applications, essays, references, and financial-need documents.

In response to the need for information and guidance on colleges, Coplan and the Markus Foundation created a nonprofit organization, the Cleveland Scholarship Programs. The foundation hired a team of financial aid advisers, a fund-raiser, and an administrator of the scholarship program, Clarence Mixon. They sought funds from Cleveland-area foundations, businesses, and individuals. Over time, the annual fund-raising activity resulted in a yearly flow of $600,000—almost one-third of the funds raised from family or metropolitan-area foundations.

During the 1970s the CSP operated on two important assumptions: first, students need not only money but also detailed advice on how to apply for college and on when and how to qualify for financial aid, along with encouragement to stay in school. Second, private scholarship funds are required to fill any remaining need or cost-of-education gaps after all other public grants, work-study money, and loans have been authorized by campus and state aid offices.

How successful has the CSP been over a twenty-year period? By 1989, more than sixty thousand students had been assisted in their efforts to pursue higher education. The percentage of Cleveland public school students pursuing college or vocational training rose from 12 percent to 52 percent. Cleveland leaders raised almost $6 million over twenty years in college scholarships for the further education of disadvantaged students. CSP provided more than $4 million for specialized counseling services by twenty-one part-time financial aid advisers and for payment of college test fees, application fees, acceptance fees, and housing fees if they could not be deferred or waived.

In addition, the above efforts leveraged another $70 million in state, federal, and institutional sources for Cleveland students over the two decades.

President Reagan's Task Force on Private-Sector Initiatives saluted the CSP as a model program, and the U.S. Department of Education invited twenty-three cities in 1985 to a Washington conference to discuss similar strategies for other cities. The CSP model was adopted by, or influenced programs in, Boston; Baltimore; New York; Columbus and Dayton, Ohio; Richmond, Norfolk, and Alexandria, Virginia; Miami, Florida; and elsewhere. The Cleveland model also attracted the interest of several Cuyahoga County suburbs, smaller cities, and private high schools in Ohio. The CSP serves these schools, provided they pay a fee for the support of additional counselors.

In sum, the pioneering efforts of the CSP provided the background and a model for development that inspired the major undertakings for education by Boston and Cleveland in the 1980s.

Boston's Initiatives

The Boston public schools in 1981 attracted a new superintendent of schools, Dr. Robert Spillane, then the deputy commissioner of education in New York State. Responding to a *Time* magazine description of the Boston schools as "national disgrace," Spillane sought help from the business community and universities, many of which had already signed on as partners to the city high schools.

The Greater Boston Chamber of Commerce had just formed a new education committee and was searching for ways to assist the schools. Harvard's Francis Keppel, former U.S. Commissioner of Education, suggested that chamber leaders be asked to provide private scholarships, perhaps on a matching-grant basis, along with government or colleges.[1]

During 1982 the Boston Private Industry Council (PIC) announced a new initiative to bring the city schools and the corporate community together. The PIC proposed the Boston Compact, which promised summer jobs and consideration for full-time jobs after graduation from high school as long as Boston schools raised attendance rates and test scores and lowered the dropout rate each year for five years. The PIC established fourteen work groups, one of them a higher-education task force that enlisted school volunteers to counsel students about college financial aid.

The Greater Boston Chamber of Commerce helped recruit four hundred companies to sign the Boston Compact and to provide the summer and full-time jobs. During 1983 and 1984 its education committee discussed ways to raise more corporate funds for higher-education scholarships. One advocate was Kenneth Rossano of the Bank of Boston, who had raised funds for STRIVE, a private scholarship program for vocational students. The chamber also raised college scholarship funds for the Program for Academic Youth in School.

Institutions of higher education in eastern Massachusetts also proposed and signed a compact with the Boston public schools. Presidents of twenty-five colleges and universities offered to increase the number of graduates enrolling in postsecondary education by 25 percent over a five-year period in return for stronger academic preparation by the Boston public schools.

The presidents' steering committee separately agreed to help finance the Higher-Education Information Center (HEIC), to provide pamphlets, financial aid application forms, and advice on colleges and careers generally. The center, which opened in October 1984, was financed by a start-up grant from the Jessie Cox Fund; by a variety of city, state, and federal sources; and by the twenty-five colleges. Since signing the Boston Compact, the higher-education institutions have contributed an additional $15 million in scholarships to Boston school graduates.

One serious barrier to college attendance encountered in the early stages of Boston's efforts was the multiplicity and complexity of financial aid application forms and the limited time Boston high school counselors could give to each student. Money was also a problem for students in 1983. Students who might have been eligible for aid were not getting aid, and students without aid who did go to college were dropping out at alarming rates. Of Boston public school graduates receiving no financial aid, 27 percent dropped out during the first semester, and only 51 percent registered for the second semester. Those with financial assistance were much more willing to remain in degree programs. "Students without any form of aid have significantly lower chances of staying in college," concluded one report on college retention.[2] Both money and information on how to get it make a difference.

Much more help was needed. Dr. Robert I. Sperber of Boston University (and director of the Higher Education Partnership Steering Committee) and Harry Johnson of Polaroid offered to lead a Chamber of Commerce committee to create new scholarships with the Boston public schools linked to the Boston Compact.

The new chamber subcommittee on scholarship programs invited Dr. Mixon of Cleveland to provide a briefing on the CSP. He explained how funds could be raised for up to five years of undergraduate education—important because some students needed extra time to cope with family and personal crises. Mixon reported that each private dollar generated ten times as much in public and campus financial aid because of the counseling and advising services. He also noted that only one in every five students helped by the CSP actually needed the last-dollar assistance.

Harry Johnson arranged for a small grant from Polaroid as a first step in developing a similar program for Boston. School officials were consulted, and the cooperation of Boston's high school guidance counselors was solicited. The early efforts of Boston's program were located in the HEIC in the Boston Public Library. The city donated the space. All of the information to prospective students was provided at no cost to those who sought help.

In the early 1980s, Boston's climate of business support for education was moving from good to excellent. The Bank of Boston, on the occasion of its two-hundredth anniversary, had just created an urban education endowment called the Boston Plan for Excellence in the Public Schools. A gift of $1.5 million in stocks was designated for school improvement grants to fund proposals submitted by teachers and principals. A major life insurance and financial services company, the New England, decided to celebrate 150 years of success with a series of gifts to Boston. The largest was a $1 million donation to endow the ACCESS program.

Kenneth Rossano, chairman of the Greater Boston Chamber of Commerce and an official of the Bank of Boston, announced the creation of ACCESS at the annual chamber dinner meeting in May 1984. The purpose of ACCESS was to assure that any academically qualified student in the Boston public schools had a chance to go to college.

Mario Pena was hired as the first ACCESS director in 1985, later moving to the executive directorship of the entire Boston Plan for Excellence. From the start, the ACCESS effort emphasized financial aid counseling as an ingredient just as important as the last-dollar scholarships. Although volunteers were helpful and regular counselors wanted to provide more assistance, the initial ACCESS counselors were offered pay equivalent to substitute-teacher per diem salaries in the Boston schools.

Edward ("Ted") Phillips, chairman of the New England, saw the need to build a larger endowment for ACCESS to provide enough funds to pay for a second, third, and fourth cohort of students. It would not be enough to help freshmen for one year or to fund only one class of high school seniors. Funds were needed to renew the assistance in subsequent years. An imaginative fund-raiser for his own college and for the fine arts, Phillips developed a plan to raise $5 million for ACCESS. He persuaded the Boston Foundation, a community philanthropic organization, to authorize a challenge grant of $1 million on a two-to-one match. He sought the participation of other financial institutions and corporations, large and small. As the pledges poured in during a vigorous campaign, the Private Industry Council agreed to a novel amendment to the Boston Compact—that all Boston public high school graduates who completed postsecondary programs would be given the opportunity to interview for professional and management positions in the same companies that had agreed to hire summer employees and high school graduates.

The public announcement of this commitment to provide inner-city public school students access to higher education and professional careers brought immediate acclaim from the Boston press, the *New York Times*, the *Wall Street Journal*, *USA Today*, and the major television networks.

So warm was the reception that a nonprofit organization, the Massachusetts Higher Education Assistance Corporation (MHEAC), contributed $1 million to endow the counseling and information component. The unanimous vote of the MHEAC board brought the total contributions and pledges to $5.5 million.

In 1985, the first year of operation for ACCESS, one hundred Boston high school seniors received last-dollar scholarships averaging $500. Almost one thousand seniors received advice on attending college and obtaining financial aid. The average ACCESS award in 1986 rose to $535 and was even higher in 1987, as pledges were fulfilled. Some individuals in 1988 received $1,500 or more, in part to reduce reliance on student borrowing during freshman year.

Last-dollar scholarships were increasing, but was information about sources of aid for college sufficient? Leaders of the HEIC and ACCESS efforts felt that much more needed to be done and developed several new strategies to inform students and parents about postsecondary education. First, city children know very little about colleges, and their parents often lack both information and transportation to colleges ten miles from the city. The HEIC used the Fund for the Improvement of Post-Secondary Education (FIPSE) grant for college students to provide early awareness information to ninth-graders. The Boston schools supported student trips to nearby suburban colleges willing to recruit more urban students. Later, a private corporation, the New England Education Loan Marketing Corporation, provided a small grant for these trips.

A second strategy was to help students recognize that crucial decisions about courses must be made early. During 1988, The Education Resources Institute (TERI) agreed to finance an early-awareness booklet to be prepared in English and Spanish by the Association of Independent Colleges and Universities of Massachusetts. Within weeks, the first fifty thousand copies were spoken for and a second edition of twenty-five thousand was ordered.

A third step involved helping urban students to practice in preparing for SAT and ACT tests. The regional office of the College Board helped the HEIC schedule practice examinations by providing copies of previous entrance exams and advice on how to score and report any patterns of academic weakness to students.

A fourth tactic was to develop a comprehensive support system for college students that would provide inner-city students, once admitted to college, with advice on how to stay in school and cope with numerous challenges.

The College Board Commission on Pre-College Guidance and Counseling recommended early-awareness programs of guidance and urged stronger collaboration among schools, agencies, colleges, businesses, and other community resources for these purposes. The College Board concluded, as had Cleveland and Boston teachers, that high schools have "too few counselors trying to do too much for too many."[3]

Boston remains particularly active in promoting higher-education opportunity. Recently, the Boston Plan for Excellence arranged for the *Boston Globe* to print several hundred thousand copies of a brochure on ACCESS and the other school-improvement programs available for students in the Boston schools.

The New Cleveland Initiative for Education

Many cities around the world read or heard about the Boston Compact, ACCESS, and the Boston Plan for Excellence in the Public Schools. Business and foundation executives from dozens of cities sent for information or visited Boston during the 1980s.

Late in 1986 the new Cleveland superintendent of schools, Alfred D. Tutela, announced an intention to increase the holding power of the Cleveland schools, whose dropout rate was around 50 percent. He also asked for help on a School-to-Work Youth Employment Transition program, including summer jobs and priority hiring for Cleveland public school graduates. A nonprofit organization, Youth Opportunities Unlimited, conducted the job-readiness training and arranged summer jobs for two thousand students and arranged community service projects for another six hundred students. This variation on the Boston Compact was named the Cleveland Initiative for Education.

The other component was a new incentive plan to reward pupils who studied hard for good grades in academic subjects in middle school and senior high. Called the Scholarship-in-Escrow (SIE) program, the incentive plan enabled students to earn $40 for each A grade, $20 for each B, and $10 for each C in a core academic subject, with a $10 bonus for each honors class. Cleveland students qualified for $1.8 million in credits during the last two quarters of the 1987-1988 school year. A task force of the Greater Cleveland Roundtable worked out the SIE program details, and Ameritrust, a Cleveland bank, helped devise a system of accounts for each student.

No one in Cleveland feels that success will come easily or automatically. In 1987 almost 40 percent of the students in grades 7 through 12 earned only D's and F's in the core academic subjects. In 1988 any student with straight A's from the seventh grade on could build up as much as $4,800, whereas a C student could earn $1,000, assuming thirty courses and four quarters of grades in each course. The bank will issue a statement to each student periodically, showing how much money has been earned. A student will have up to eight years to spend the money on continued education. If the student leaves the system, the money is lost to that student.

The Cleveland Foundation committed $3 million to stimulating a drive to raise an endowment for SIE from corporations and other foundations. Two major Cleveland companies, TRW Inc. and the Eaton Corporation, pledged $2 million in 1988 to the Payment for Grades program. Joseph T. Gorman, president of TRW, led the fund-raising drive for the Cleveland Initiative, and James R. Stover, Eaton's chairman and chief executive officer, explained that their large gift "reflects our conviction that education is the answer and the essential ingredient for a healthy future for the young people of this city." Their goal was to raise $16 million through pledges of funds payable over five years.

Higher-education institutions also agreed to support the Cleveland Initiative. Oberlin College has offered to put up matching scholarships to any Cleveland student who earns such a scholarship. So will Case Western Reserve University. This happens independently in Boston, where Boston College and Northeastern University offered packages of full-tuition scholarships to Boston students. Boston College and Northeastern also raised private funds for summer enrichment programs for eighth-graders in the Boston Schools. Later the *Boston Globe* pledged scholarship aid to the University of Massachusetts at Boston.

Early Awareness: A Philanthropic Frontier

Gallup polls show that 20-40 percent of the population do not feel they could qualify for financial aid, that only smart people or athletes will get scholarships and grants. Most news about financial aid is bad news—drastic reductions in federal grants or state scholarships. Good news, when Congress or state legislatures complete work on aid budgets, is often lost in July or September news accounts, and by then, many people feel that "it is too late to apply."

In truth, every state and campus can take a very needy student and prepare a package of from $5,000 to $10,000 of grants, below-market rate loans, and campus work-study. Residents of public housing projects or welfare hotels do not know this, nor do many farm workers or immigrants. They give up early or fail even to consider that college is discussable and, in fact, must be planned for as early as the sixth or seventh grade in school.

To think that college is too expensive or unattainable is to make this negative prophecy come true. Also, unless students elect algebra in grades seven or eight, their sequence of math courses may not qualify them for admission to a selective college. This is especially true because many states responded to *A Nation at Risk* and other reports critical of soft pedagogy by raising the high school graduation and public-college admission requirements.[4] Thus, the costs of early decisions to rule college out are compounded by parental or student decisions to accept a general or nonacademic course of study in high school.

The College Board, the National Association of Student Financial Aid Administrators, TERI in Boston, and several states and foundations have decided to combat precollegiate defeatism and despair. Hundreds of projects were launched in the 1980s, including "stay in school" campaigns, expanded college visit programs, academic-success contracts (such as Cleveland's or Lang's), and the use of videotapes or pamphlets. Many are simple low-budget efforts. The Cleveland and Boston initiatives are comprehensive, visible, and most complex because the problems of parental and pupil pessimism about the future are themselves so complicated.

Companies, foundations, state agencies, and colleges working together can make a difference—just as federal outreach programs such as Upward Bound, Talent Search, and Educational Opportunity Centers in the federal TRIO programs for support services have made a substantial dent in the higher-education awareness problem.

SOME MAJOR EARLY-AWARENESS EFFORTS

Some examples can illustrate the diversity of private-sector support of early-awareness activities. In 1987, Eastern Michigan University (EMU) began a College Day (actually a two-a-half-day) program for at-risk eighth-graders in several cities, including Detroit, Lansing, and Ypsilanti. EMU intends to add two hundred minority students to the entering class of 1991. Although initial funds came from the King-Chavez-Parks state program, EMU also created a private $500,000 endowment to provide a loan-free freshmen year and will raise $400,000 from the private sector to expand College Day and follow-up programs, including academic-skill development. Three other colleges participate in the program to provide the six hundred students a choice.

Another private-sector initiative was developed in Atlanta. Atlanta offers several programs, including a mentor or adopt-a-student program wherein one hundred black donors guarantee funding for college to those from a school whose graduates meet college entrance requirements. Another project raises funds for twelve middle schools and sponsors the Atlanta Dream Jamboree.

Columbus, Ohio, organized I Know I Can, Inc. to promote academic preparation for college and to offer financial aid form-filling assistance and last-dollar financial assistance.

Dallas offers Project Early Option to help first-generation college students plan for college as early as possible, prepare for standardized tests, and enroll in summer school, community college, or advanced placement courses. The Dallas public schools and the Meadows Foundation cosponsor this project.

The Washington (State) Private Industry Council, in cooperation with several state agencies, offers at-risk fourteen- and fifteen-year-olds an eight-week summer course at two state universities to develop career goals, academic skills, and community-service values.

The West Virginia Education Fund sponsors college awareness programs in the fourth through ninth grades and school business partnerships to create scholarship opportunities in local communities or counties.

OTHER CITY AND STATE EFFORTS

A dozen other urban communities and several states have also decided to raise funds to encourage urban youth to prepare for and finance a college education.

Baltimore has begun a five-year $25 million fund drive, creating the College Bound Foundation, which has a permanent endowment and aims principally at helping economically disadvantaged graduates of the city public schools. The format includes underwriting costs of preparing for college, including college entrance exams, application fees, and SAT-exam preparation courses. It also provides full and partial grants, including last-dollar financing; help in applying for college admissions and financial aid; payments for college acceptance and dorm reservation fees; and continuing mentors, including paid student tutors and peer counselors at college.

The Greater Baltimore Committee organized the College-Bound Foundation, with a board consisting of the mayor; the superintendent; the president of the University of Maryland; Baltimore County; a foundation president; and six corporate executives. As in Cleveland and Boston, one goal is to prevent students from dropping out, and a major tactic involves the hiring of special college counselors. Businesses—as many as 150—will provide tours to introduce pupils, as early as the sixth grade, to the business world. Ultimately, the businesses will provide summer internships and part-time after-school jobs.

Meanwhile, the state of Florida received funds from the McKnight Foundation (established by the president of the 3M Corporation) to finance Centers of Excellence, to develop academic talent, support parent training, and encourage personal enrichment. There are thirty-five such centers in Florida. During 1986, McKnight provided $100,000, and the Florida state legislature, $150,000.

The explicit McKnight-Florida strategy is to create a black community support system for minority youth. The tactics include heavy reliance on black churches—seventy-five of them—to instill a sense of heritage, cultural pride, and moral purpose and to provide homework centers. Moreover, the strategy creates McKnight Achievement Societies in each county or community and provides distinctive jackets and a logo for honor graduates earning A's and B's and for those who achieve musical or artistic work of distinction. The support system involves enlisting adult sponsors/mentors, who link the students to successful adult professionals in the community. It also entails sponsorship of a statewide "Brain Bowl," an academic equivalent to highly visible athletic recognition.

The National Urban League has endorsed this program, and the state has pledged to help support creation of a $25 million endowment fund. The McKnight program, with its reliance on churches, mentors, academic competition, and young Black Achiever clubs builds a support structure for black, Cuban, and Haitian youth that could help many thousands of students each year.

OTHER CORPORATE, COMMUNITY, AND PHILANTHROPIC MODELS

The Citizen's Scholarship Foundation of America (CSFA) manages more than 220 scholarship programs for 350 local community chapters and more than 100 corporations and smaller foundations. Dr. Irving Fradkin of Fall River, Massachusetts, an optometrist with vision, created what he called the "Dollars for Scholars" program, which, has branched out from Massachusetts since the 1960s to many other states.

Originally, local CSFA chapters raised annual scholarship funds for needy students from citizens and companies in a town or city. Also, a number of companies, from Bumble Bee Seafoods to General Motors and Levi Strauss, asked CSFA for help in administering scholarship programs for the children of their own employees. A total of more than $10 million a year is provided in scholarship aid to good students. CSFA chapters encourage recipients to repay their scholarships later in life, in effect an "honor loan" or moral obligation to help the next generation of students.

During 1988 the Lilly Foundation provided $300,000 to CSFA to create the Indiana Dollars for Scholars project. Their challenge grants helped start eleven new community chapters. CSFA also helps smaller community foundations to administer a scholarship program. Usually, CSFA chapters rely on volunteers to screen student applications prior to the decision, and a small central office mainly coordinates the expansion efforts.

Ever innovative, CSFA has developed with the Blandine Foundation a parents' college savings plan in Minnesota. It also administers endowments for scholarships in two communities and runs two inner-city programs for individual high schools in Los Angeles and Cincinnati. New programs include the Larry Bird Pro All-Star Scholarship game, an Indiana fund-raiser. The Lutheran Brotherhood asked CSFA to distribute $1 million a year in scholarships. More than 175 colleges will match CSFA scholarships for students admitted to their college.

Now headquartered in St. Peter, Minnesota, CSFA has grown from $2 million in awards in 1984 to almost $10 million in 1988. Program administration, volunteers, and fund-raising expenses amount to about 17 percent, much of which in recent years represents management fees to help corporations run an employee or community program. CSFA activity is especially strong in New England, New York, Minnesota, and Indiana, but CSFA has hired program development officers in California and New Jersey to expand services to other regions. Supporters include Independent Sector and the National Association of Student Financial Aid Administrators.

TRADE FOR AID

In one of the most unusual philanthropic college financial aid programs, companies donate products or facilities to a college that then transforms the "savings" into additional off-campus aid for students. This program, Education Assistance Ltd. (EAL), was devised by V. R. Roskam, who recalled how his own college tuition was paid by a family who lost a son in World War II.

To make the project work, Mr. and Mrs. Roskam recruited 130 corporations, which have contributed such goods as office furniture, steel shelving, plastic bags, computer equipment, and even horses for equestrian programs. Moving companies helped transport the donated goods, and a Wisconsin resort offered space for faculty conferences.

The college has translated savings into scholarships that so far have helped five hundred students. Monsanto Agricultural Company and the Oil-Dri Corporation, where Roskam is a vice-president, are two of the major industrial sponsors. Companies receive a tax deduction for the donation.

Under the Roskams' EAL Eighth Grade College Opportunity plan, four communities decided to help disadvantaged junior high school students. Each community forms a board, hires a counselor, and will raise scholarships for students who complete the program. In 1988, President Reagan saluted EAL with a Volunteer Action Award.

COLLEGE SEARCHES BY COMPUTER

New York City offers the Job and Career Center on West Fifty-fourth Street, with seven IBM Infowindow touch-screen computers. The Rudin Foundation, the New York State Department of Labor, and the Association for a Better New York helped launch this "College Town Center," which provides computer printouts of varying length and detail, according to the size of a college and intended major field of study. Students can also select videos of a dozen or more colleges.

A similar service is offered to Massachusetts citizens by the Higher-Education Information Center in Boston, which is financed by colleges, several nonprofit loan agencies, and support from the College Board and Houghton Mifflin. The HEIC serves adults and children, more than forty thousand prospective students a year, an indicator of the need for similar services in every U.S. metropolitan area.

BEYOND THE LANG MODEL

Eugene Lang's example and his I Have A Dream Foundation, described elsewhere in this volume, have captured the popular imagination and won supporters in other cities. Just a few examples of the offshoots include Philadelphia's initiative by George Weiss, a stockbroker, to help 112 students graduating from the Belmont Elementary School finance a college education. Weiss has challenged his business colleagues to provide more counselors, tutors, and an endowment for 35,000 children in West Philadelphia.

Baltimore's Robert Bonwell, a retired businessman, offered $5,000 in tuition to attend any state-approved college or university in Maryland to fifty-four students at a Baltimore senior high. Bonwell also hired five minority mentors to advise them.

Virginia multimillionaire George Kettle offered to pay college costs for a sixth-grade class at the Winston Educational Center in Washington, D.C., if they finish high school. Also in the District of Columbia, the Federal National Mortgage Association ("Fannie Mae") will place $500 per semester in a special savings account for Woodson High School students who earn all A's or B's—up to a $4,000 total.

By 1987, Lang grant college programs had spread to fifteen cities. During 1988, Merrill Lynch, in cooperation with the Urban League, contributed $500,000 to be used in ten cities for twenty-five first-grade students. Each student would have $2,000 invested in a way that would yield $25,000 twelve years later.

Not all the Lang programs have been as open-ended in pledging full support of college costs. One reward program offered $50 gift certificates at the end of the sixth and seventh grades; $100 after the eighth, ninth, tenth, and eleventh; and $500 at high school graduation. This might be called a "pay to stay" program linked to career awareness and potentially to college attendance.

SOME COMMENTS ON SPONSORED PROGRAMS

Each of the sponsored programs was dramatic, highly visible, and motivating to the students in the school and grade selected. When combined with care and attention from adult sponsors, the increase in student ambition and attention was impressive.

Unfortunately, the effect is limited to those who are in the chosen grade or school who have spun the wheel of fortune and won the collegiate lottery. In an urban desert, they and their classmates have found an oasis—one school in an entire system. What of other schools? Other grades? Can we find a million millionaires or companies to adopt individual grades? Should we? Instead, we need the citywide efforts of the Cleveland and Boston models combined with early-awareness efforts and mentoring such as Eugene Lang's personal interest and visible commitment.

Governor Mario Cuomo's original Liberty Scholarship proposal was designed to build on the Lang model and to provide the early-awareness incentives needed. Other legislatures should endorse and adopt a statewide system of early financial aid pledges to provide encouragement to fourth- and fifth-graders. Any corporation, philanthropy, or wealthy individual considering the Lang model should build on the Cleveland and Boston experience and incorporate these valuable ingredients:

1. availability to all of the needy students in a city, county, or state;

2. linkage to existing state, federal, or campus financial aid;

3. early awareness and encouragement, such as through advisers or mentors;

4. support from colleges, universities, and other groups that assist higher education.

To build a scholarship program in isolation from other efforts can create confusion. Some cities find two or more positive higher-education support programs in competition for scarce corporate and philanthropic resources. Coordination and cooperation are essential.

Evaluating the Programs

To understand how the citywide and statewide initiatives represent substantial advances over isolated individual philanthropic efforts and to improve their ability to deliver financial and educational assistance to traditionally underserved populations, we need to measure their performance in more specific detail.

EVALUATING THE CLEVELAND PROGRAMS

Although the Cleveland Scholarship Programs have a long history and an adequate sample for evaluation, the newer Scholarship-in-Escrow plan poses a challenge for evaluation.

THE CLEVELAND SCHOLARSHIP PROGRAMS. In an early study, the Markus Foundation discovered that one reason students did not claim student aid in the 1954-1967 period was that they did not know how to fill out the forms and did not believe they could qualify for assistance. In the 1970s, to measure its own efforts in countering the problems of inadequate information and aid, CSP leaders called in an outside expert, who showed them how to leverage other sources of student aid more effectively. Finally, and most important for our purposes, the Cleveland programs were assessed in 1988 by Case Western Reserve sociology professor Eugene Uyecki, who surveyed a random sample of 633 students who had been assisted by the CSP. The Cleveland Foundation and Picway Stores paid for this study of recipients from 1967 to 1983.

The 1988 evaluation asked questions about completion of college, subsequent employment and degrees, and attitudes toward the services received. The finding revealed that more than 90 percent of the respondents attended a four-year college, and 77 percent finished college (80 percent of the four-year college students, 64 percent of the two-year students). The survey also showed that 85 percent attended Ohio colleges, 62 percent at public colleges; that more than half of the students were the first persons in their family to attend college; that 56 percent were black, 4 percent other minorities, and 39 percent white; and that the more aid received from CSP, the more likely students were to graduate from a four-year college; and that the graduation rate was 85 percent for white respondents and 75 percent for black respondents, substantially higher than the 50 percent reported in other national studies.

In addition, Professor Uyecki's research revealed that whereas 21 percent studied business, 28 percent studied the humanities or social sciences, 15 percent studied education, and 12 percent took up science and engineering. At the time of the survey, 40 percent were working in private industry, 23 percent worked in government (one as an Ohio state senator), 15 percent worked for nonprofits, and 5 percent were self-employed.

In response to questions about the usefulness of CSP services, 82 percent of respondents said CSP assistance was important in getting to college, and 63 percent believed it was important in finishing college; 65 percent benefited from assistance with forms; 49 percent cited counseling support; 41 percent cited information about specific colleges and universities; and 19 percent cited assistance in paying application fees and housing deposits.

CSP aid did not stand alone as a support for these students. It was augmented for 76 percent by earnings from students' work, for 62 percent by federal grants, for 60 percent by campus scholarships, for 55 percent by state grants, for 45 percent by bank or college loans, and for 43 percent by family assistance.

Of those who received aid, 54 percent came from families with an average annual income of under $15,000. Those from families with an income of more than $25,000 were typically from large families. The evaluation report included biographical case studies. One Hispanic attorney now in his early forties serves on the CSP board. Another former recipient is a financial administrator for two foundations. Others include a medical doctor, an electrical engineer, a research chemist, a special-education teacher, and a neighborhood housing specialist.

The collection of longitudinal data is important in evaluating all corporate and philanthropic efforts to assist education, especially in the cities. The Case Western study had a response rate of 38 percent, which reflects in part the difficulty in keeping track of thousands of past recipients, many of whom became more mobile because of their education. Especially in the early years, it was more important to get new groups into college than to track the progress of alumni. Some funds must be raised or set aside, however, for program evaluation and for maintaining a file on recipients after they leave or graduate.

THE CLEVELAND SCHOLARSHIP-IN-ESCROW PROGRAM. The Cleveland Scholarship-in-Escrow program presents a different evaluation challenge. After three years, the principals and teachers will know whether the extra payments for honor grades actually motivated the low-achieving students or merely rewarded those already doing well. Were there any pressures on teachers to inflate the grades? What extra assistance was offered to students who earned D grades but were considered low achievers?

The L. G. Balfour Foundation in 1988 provided a grant of $1 million to the Northeastern University Academy (now the Balfour Academy) that provides a six-week academic and tutoring program for junior and senior high school students whose grades are too low to get into college. Students subsequently go to colleges across the nation. The policy and evaluation questions include how much of a "carrot" to provide students already doing well in urban high schools and how much extra help to offer high-potential students who have not done well in the middle grades.

EVALUATING THE BOSTON PROGRAMS

Annually, as well as at the end of five years, the organizers of the Boston Compact completed program evaluations. Indicators of success included a higher student attendance rate and some improvements in student achievement scores in four out of five years. The dropout rate, however, showed signs of worsening in a decade of full employment, rising teenage pregnancies, and slightly increased drug traffic in the city. The corporate community, for its part, met or exceeded all of the employment goals as promised at the outset of the Compact.

The ACCESS program is just graduating the first class of college seniors. ACCESS retention figures show that the percentage of ACCESS-assisted college freshmen going on to sophomore year exceeded 80 percent, a dramatic improvement over nonassisted students. The number of Boston public high school graduates going on to some form of postsecondary education rose from 50 percent early in the decade to almost 60 percent in 1988.

ACCESS program administrators met a constant barrage of difficulties, however. For example, a few campus aid officers wanted to deduct the ACCESS award from the total funds provided by the college. Although aid officers must eliminate any excessive awards, some students may be stranded with a gap of $500 or $1,000. Even a relatively small amount of "unmet need" can make college impossible for a youth living in a family at, or below, the poverty line. Unlike the suburban youth, the low-income student usually does not have an uncle or grandparent to fill the dollar gap or pay the ever-present college fees.

Besides money, another key ingredient to ensure that urban at-risk students stay in college is emotional or survival support. Large urban universities can be cold, faceless, impersonal places. There "advisers" may simply be instructors or professors who sign a course registration card but are too busy with other duties to notice or help an insecure urban student. ACCESS has great value in that it recruits mentors and provides a constant flow of advice and encouragement.

OTHER POLICY AND RESEARCH QUESTIONS

Well-educated middle- and upper-income individuals may conclude that any inner-city at-risk student would be fortunate indeed to have the types of assistance and encouragement offered in the several cities and states. Yet some fundamental questions remain.

First, how much can be done to increase college participation if the basic preparation for college is weak? Or if a high proportion of urban youth is malnourished and lethargic in school? Too few city high schools offer a fully comprehensive curriculum with enough well-trained and experienced teachers of mathematics and science. Too few students practice writing often enough to write well. Preparation for college requires much more than practice during junior year on college admissions examinations. In sum, the twelve or more grades preceding college must provide a solid academic foundation.

Second, can the safety of students in urban schools be assured? Raymond Flynn, mayor of Boston, in 1986 warned those raising funds for ACCESS that too many students in cities would succumb to cocaine addiction to benefit from further education. Other education workers report of gangs and drug dealers in the streets and school yards.

Third, will early-awareness efforts in middle schools be early enough and potent enough to counteract the influence of peers and neighborhood persons who scoff at college attendance as a waste of time and otherwise actively discourage thinking about staying in school? Some intelligent students are suspended often, held back in the grade, and tracked into noncollege programs by educators who feel that only students conforming to typical norms should have the right to apply to college. How can we work with parents of students to raise their expectations, to make them realize college is affordable, to make them understand their aspirations for their children can be realized?

Fourth, can foundations and corporations make enough of a difference beyond indicating support of major changes in urban education and talent development? Robert Reich, in *The New American Frontier*, warns about the limits on "the ideology of charity" when a national strategy of economic development is required to shift efficiently the labor force to higher-valued production. William Julius Wilson, in *The Truly Disadvantaged*, documents a dramatic drop in urban demand for unskilled labor and a surge in demand during the 1980s for graduates with technical and professional skills.[5] If so, students need more help than pretax dollars can provide. Thus, the interest by Florida, New York, Massachusetts, and other states is crucial in expanding state-supported centers of excellence, talent search, early awareness, and other interventions, along with lifelong retraining strategies. But what may be even more crucial is the use of private venture capital to demonstrate the worth of new approaches that then can be followed up in collaboration with government agencies and with consortia of colleges and universities.

Frequently the solution includes advice to students either from an adult mentor, perhaps from a donor corporation, or a slightly older student from the same city neighborhood or comparable circumstance. Support from a caring individual can be crucial to a student's decision to remain in school. This fact persuaded the ACCESS staff to provide newsletters and frequent follow-up help to those students moving through the college years.

Higher education by the year 2000 will cost more than $100,000 for many selective independent colleges and $50,000 at residential public universities. The stakes are very high. Not every student in the seventh or eighth grade will earn enough A's to assemble $5,000 or $10,000 in accumulated cash, and if they do, it may pay for only one semester. Some students will survive family crises or neighborhood temptations and will graduate, but they will need help, and they deserve as much assistance as our combined philanthropic and governmental systems will provide. What is important is that all children in a city or county have the opportunity to benefit from higher education.

"It was the best of times, it was the worst of times." The tale of two cities, Cleveland and Boston, in the 1980s is a story of corporate commitment. That story should influence dozens of other cities in the 1990s to strengthen access to higher education and to enrich the choices for America's disadvantaged youth.

Notes

1. In 1973 Boston University had initiated full scholarships to graduates of Boston's seventeen senior high schools each year—fifty-eight a year. The program has provided 702 Boston University graduates with $17 million in scholarships in fifteen years of operation.
2. Peter Langer, "Patterns of Enrollment, Year 3: The Local College Enrollment of Boston Public School Graduates," paper presented to the Fenway Retention

Consortium Symposium, Simmons College, June 1987.

3. Harold Howe III and Aaron Fink, *Keeping the Options Open* (New York: College Entrance Examination Board, 1986).

4. United States National Commission of Excellence in Education, *A Nation at Risk: The Imperative for Educational Reform* (Washington, D.C.: U.S. Department of Education, 1983).

5. Robert Reich, *The New American Frontier* (Chicago: University of Chicago Press, 1987); William Julius Wilson, *The Truly Disadvantaged* (New York: Penguin, 1983).

11

Public Service and Student Financial Aid

KATHRYN MOHRMAN and SUSAN STROUD

Higher education and public service* have long been linked in the United States. From the earliest colleges founded to train ministers and community leaders in New England, to the land-grant universities created in the nineteenth century to develop the mechanical and agricultural arts in the states, to the GI Bill enacted to provide access to education for those who served their country in World War II, higher education has been publicly supported because it provides service to the nation. Today many policymakers are discussing ways to link the concept of service by individual students to their need for financial support to pay for college.

We explore the ramifications of different links between service and financial aid and suggest ways in which students, colleges, and communities can benefit. First, we discuss two traditions in federal student financial assistance. Then, we turn to policy questions that arise in efforts to link service and financial aid. Next, we summarize current programs and recent propos-

---

*By "public service" we mean governmental services to citizens; "community service" includes nonprofit and voluntary organizations aiding people in need. We include both in the focus here. Students frequently participate in service activities sponsored by both public and nonprofit agencies for the good of individuals and communities, so "public service" and "community service" are often used interchangeably in legislation and in programs on campus. "National service" implies a full-time commitment to military or civilian service and a nationally organized program; some advocates also call for mandatory national service by all young people. Except when explicitly stated, we are not talking about national service when discussing links between service and financial aid.

als to encourage public and community service while assisting students with college costs. We close with our recommendations for action by federal, state, and local governments, institutions of higher education, and corporate and foundation donors.

Existing Policies Linking Financial Aid and Service

Federal student assistance policies reflect two strong American traditions— rewarding service and supporting equal opportunity—and the shifting balance between the two over the last four decades. The tradition of service has a long history. The GI Bills of World War II and the Korean War were the first large federal programs providing student aid to college students. In them, the link between military service and *subsequent* reward was clear and well supported by the public. Later, grants and loan forgiveness to students who entered teaching or health professions provided financial aid to students *prior* to service in areas of national need. Some aspects of the Reserve Officers Training Corps (ROTC) and College Work-Study (CWS) programs combine federal support and service *while* students are enrolled in higher education.

The tradition of equal opportunity came to the fore in the 1960s with Great Society programs designed to improve the social and economic conditions of disadvantaged groups through access to education. Need-based aid, such as Pell Grants, Guaranteed Student Loans (GSL), and campus-based programs, targeted individuals whose family circumstances were likely to limit opportunities for college. Americans' belief in education as the vehicle for social mobility, combined with a heightened sense of responsibility for providing equal opportunity, especially to blacks, focused these new programs on need rather than service. Throughout the dramatic growth of the 1970s, as well as the tighter restrictions of the 1980s, the fundamental policy of aid based on economic need remained unchanged.

The dollar investment of the federal government in service and need-based aid has shifted as policy priorities have changed. In 1973, veterans' educational benefits under the GI Bill accounted for 55 percent of all federal expenditures for student financial assistance. Twelve years later, as the number of eligible veterans declined and the volume of student grants and loans soared, the GI Bill represented only 9 percent of federal student aid expenditures. Similarly, loan forgiveness for teachers was dropped as the demand for teachers declined in the 1970s, and scholarships for health professionals were curtailed as the national need for doctors diminished. Need-based aid accounted for most of the student aid provided by the federal government.

In the mid-1980s, however, interest in service increased in higher-education and policy circles because of the interaction of a number of factors.

Nationally, the general concern about education rose with the publication of *A Nation at Risk* and other reform reports.[1] United States National Commission in Excellence in Education, A Nation at Risk: The Imperative for Educational Reform: A Report to the Nation and the Secretary of Education (Washington, D.C.: U.S. Department of Education, 1983). The patriotism fostered by the Reagan administration helped to make national service an acceptable topic for public debate. Serious books such as *National Service: What Would It Mean?* provided additional intellectual arguments for public support for public service.[2] At the same time, 150 college and university presidents joined together to form the Campus Compact, an institutionally based consortium to foster public and community service projects on campuses across the country. The Campus Outreach Opportunity League (COOL) was founded in 1985 by two recent Harvard graduates to assist students in organizing public service programs on 350 campuses across the nation.

The interest in public service rose at the same time that students, parents, and policymakers became increasingly concerned about rising college costs and the debt burden faced by many undergraduates. Thus, for the first time in the 1980s, the desire to limit student indebtedness became linked with the benefits of public service, with proposals for new forms of financial aid, for modifying existing programs, and for permitting students to acquire additional resources for college through service. The debates about the extent to which the federal government should provide benefits to citizens, and especially the extent to which federal aid programs ought to be viewed as entitlements, reinforced the interest in student financial assistance linked to service as a substitute for, or supplement to, assistance based on economic need. The reauthorization of the Higher Education Act in 1986 allowed the first formal connection between service and aid through a provision allowing colleges to use a percentage of CWS and State Student Incentive Grant (SSIG) funds to support community service activities.

Proponents of current proposals linking public service and financial aid cite several benefits beyond providing additional assistance to college students. One is the educational advantages that derive from engaging college students in public and community service activities. Research shows that students involved in both work and study are more likely to stay in school and have higher academic performance than their peers who merely attend class. Also, in the best-designed programs, students learn about the communities in which they live and discover effective ways to address the problems of those communities. Students also learn responsibility and good work habits, develop a sense of connection with others, and discover useful ways to apply their intelligence and talents to real problems.

Community service also benefits people in need. Government, nonprofit organizations, and citizens' groups all have larger agendas than their resources allow them to address. Although most programs of student aid and service focus primarily on economic and educational benefits to students, there are committed students in soup kitchens, tutoring programs, service to the elderly, and other projects benefiting many people beyond the bounds of the university.

Current Policy Perspectives

The idea of linking public service and student financial assistance requires attention to the same questions that any aid program should encounter: Does this program encourage equal opportunity? Does it provide horizontal and vertical equity? To what extent might it foster greater social mobility? Who should provide the funds—federal government, states, communities, private sources, colleges and universities, or a combination of the above? At the same time, the particular characteristics of public service generate questions specific to the type of aid being considered: To what extent are educational objectives and social benefits as important as financial aid goals? Should aid be a reward for service already rendered, a payment for service performed concurrently with education, or a support for training for a public service career?

We address both types of questions—about programs and aid—in describing the policy context in which financial aid and community service might be linked. In general, we believe that the most effective approach is a multifaceted, multiprogram scheme, because students in higher education are heterogeneous, public and community service activities are diverse, and various providers of student assistance play quite different roles in the financing of higher education.

Should aid linked to community service be need-based only? Those who approach the issue from the financial aid perspective tend to focus on needy students who are unable to get sufficient support to consider college or to attend the college of their choice. New proposals thus build on the tradition of aid based on need, with service as a funnel for support to poor students. On the other hand, those who begin at the service end of the spectrum focus on the educational and social benefits of engaging more undergraduates in public and community service, regardless of the economic circumstances of the students involved.

Questions of equity arise, whatever the starting point. Federal grants and loan programs target students from needy families, but the issue of service clouds the focus on economic circumstances as the chief criterion for distribution of aid. Few analysts would support a financial assistance program that made service the province of the poor, but few would also want to create a de facto barrier to service by needy students. Yet if needy students are forced to work many hours or to assume heavy debts to go to college, they may find that their obligations virtually prohibit their participation in public and community service programs. This outcome would limit service to affluent students who did not require grants and loans for college attendance, with the concomitant danger of reinforcing outdated images of noblesse oblige.

Precedents from existing federal programs provide some helpful models. The focus on need-based aid is most clear in the programs that provide assistance *while* the student is in college: Pell Grants, Stafford Loans, CWS, and the like. Of these programs, CWS is the best parallel to a service-linked aid structure for current college students. Under certain circumstances, undergraduates can receive financial support when they work part-time in approved community and government agencies.

The link between economic need and service goals is less clear with aid that either precedes or follows college enrollment. The GI Bill, for example, provides benefits for all qualifying members of the armed services, regardless of financial circumstances. Poor and wealthy alike accrue credits toward college costs through service to their country. Similarly, medical students who agreed to work in public health agencies after graduation in return for financial support during medical school were not subjected to a means test under the National Health Service Corps Scholarship Program. Although in fact many of the students who exercise such options are from poor and modest backgrounds, the policy structure focuses on the service the students have rendered or will provide, not on their economic status. Such precedents will lead us to make a series of recommendations that draw on both need-based and need-blind financial aid programs linked to service activities.

Should financial aid be linked only to public and community service? In May 1988 the Democratic Leadership Council (DLC) issued a report entitled *Citizenship and National Service: A Blueprint for Civic Enterprise.*[3] The document called for a voluntary program of national service, both civilian and military, primarily for young adults. In exchange for service at subsistence wages, participants in the Citizens Corps would receive vouchers that could be used to pay for college, vocational training, or purchase of a home. The DLC proposed phasing out current federal grants and loan programs and, instead, applying the dollars now spent on student financial assistance to this new program of aid and service.

This radically new approach to financial aid has raised both practical and equity concerns. On the practical side, the dollar amounts recommended by the DLC will fund many fewer students than current federal programs now assist. Janet Hansen of the College Board estimates that the current recipients of all federal grant and loan programs are more than five times the number the Citizens Corps would aid. The shortfall represents a significant policy shift to a much smaller pool of Americans eligible for educational assistance.[4]

On the equity side, the proposal to restrict federal aid only to service programs suggests that certain students,—the most needy—should also carry the burden of public and community service. The DLC recommends that only individuals willing to invest a year or two of their lives in public service would be eligible to receive assistance for college or vocational training. Yet the history of federal student aid is one of multiple approaches, even an over-abundance of programs, rather than a single model for delivering financial assistance. The proposal provides an exciting challenge when viewed as a new or supplemental method of helping students earn their way through college, but it is restrictive when seen as a replacement for many or all of the student assistance programs now on the books. We favor Pell Grants as the base of financial aid for needy students, with service and work programs building on that base to help students pay for college, reduce their debt burdens, and contribute in other ways to their own development and that of their communities.

How should adult and part-time students be considered in programs linking financial aid and service? The reality in higher education today is that full-time students aged eighteen to twenty-two are the minority on college campuses, yet these traditional students are the undergraduates for whom many service proposals seem most feasible. For many adult and part-time students, college is only one component of their lives, in which work, family, and other responsibilities place strong demands on their time.

Community service activities for these students will be most effective if linked in some way to the realities of their lives. The GI Bill or other programs using that model have obvious appeal because they provide cash grants based on previous service. Students have lower financial obligations when they attend college. Grants for future service, such as ROTC or health professions grants, also provide cash incentives and thus ease the costs of higher education, although older students are probably not as likely as their younger peers to be attracted to long-term future commitments. The most difficult problem arises with service expectations concurrent with study, because service is then competing with students' other responsibilities.

One effective link responds to the reality of work for most part-time students. If CWS funds, for example, are available for service activities as well as for campus jobs, then students who need to earn money for educational expenses have an opportunity to contribute to their communities while meeting their financial obligations. Such work opportunities, in addition to providing financial assistance, can contribute to student retention. Recent research shows that work on campus or linked to campus is correlated with persistence in college, whereas work off campus and work of more than twenty hours per week is negatively related to retention. Campus student aid funds, whether from CWS or other sources, can address both the financial aid needs of students and the institutional interest in encouraging student persistence to graduation.

A second approach that addresses the needs of part-time and adult students is stronger ties between service and academic programs. If courses include field-based or service requirements, more students will benefit from involvement in the community. The traditional model, of course, is education, in which student teaching and other practical experiences are integral components of the undergraduate curriculum. Yet other subjects, from sociology to journalism, to environmental studies, could integrate service effectively in their courses. In such cases, students would not be likely to earn additional stipends for their service activities, but if community-based experiences were included in course requirements, students would not be forced to choose between community service and academic demands on their time.

Just as service should not be restricted to needy students, it should not be limited to full-time residential traditional-aged students. Existing models suggest that public service opportunities can be expanded in ways that link service to the financial and academic realities of part-time and adult students.

Should service programs be designed consciously to foster social and educational objectives in addition to financial aid goals? Public service is not the only way to help students finance their higher-education expenses. The long tradition of financial aid linked to service, beginning with the GI Bill, speaks to the expectation that students will contribute to their education through their own efforts, in addition to support received from outside sources. Thus, financial aid linked in some way to service, whether before, during, or after college, addresses public expectations that students must help themselves through school. Such aid also responds to general concerns that today's undergraduates are overly focused on vocational success and insufficiently attentive to public problems.

Frank Newman has argued that different forms of financial aid provide different incentives for college students.[5] Each student assistance program, whether intended or not, reflects inherent values. A federal student aid plan that says to a student, "There is help available if you work," places work in service to learning. This is quite different from a program that says, "You may borrow money and pay it back out of the higher earnings you can expect." Such a program places learning in service to work. According to Newman, the values that each of these programs promotes are almost exactly reversed.

The priority placed on financial aid goals in comparison with social and educational benefits will vary with the provider of funds. The federal government, for example, puts a clear priority on providing equal opportunities for disadvantaged citizens and on providing access to college through financial aid. The values of service to students or communities would be attractive but secondary objectives. Institutions, however, may place the educational development of individual students or increased retention rates as the primary focus of service, with financial assistance a strong, but not predominating, objective. State and local programs of service, as described below, fall somewhere in the middle, with their focus on community development and remedial education. Although they often provide assistance for further education, the target populations of most programs are high school dropouts or graduates who are not likely to apply to college.

Focusing on innovations in student financial assistance, our first priority clearly is to help students pay for college through service-related programs. The social and educational benefits, although real, are secondary. But because we believe that the best approach to service-based aid is multifaceted, we call below for state, local, and institutional programs that build on a federal base and that may put greater emphasis than the federal government on the nonfinancial benefits of the connection between public service and financial aid.

Current Programs and Proposals

Many programs at the federal, state, and institutional levels link student financial assistance to public and community service. Some programs, such as the GI Bill and ROTC, are well-established federal programs with broad public support. These military programs often serve as analogies for new proposals that link financial aid with public service. Other federal programs, such as College Work-Study, are not frequently used for service objectives, but they provide an option for institutions to offer opportunities to students to earn part of their college expenses by working in the community.

Most of the programs instituted or proposed at the state and campus levels have been created within the past three years. These programs engage a relatively small number of students, so that in most cases they function as pilot or demonstration programs. Few, if any, have been adequately evaluated, although the staff of the Campus Compact is compiling a comprehensive inventory of programs that link financial assistance with community service.[6]

FEDERAL PROGRAMS

Federal programs can be classified in three categories: established programs, new initiatives, and proposed legislation.

ESTABLISHED PROGRAMS. At the federal level, existing legislation authorizes several programs that provide financial assistance to students through (1) grants after a period of service, (2) grant assistance with a subsequent service payback, or (3) loan deferment and cancellation. The best-known service program is the GI Bill, which provides college assistance after a period of national service. Although the original GI Bill is currently being phased out, as the last of the Vietnam veterans pass through the system, the new GI Bill, according to a recent study, could account for as much as a 25 percent increase in the number of veterans and reservists enrolled in college by 1993.[7]

Programs that provide assistance to students in return for students' commitment to provide services in the future include the ROTC, the National Health Service Corps Scholarship Program, and the Congressional Teacher Scholarship Program. Congress established these programs in response to critical needs—the preparation of military officers and the shortage of medical doctors and teachers in underserved areas. In these programs, students make a commitment to serve for a time after receiving their undergraduate or medical degrees. In return, they receive tuition assistance, a living allowance, and educational fees. The size of these programs and public commitment to them may change in response to the realities of demographic and labor market fluctuations.

Loan-forgiveness and -deferment plans encourage graduates to serve in certain critical areas. Currently NDSL and GSL loans are deferred while students engage in military service or do antipoverty work in low-income communities. Full-time teachers serving in low-income communities and full-time teachers of handicapped students can obtain partial cancellation of NDSL loans—15 percent during the first and second years of service, 20 percent during the third and fourth years, and 30 percent for the fifth year. Under the Higher Education Act amendments of 1986, the loan cancellation provisions were extended to Peace Corps and Volunteers in Service to America (VISTA) volunteers.

NEW FEDERAL INITIATIVES. Congress has also created financial aid programs that were not intended primarily as vehicles for compensating students for community service but that contain special provisions for that purpose. The 1986 reauthorization of the Higher Education Act included changes in existing programs to encourage the use of those programs to support student community service.

College Work-Study legislation was amended in 1986 to encourage higher-education institutions to place work-study-eligible students in jobs in which they improve services for low-income communities, work to resolve the social problems within these neighborhoods, and enrich the quality of their own education as well as earning money. Incentives are offered to institutions to facilitate these placements by allowing a 90 percent federal share of the students' salaries. Institutions are also allowed to use 10 percent (or up to $20,000) of their CWS allocation for administrative expenses to develop placements in community service jobs. Additionally, 25 percent of unused work-study funds returned to the Department of Education are to be reallocated to higher-education institutions for initiating, improving, and expanding community service-learning programs. In 1988-1989, at the discretion of the secretary of education, additional returned CWS funds were reallocated to provide supplemental grants to institutions specifically for students performing adult literacy work. The future of this program beyond 1989 is uncertain.

Also during the 1986 reauthorization, Congress added language to the Higher Education Act allowing 20 percent of SSIG funds to be used for need-based state work-study programs and grants to eligible students for campus-based community service work.

The most significant new source of funds for developing student community service opportunities is a new program of the Fund for the Improvement of Post-Secondary Education (FIPSE) called Innovative Projects in Community Service and Student Financial Independence. In fiscal year 1987, the sum of $1.537 million was appropriated for innovative demonstration projects to determine the feasibility of student participation in community service in exchange for educational services or financial assistance. FIPSE guidelines require projects established with these funds to address ways to help students reduce their loan indebtedness. No evaluation of those programs has been done yet.

PROPOSED LEGISLATION. The growing interest in public service linked to financial aid has led to a number of legislative initiatives at the federal level.

Voluntary National Service and Education Demonstration Program. In 1987, Senator Claiborne Pell of Rhode Island introduced the Voluntary National Service and Education Demonstration Program Act (S. 762). When originally introduced, Title I of the bill was based on the principle that high school graduates sixteen to twenty-five years old who serve their country for a period of two years in either a military or civilian capacity should receive educational benefits in return for their service. In effect, the bill extends the notion of the GI Bill to include civilian as well as military service. The bill would authorize $30 million per year for five years in new federal funds to fund demonstration programs.

Title II of S. 762, authorized at $5 million per year, would provide demonstration grants to colleges and universities for educational training programs for participation in the Peace Corps. First discussed by Father Theodore Hesburgh, who argued that the federal government should provide educational assistance to young people who serve their country in either military or civilian capacities, the bill would provide benefits for Peace Corps volunteers roughly equivalent to those provided to veterans. Based on the ROTC model, this training program would enroll students after two years of college to prepare to serve in the Peace Corps for two years following graduation. Participating students would study a special curriculum to prepare them for service in developing countries and would be expected to spend some weekends during the academic year and the entire summer in service to needy communities in this country and abroad. Norwich University in Vermont has undertaken a demonstration program based on this model, offering it as an alternative to the regular military ROTC program offered by the university. Grinnell College plans to establish a demonstration program on this model.

A bill similar to Title II of S. 762 was introduced in the House in the 100th Congress by Representative Constance Morella of Maryland. Modified by the Foreign Affairs Committee to call for a feasibility study of the program described above, the bill was passed by the House near the end of the 100th Congress.

CITIZENSHIP AND NATIONAL SERVICE ACT. The Democratic Leadership Council's 1988 proposal, *Citizenship and National Service*, is based on a concept similar to the one that underlies the Pell bill: educational benefits should flow from a period of civilian or military service. Under this plan, based to a large extent on the work of Northwestern University sociologist Charles Moskos, participation in national service would be voluntary but strongly encouraged through access to student aid.[8] The DLC proposal was introduced in the 101st Congress by Senator Sam Nunn of Georgia and Representative Dave McCurdy of Oklahoma as the Citizenship and National Service Act (S. 3 and H.R. 660).

Citizens Corps volunteers would fall into three basic categories: (1) young civilians who provide a variety of social services in the U.S. or abroad for one or two years, (2) citizen soldiers who serve in the military or reserves, and (3) senior citizens who perform service tasks on either a full- or part-time basis. Young volunteers would receive a modest monthly stipend and, on completing service, would receive a voucher for education, job training, or housing. For each year of civilian service, a volunteer would receive a voucher worth $10,000. Citizen-soldiers would receive $12,000 for each year served. Those who serve in the reserves would receive only one voucher.

By DLC estimates, a Citizen Corps with 700,000 civilian volunteers would cost approximately $7.07 billion per year. The DLC further estimates that one-quarter of this total ($1.8 billion) would be shared by state and local agencies and by private sponsors, which would reduce the federal cost to $5.3 billion. This could be met through the present funding of other federal student aid programs.[9]

When initially introduced, the proposal was radical in its position that *all* federal student financial aid should be contingent on service and that service would replace all existing student aid programs, including need-based financial assistance. As the debate on the proposal developed, the sponsors of the bill allowed for numerous exceptions that would have required present financial aid programs to be kept intact while creating an entirely new and expensive financial aid program. Throughout the debate that followed the introduction of this proposal in Congress, proponents of the Nunn-McCurdy bill argued that student aid should be viewed as an earned benefit rather than as an entitlement and that the proposal was an attempt to shift the federal role in student aid in that direction. Although the bill had support in Congress, it was largely opposed by the higher-education community, which remains committed to a financial aid system that is significantly need-based.

NATIONAL COMMUNITY SERVICE ACT. The legislation proposed in the 101st Congress by Senator Barbara Mikulski of Maryland and Representative David Bonior of Michigan as the National Community Service Act (S. 408 and H.R. 1000) draws from the experience of the National Guard. Participation in the proposed program would be voluntary, part-time, and open to all ages. Volunteers organized in teams would work with existing or newly created community agencies in their own communities on human service projects. Participants would make a three- to six-year commitment to serve two weekends each month and two weeks in the summer and would receive at the end of their service a $3,000 nontransferable voucher, excluded from taxable income, for each year of service for use only for payment of federal student loans, down payment on a home, or for tuition, fees, room, and board paid directly to the educational institution subsequently attended by the participant. The legislation authorizes $250 million for fifty thousand participants in the first year and increases over four years to $2 billion for four hundred thousand participants. This program would supplement existing federal student aid programs.

Higher Education Volunteer Amendments. Two bills (S. 759 and 760) introduced by Senator Dale Bumpers of Arkansas would tie repayment of loans to service in charitable and community service organizations. S. 759 directs the Department of Education to publicize existing provisions under which college graduates serving as full-time low-paid employees with tax-exempt organizations may defer repayments on their student loans. S. 760 would supplement the current loan repayment program by partially forgiving repayment of NDSL loans up to 70 percent of loan debt over four years in exchange for full-time low-wage positions with community service and other tax-exempt organizations.

YOUTH SERVICE CORPS. Representatives Leon Panetta of California and Christopher Dodd of Connecticut have introduced the Youth Service Corps Act (H.R. 717 and S. 322) to create a national youth service and conservation corps and a two-year commission to study and make policy recommendations regarding opportunities for youth service. The legislation would significantly extend support for existing local and state youth service corps. The bill mandates both in-service and postservice education benefits for volunteers sixteen to twenty-one years old (summer participants fifteen to twenty-one years old). The bill authorizes $152.4 million for the first year and "such sums as necessary" thereafter. States would be required to match federal funds.[10] The impact of these programs on the federal higher-educational financial aid budget would be fairly small, because participants in these programs at present typically do not expect to pursue higher education.

SERVE AMERICA. Several other bills were introduced in the 101st Congress, but only the bills that have the greatest implications for the federal role in financial aid have been described here. In the Senate all of the national service bills have come under the jurisdiction of the Committee on Labor and Human Resources, chaired by Senator Edward Kennedy, who has expressed a keen personal interest in youth service legislation.

His own bill, Serve America (S. 650), attempts to combine the key elements of the bills described above in an omnibus bill divided into five major titles.

> Title I of S. 650 would provide funding for support of community service programs in elementary schools and colleges. This provision is Senator Kennedy's major contribution to the bill.

Title II would provide funding to develop full-time youth service corps in states and local communities, essentially incorporating the Youth Service Corps proposal of Representative Panetta and Senator Dodd.

Title III would provide funding for pilot projects that demonstrate the connection between federal student aid and community service. This provision requires the greatest effort at compromise and is drawn from the bills introduced by Senators Pell, Mikulski, Dodd, among others. Participation in pilot projects would result in earning federal vouchers for education, first-home purchases, or job training in exchange for one or two years of full-time service and/or substantial monthly hours of part-time service.

Title IV would provide for expansion of VISTA.

Title V would provide financial support for senior citizen service programs.

Representative William Ford of Michigan has expressed some interest in introducing a House version of the Kennedy omnibus bill.

PRESIDENT BUSH'S INITIATIVES. In June 1989, President Bush announced the creation of a foundation to administer two related national service initiatives: Youth Engaged in Service to America (YES) and the Points of Light Initiative. The president will serve as honorary chairman of the foundation, and he has included in his budget proposal to Congress a request for $25 million a year for four years to support the expenses of the foundation. Tom Kean, former governor of New Jersey, has agreed to chair an advisory committee to make recommendations regarding the structure, composition, and legislation needed to achieve the foundation's goals. Although the content of both efforts is still vague, YES will direct its efforts specifically at young people to engage them in a wide range of service activities. The president's announcement of the Points of Light Initiative mentioned four specific activities it will undertake: (1) a technical assistance effort called the ServNet Project, (2) a massive clearinghouse of service opportunity called the ServLink Project, (3) sponsorship of Presidential Leadership Forums, and (4) a program of President's National Service Youth Representatives, which will recruit two college-aged youths from each state to spend one year traveling around the state encouraging other young people to become involved in service activities.

The implications for legislation of President Bush's initiatives are unclear, although Senator Kennedy has stated that he hopes to include the president's legislative proposals as part of his omnibus bill, Serve America. The president's staff in the Office of National Service has stated repeatedly that the president does not believe there should be any compensation or other financial incentive for young people to participate in community service activities. This statement indicates that the president's initiatives will have little or no impact on the student financial aid budget and federal student aid policy, and it sets the president at odds with the key Democratic proponents of national service in the Senate.

STATE PROGRAMS

Many state programs that link financial assistance and community service parallel federal programs in design and funding. Examples listed below indicate the range of activities in the fifty states and four territories.

YOUTH SERVICE CORPS. Youth service corps in states and cities across the country have multiplied by a factor of twenty-five in the past ten years, growing from two programs ten years ago to more than fifty now. The largest is the Michigan Youth Corps, with a budget of $25 million. The smallest is the New Hampshire Conservation Corps, budgeted at $25,000. The oldest is the California Conservation Corps, which employs young people at subsistence wages to perform conservation and environmental disaster relief work. Other youth service corps focus on meeting the human needs in their communities; some combine both. Almost without exception the corps provide remedial education and job-training services as well as postservice educational benefits to participants. The most generous postservice program is the New York City Volunteer Corps, which gives participants either a $2,500 cash bonus or a $5,000 tuition voucher on completion of a year of service.

New youth service corps proposals on the drawing boards include former Massachusetts state representative Mel King's Future Corps, which would provide two years of college or technical-education benefits in exchange for two years of service to the community. The intention of the bill is to establish a program of peaceful public service as an alternative to military service.

Most of the youth service corps employ young men and women (primarily from minorities) who are not successful in school and are not intending to pursue higher education. A significant number have not completed secondary school. The youth service corps exist in many cities and a number of states, but the aggregate number of participants in any one year is estimated at sixty thousand, a number far smaller than the number who are sixteen to twenty-four years old who are not in school and are not employed full-time. In this light, the expansion of youth service corps would have little effect on the financial aid landscape in higher education.

MANDATORY SERVICE PROGRAMS. In 1986, John Vasconcellos, chairman of the Ways and Means Committee of the California Assembly, introduced a bill to establish the Human Corps and to require every student in the California State University and the University of California system to perform community service as a requirement for graduation.[11] Vasconcellos argued that students who benefit from the low-cost quality education provided by the state owe something to the communities that generated the support for their education. The mandatory aspect of the legislation was removed before the bill passed, but the final bill included provisions requiring campuses to establish task forces and to report annually on the progress being made to involve students in community service. The first report to the legislature by the California Postsecondary Education Commission indicated that the campuses in both systems had established task forces of community representatives, faculty, staff, and students to assess current policies and programs and to plan for expansion of activities related to community service.

This legislation was important in itself for generating a great deal of activity—and resistance in some quarters. It also gave rise to several copycat bills. Representative Nick Paleologos, chairman of the House Education Committee in Massachusetts, proposed a bill that would require all students attending public colleges and universities and students receiving state aid at private colleges and universities to perform community service as a condition for receiving state financial assistance.[12] These mandatory provisions parallel the DLC proposal that all federal financial aid would be conditioned on performance of service.

STATE COLLEGE WORK-STUDY. Jim Mingle, executive director of the organization of State Higher Education Executive Officers (SHEEO), surveyed state CWS programs for their connection to community service. In 1985, seventeen states had work-study programs and another fifteen had plans for programs in various stages of development. Mingle found a growing interest in the states in work-study programs because they are less expensive than grants or loans and because research shows "a positive relationship between work-study and both retention and academic performance."

Several states have also found work-study programs useful in providing incentives for student community service. The Florida State Work-Study Program and the Florida Public School-Work Program both provide paid public school work opportunities for college students. Minnesota's State Work-Study Program funds a $4.4 million program that allows handicapped individuals and persons over sixty-five to employ work-study students. Connecticut passed legislation in 1987 approving 5 percent of state CWS funds for community service work-study placements.

California Assemblyman Tom Hayden has proposed a Robert F. Kennedy Memorial Service Scholarship program that would match federal work-study funds with private-sector funds for public service positions. The program would help to redirect the use of work-study funds as institutional budget relief and, instead, would employ students to help meet community needs.

State-funded CWS programs are an increasingly important source of financial aid. New provisions in the 1986 reauthorization of the Higher Education Act allow greater flexibility in the use of SSIG funds and could provide sufficient support to fund other programs that are on the drawing board. Many existing or new programs could be targeted at supporting students, to address a range of community needs.

LOAN FORGIVENESS AND DEFERMENT. The most common loan-forgiveness and -deferment programs are those designed to attract and retain more-qualified classroom teachers. According to a 1985 College Board study, loan-forgiveness programs had been enacted or proposed in over half the states.[13] The school district of Jefferson County in Colorado passed a loan-forgiveness program for its own high school graduates who promise to return to the county to teach after graduating from college. The amount of funds appropriated by state legislators varies widely, as does the size of the loans forgiven under the various programs. Most states do not base eligibility on financial need.

Many of the incentive programs were put in place in states in the last several years in response to the school reform movement of the early 1980s. Other loan-forgiveness or -deferment programs could be based on these established models in response to the perception of other important community needs—for example, affordable low-income housing, care for the elderly, and day care. In Minnesota, Governor Rudy Perpich has requested funding from the legislature to provide tuition forgiveness to college students who would volunteer for a range of community service programs. The College Board has raised a number of policy issues regarding the efficacy of loan-forgiveness programs as a way to attract and retain elementary and secondary school teachers.

OTHER STATE-INITIATED COMMUNITY SERVICE PROGRAMS. Other new state initiatives creatively use state funds to meet important community needs and to encourage college students to participate in public service activities. The Kansas state legislature funded the pilot program of Youth Education Service (YES), in which students from three colleges serve as mentors for children at risk of dropping out of school. In exchange, the college students receive a stipend to reduce their financial aid debt.

In California, "bottle bill" legislation allocates 10 percent of funds collected from a surcharge on bottles to be used to support local conservation corps. Seven new local corps are either under way or are being planned with a pool of funds from this revenue source, starting at $1.5 million. Other states could adopt this model as a source of financial aid for students participating in community service programs.

INSTITUTIONAL INITIATIVES

In the past three years, individual institutions have initiated or expanded community service programs, many of which provide some financial assistance to participating students as fellowships, work-study funds, scholarships, tuition remission, or loan reduction. In 1986, Stanford University conducted a survey of Campus Compact members to determine the extent of student involvement and to catalog institutional policies that support student involvement in public service. Respondents were asked to identify factors that prevent more students from participating in public service activities; 70 percent cited financial deterrents as the most significant reason for not participating. Many institutions in the Campus Compact have responded to this information by establishing a range of programs to link financial aid and service. Several of the new programs mentioned below have been the result of grants from FIPSE's Innovative Projects in Community Service and Student Financial Independence.

Westmont College in California has begun a community service program through which a student can receive a tuition credit based on the numbers of hours per week the student has been active in a community service program the previous semester. The amount of the credit ranges from $400 for eight hours of service each week to $800 for sixteen hours. At Bethany College in Kansas, a special grant program is funded by the college and local public service agencies. Financial assistance is provided by the service agency in tuition grants based on a percentage of the tuition rate and the number of hours a student agrees to contribute. The formula allows an agency to secure a qualified worker at a cost approximately equal to minimum wage. Students participating in this program can work up to twenty hours per week and receive up to 50 percent of their tuition costs. The University of Southern California provides grants, renewable for up to four years, through the Norman Topping Student Aid Fund to replace 5 percent of students' loans or CWS aid. Students must provide more than 20 hours of service per semester and maintain a 2.0 grade point average. The program is funded by a student activities fee matched by university funds.

Brown University created the Starr Scholarship Program to recognize and reward students who have made a commitment of the equivalent of one year to public service work, either before entering Brown as a first-year student or while on a leave of absence from the institution. The grants, normally $1,000, are awarded on a competitive basis. The Public Service Scholars Program at Hunter College provides funds for twenty-four competitively selected students a year to consider public service careers. The program enables talented students, particularly women and minorities, to hold year-long internships in the public sector while attending a seminar on issues important to the future of New York City. Students receive a stipend of $4,000 and earn nine credits for the seminar.

The Service Opportunity Stipend program at Wellesley is funded by an alumna to encourage direct student involvement in public service. Stipends of $750 to $1,500 support students who undertake public service projects in this country and abroad. Other students were awarded funds to work during winter session with Boston-area organizations focusing on the homeless, hungry, and elderly. Grinnell College, through the Rosenfield Program in Public Affairs, Human Rights, and International Relations, awards $2,700 to selected students each summer to pursue internships in public service. Brown University has a summer public service fellowship program in honor of its former president and his wife, Howard and Jan Swearer. Approximately twelve $2,000 fellowships are awarded to students who design projects with a community organization either in this country or abroad.

At the University of California at Berkeley, $200,000 in university funds were set aside to fully or partially repay student loans for any financial aid recipient who participates in approved community service projects either while in school or following graduation. Students are responsible for finding community service placements through the clearinghouse on the campus. Dartmouth College offers a loan-forgiveness program for graduating students working in lower-paying public service jobs. Berea College has no-interest loans for graduating students who work in the mountain areas of Kentucky. The University of Rochester Reach Experienceship subsidizes 50 percent of salaries for students who work ten to fifteen hours per week during the academic term or full-time during the summer. Students who participate for a second year in the program receive a need-based debt-reducing grant of up to $2,500.

CORPORATE PROGRAMS

A program established in 1983 by the Stride-Rite Corporation provides ten scholarships each year to needy first-year Harvard students from inner-city Boston. Each student selected for support receives a $1,500 scholarship, $3,000 work-study subsidy, and $500 for books. In return, students work in social service agencies a certain number of hours each week during all of their undergraduate years. Arnold Hiatt, chief executive officer of Stride-Rite, hopes that the program he initiated will serve as a prototype for similar corporate programs at other colleges and universities. The program has many strengths: it can be funded at any level; it provides generous aid to give lower-income students access to college and encouragement to work with community agencies at the same time; its participants act as role models to younger students in the community and build links to high school students; and it is an example of college, community, and corporate cooperation.

FOUNDATION PROGRAMS

In 1984 the Charles A. Dana Foundation established a competitive grants program called Student Aid for Educational Quality to help institutions, principally liberal arts colleges in the eastern states, increase their total financial aid resources in ways that enhance the quality of students' education. The foundation hopes that increased student aid, strategically applied, will help these colleges remain a viable choice for students with limited financial means. To date, the foundation has provided almost $6 million to twenty-eight colleges, leveraging $17 million in matching funds supporting five thousand student jobs.

Recipient institutions have applied the Dana funds to a range of interesting programs. For example, at Wheaton College in Massachusetts, the funds were used in 1987 in part to underwrite twelve students on financial aid to work full-time on summer community service projects with local human service agencies, including projects on urban justice, economic development for minority populations, and displaced homemakers. Several service positions were also funded in Kenya, complementing Wheaton's emphasis on internationalizing the curriculum.

Conclusions and Recommendations

Student financial assistance linked to service in the national interest goes back to the GI Bill of the 1940s. In the 1980s, governmental and institutional policymakers have renewed their interest both in helping students find new ways to pay for college and in encouraging them to develop a sense of civic responsibility. The ability to pursue both goals through the same programs lies behind much of the recent interest in service-based financial aid. The roster of current programs and new initiatives presented above is testimony to the appeal of public and community service for young people.

We have suggested that public and community service is an appropriate policy objective at many levels: federal, state, and local governments, colleges and universities, corporations, foundations, and other private-sector groups. Each can expand its responsibility for financing higher education by incorporating public and community service programs in ways appropriate to its role. Thus, we do not call for a service link in every financial aid program, nor do we advocate that all federal student assistance be dependent on service. Instead, we believe that a multifaceted, multiprogram approach will bring the greatest benefits to both students and the nation.

The federal government should act on both of its long-standing traditions for student financial assistance—reward for service and equal opportunity. The foundation should be a strengthened program of Pell Grants to provide access and opportunity for students whose financial circumstances might otherwise deny them further education. But all students should be expected to provide a self-help component. Rather than demanding self-help in the form of ever higher levels of borrowing from students, we should direct new federal dollars toward CWS and other need-based programs that reinforce sound educational goals, encourage retention, and develop citizenship while providing the means for students to contribute financially to their own education. The Pell Grant program could also include a kicker clause: eligible recipients who engage in service would receive a larger Pell Grant than their nonservice peers. Evaluation of the FIPSE experiments described above should provide models on which new public, as well as institutional, policies can be based.

In addition to achieving equal-opportunity goals, the federal government seeks to provide financial aid as a reward for service through the GI Bill, health professions, and teacher corps programs, and other responses to labor market needs. The level of investment in such programs will vary with projections of shortages in critical occupations. The current focus on support for doctors and teachers who serve in inner cities or poverty areas targets federal funds on national needs that are unlikely to disappear even with the increase in supply of doctors or the general rise in teachers' salaries. Although these financial assistance programs are related to service from the students' viewpoint, they address equal-opportunity goals in a national perspective.

There are serious problems with the growth of loans, not only for federal obligations in future years but for needy students facing increasing debt loads. Within the constraints of the current federal fiscal situation, expansion of service-based aid programs will be limited to replacement for current expenditures on other types of financial assistance. The proposal for one modeled on ROTC—with prior training and subsequent grants for education— for Peace Corps and VISTA volunteers becomes a high priority for redirected funds. Creating parity in the treatment of young people performing military and civilian service to their nation also addresses issues of equity not heretofore raised in debates on financial aid.

If new federal dollars for student financial assistance become available, we place a high priority on programs that link aid to work and service and thus reinforce positive educational and social values while decreasing reliance on loans as the primary vehicle for providing equal opportunity.

State governments have assumed a greater role in providing student aid in recent years, while federal appropriations have remained constant at best. All the arguments on behalf of service-related programs at the federal level can be repeated at the state level. The increases in state work-study programs are an example of state initiatives mirroring federal programs. In addition, the incentives provided by the federal government through SSIG have stimulated substantial new investment in financial aid, including service-related aid, by states.

The second type of investment in service at the state level has been the establishment of youth service corps. Many state-sponsored youth corps tend to emphasize service projects for young people who are not college-bound, and most programs share the federal focus on economically disadvantaged students, although at the state level service to the community gets higher priority.

States can also encourage links between service and financial aid by the expectations they place on public institutions within their jurisdiction. Whether public or independent, however, colleges and universities may have the greatest impact on service activities of their students. Campus decision makers can target their own scholarship and loan programs to reward service; they can give priority to service in admissions decisions; they can create centers for public service; they can modify curricula to add service components; and they can encourage undergraduates, regardless of economic circumstances, to participate in activities that enhance public and community objectives. As noted earlier, institutions may choose to focus on the educational and social benefits of community service, making the link to financial aid an important, but not overriding, consideration. It may also be easier at the campus level to create loan-deferment or loan-forgiveness programs to provide incentives for particular types of service, using institutional funds to achieve these objectives. Colleges and universities have the ability to involve all students in service goals, regardless of financial need.

The role of other private-sector groups, such as corporations and foundations, is largely untested. The few examples listed above suggest a rich opportunity for organizations concerned about both educational and community needs to support programs that bring students into service beyond the bounds of the campus. Corporations and foundations could play a significant role as providers of matching funds for institutional programs of financial assistance linked to public and community service.

The interest in service among federal officials, state governments, colleges and universities, and private entities suggests that new policies for financing higher education should certainly include a component of public and community service. Such programs not only help students reduce their dependence on loans but provide self-help components to financial aid that foster student retention, academic achievement, and citizenship development.

Notes

1. United States National Commission on Excellence in Education, *A Nation at Risk: The Imperative for Educational Reform* (Washington, D.C.: U.S. Department of Education, 1983).

2. Richard Danzig and Peter Szanton, *National Service: What Would It Mean?* (Lexington, Mass.: Lexington Books, 1986).

3. Democratic Leadership Council, *Citizenship and National Service: A Blueprint for Civic Enterprise* (Washington, D.C.: DLC, 1988).

4. Janet S. Hansen, *The Democratic Leadership Council Proposal for Voluntary National Service* (Washington, D.C.: College Board, 1988).

5. Frank Newman, *Higher Education and the American Resurgence* (Princeton, N.J.: Carnegie Foundation for the Advancement of Teaching, 1985).

6. See Mark Ventresca and Anna Waring, *Collegiate Community Service: Status of Public and Community Service at Selected Colleges and Universities* (Providence, R.I.: Campus Compact, 1987).

7. American Council on Education, Division of Policy Analysis and Research, *Joining Forces: The Military's Impact on College Enrollments* (Washington, D.C.: ACE, 1988).

8. Charles Moskos, *A Call to Civic Service* (New York: Free Press, 1988).

9. The DLC breaks the costs of the Citizen Corps down as follows: Senior Citizen Corps (100,000 positions), $1.4 billion; Conservation Corps (100,000 positions), $1 billion; Peace Corps (10,000 new volunteers), $200 million; VISTA (13,000 new volunteers), $110 million; and new slots (477,000 volunteers), $4.3 billion.

10. See Greg Gollihur, *Financial Aid and Public Service: A California Perspective* (Sacramento: California Student Aid Commission, 1987).

11. The Vasconcellos bill was Assembly Concurrent Resolution 158 of 1986.

12. The Paleologos bill was House bill 4907.

13. Irene Spero, *The Use of Student Financial Aid to Attract Prospective Teachers: A Survey of State Efforts. Testimony on Reauthorization of the Higher Education Act* (Washington, D.C.: College Board, 1985).

PART III

Government and Private Responsibilities

12

New Ways of Paying for College: Should the Federal Government Help?

JANET S. HANSEN and LAWRENCE E. GLADIEUX

The late 1980s found the American public deeply concerned about paying for higher education. In recent years, annual increases in college tuitions have exceeded inflation, growth in family and per capita incomes, and returns that savers can reasonably expect to receive on investments. Moreover, federal programs of student financial aid, after undergoing tremendous growth during the 1970s, leveled off just as tuition costs surged upward. Increases in state and institutional student aid could not compensate fully for rising college charges and the declining value of federal awards. Increasingly, student aid took the form of loans, with uncertain implications for young borrowers. Families who were unlikely to qualify on the basis of income for student aid also exhibited growing dismay about how to finance postsecondary education for their children.

What role should the federal government play in addressing these concerns and in fostering the development of new financing mechanisms? We approach these questions by first defining a framework for analyzing the federal responsibility for higher-education finance and then using that framework to describe how the federal government currently carries out its part in sharing the costs of higher education. We review evidence of shifts in financing patterns that have occurred in recent years. We look at the context in which decisions about the federal role will be made, particularly the financial and demographic issues, and conclude by discussing how the federal government should respond to recent concerns about college finance.

Federal Roles and Responsibilities: A Framework for Analysis

In a recent study of the financing of higher education in five countries, D. Bruce Johnstone observed that the burden of educational costs must be shared by some combination of four partners or sources of revenue: parents, students, taxpayers, and institutions (that is, colleges or universities, which in turn obtain revenues from organized philanthropy and individual donors).[1]

The United States is unusual in the extent to which the burdens of college costs are shared relatively equally among these four sources. Parents are expected to contribute to the expenses of their children's higher education to the extent that they are financially able. Students, too, are expected to work or borrow to meet a share of college costs. These costs include not just living expenses, as in many other countries, but part of the instructional costs of higher education as well. Even public institutions, which receive large subsidies from state taxpayers, charge some tuition, and private institutions are heavily dependent on tuition income. (In other countries, there are often no tuition charges for higher education or, if they exist, the government pays them for nearly all students, especially citizens.) State and federal taxpayers support both colleges and students, with states taking the lead in institutional support and the federal government providing the lion's share of student financial assistance. Finally, philanthropists and individual donors (both current and past) pick up some of the burden by providing current operating support and by contributing to endowments.

This relatively equal sharing of the burden of paying for college has an important consequence. It helps explain why access to higher education is so much wider in the United States than in many other countries. Countries that do not expect contributions from all the partners educate a substantially smaller proportion of their population.

The burden-sharing model, by highlighting the role of the various partners, refines and amplifies our understanding of the federal government's responsibilities for financing education beyond high school. For the past quarter century, Washington's responsibilities have been seen as essentially twofold: providing financial assistance to students to promote equal educational opportunity and supporting researchers in universities (and the research capacities of universities). This shorthand description of the first responsibility, while accurate as far as it goes, is inadequate to describe the full extent of federal involvement in sharing and adjusting the burden of college costs. Thus, in this essay, we use Johnstone's burden-sharing model both to describe the range of current federal responsibilities and to assess whether Washington should sponsor new financing mechanisms.

Reexamining existing policies in this light, we see that the federal government carries out its part in sharing the costs of higher education by providing grants to students from families without adequate resources to pay for college on their own. Through these outright grants, federal taxpayers pick up part of the burden of paying for college. This need-based assistance is consonant with the widely recognized special responsibility of the federal government for equalizing educational opportunities for disadvantaged, underserved populations.

Washington also uses federal tax dollars to encourage the other partners to pick up their shares of the burden of college expenses. The federal government enables students to invest in their educations through student loans. It is generally agreed that private credit markets will not make loans available to young students with no work experience or credit histories. The federal government overcomes this "market imperfection" by providing loan capital to students through Perkins Loans and, more significantly, by creating access to private credit markets through the default guarantees and loan subsidies of the Stafford Loan (formerly Guaranteed Student Loan) program. It also enhances student employment through the College Work-Study program.

In addition to encouraging the private sector to open credit and employment markets to students, the federal government encourages parents to contribute to the higher education of their children, chiefly through provisions in the income tax code. Parents with a child who is a full-time student at an institution of higher education may continue to declare the child as a dependent for income tax purposes. Savings incentives such as Clifford Trusts were cut back in the 1986 tax reform, but tax-advantaged methods of savings still exist, and a new savings incentive, college savings bonds, goes into effect in 1990 (see the discussion below). Parents can also borrow to meet educational expenses through a federally sponsored Parent Loan program that provides only minimal subsidies but carries a guarantee against default and for which there is no income limitation on eligibility.

Last among the federal encouragements, and again working through the tax code, Washington promotes philanthropic donations to colleges and universities by exempting charitable donations from taxable income.

In addition to sharing the burden of paying for college, the federal government provides counseling and academic support services to disadvantaged youth and adults, primarily through the so-called TRIO programs. These services take on added importance in the light of mounting evidence that early academic preparation and motivation are vital adjuncts to financial aid in helping at-risk students navigate successfully through high school and college.

These, in summary, are the ways in which the federal government acts to relieve the burden of postsecondary expenses and to encourage others to bear their share of the costs. Now we ask, Is the pattern of burden sharing among the partners changing in ways that might call for a federal response?

Signs of Shifting Burdens

Data about who pays how much for higher education in the United States are frustratingly elusive. Nevertheless, a brief look at some basic statistical relationships indicates that the burdens of paying for college have shifted over time.[2] Sometimes these shifts have resulted from explicit policy decisions. Especially in recent years, however, the shifts have occurred more as a result of general economic and fiscal pressures than from a strong desire on the part of policymakers to alter the balance of responsibility for meeting college costs. Whatever the reason, the burdens on parents and students have been increasing.

Figure 12.1 provides visual evidence of the increasing pressures felt by parents generally in meeting their share of college costs and suggests why rising tuition levels and the affordability of college have become major political issues in the last several years. The chart shows that college costs and median family incomes (both indexed with 1970 levels set equal to 100) rose

FIGURE 12.1 Changes in Median Family Income and College Costs: 1963 to 1987

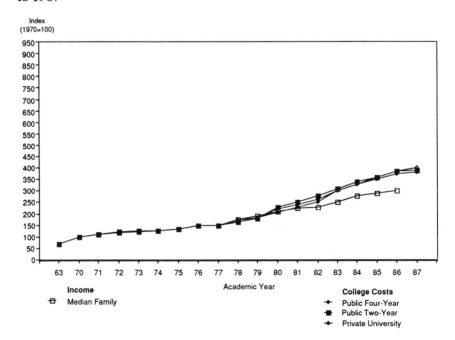

FIGURE 12.2　Changes in Grants and College Costs: 1963 to 1987

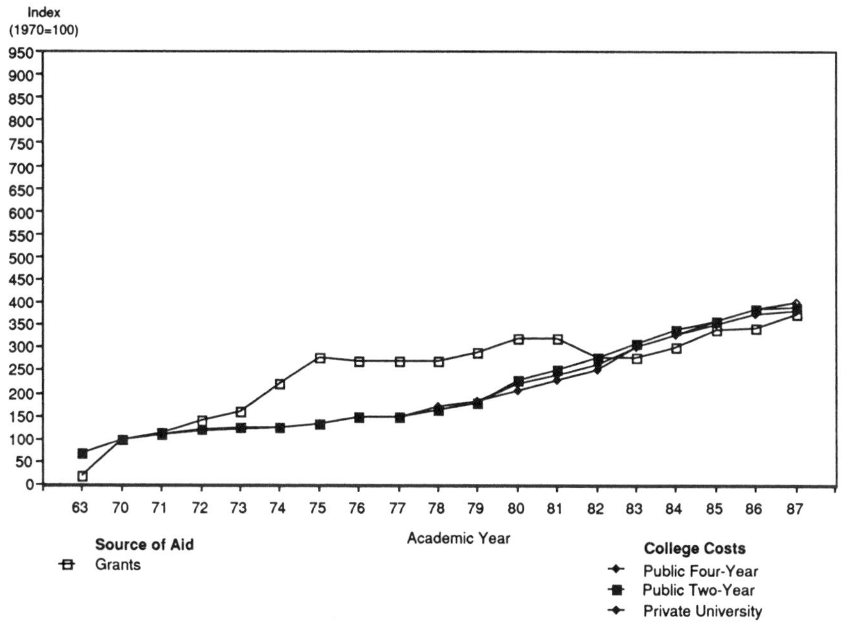

Index
(1970=100)

Source of Aid	Academic Year	College Costs
⊟　Grants		✦　Public Four-Year
		■　Public Two-Year
		✦　Private University

at about the same rate until about 1980, when family income increases began to lag behind the growth in expenses in all sectors of higher education.

Figures 12.2 and 12.3 (again indexed with 1970 equal to 100) show the growing burden on parents and students—especially those who might consider applying for need-based financial aid. Figure 12.2 shows how college costs have changed relative to grant aid. The grant index was below the index for college costs in the 1960s but then rose noticeably above the cost index in the 1970s, suggesting that the cost burden was shifting from poorer families to the providers of grant assistance. Growth in federal grant programs was largely responsible for this change. In the 1980s, however, the burden of paying for college shifted back toward families, as the grant index fell relative to the costs of attendance. Here, as in the previous decade, changes in federal grant aid were responsible. Although state and institutional grants grew in the 1980s, as federal grants languished, they did not make up for the losses in aid from Washington.

Figure 12.3 provides another view of the shifting burden, focusing on student loans. Parallel growth in the indexes for loan availability and college costs in the early and middle 1970s suggests that the student share of college expenses was generally stable. Then, in the late 1970s, after passage of the Middle Income Student Assistance Act, the loan index started growing much faster than the cost index. Grant aid had not yet begun to slow, so the immediate effect of increased student borrowing may have been to reduce the burden on parents, at least for a few years. More recently, however, grant aid fell behind the growth in college costs, and new eligibility restrictions in the Stafford Student Loan program limited its use as a replacement for the parental contribution. Hence, the growing disparity between the loan and cost indexes indicates that students, particularly at lower income levels, are assuming more responsibility for paying college bills.

FIGURE 12.3   Changes in Student Loans and College Costs: 1963 to 1987

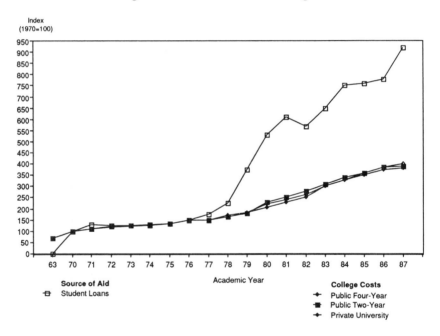

The graphic data, although oversimplified, support anecdotal evidence about the shifting burdens of college expenses over the past quarter century. Costs are outstripping income increases for virtually all families. Lower-income families who could qualify on the basis of financial need found their burdens lightened in the 1970s, as the federal government picked up a larger share. In the 1980s, however, the burden shifted back again toward parents and students, with the latter borrowing ever more heavily to make up for both slow-growing family incomes and grant aid that has failed to keep up with rising college costs. Given these changes, should the federal government respond, and how?

A Context for Decision: Deficits and Demography

Decisions about the appropriate federal role in financing higher education will not be made in a vacuum. Our views about what Washington should and should not do are strongly influenced by two critical features of the current and foreseeable national landscape: the huge federal budget deficit and the changing characteristics of the American population.

The deficit will be the overwhelming fact of political life in the period ahead. Although largely ignored during the recent presidential campaign, it surfaced as a major concern as early as the interregnum between the Reagan and Bush administrations. President Bush vows to resist any tax increase or cuts in defense and social security programs and promises to reduce the deficit through a "flexible freeze" on most other federal spending and through growth in the economy at large. Legislators from both parties doubt that meaningful reductions in the deficit can be made in such relatively painless ways. Thus, the stage is set for a major confrontation on the nation's economic future.

Our own view is that however these issues are resolved, little or no new money is likely to be available for federal education programs any time soon, and it is possible that significant cutbacks could occur. To fulfill his promise of being an "education president," George Bush may try to increase spending in this area at the expense of other social programs. Congress has demonstrated over the past eight years its support for education in general and for student assistance programs in particular, as it resisted calls for massive cutbacks from the Reagan administration. But this executive and congressional goodwill will be increasingly difficult to translate into real growth in federal education programs.

Even if new monies become available, moreover, important trade-offs will have to be addressed. Should elementary and secondary education or preschool education programs be given a higher priority for additional funding than college programs? Will uncontrollable costs in the Stafford Loan program eat into the appropriations available for financial assistance in the form of grants? What will happen to need-based financial aid programs if eligibility for federal funds is broadened to families who do not now qualify for federal assistance on the basis of financial need?

This latter question takes on special urgency in light of the demographic changes under way in the United States. Families are increasingly headed by single parents, often women, whose economic prospects are limited. Even now, a fifth of American children live in poverty. Moreover, minority-group children, who will make up a third of the U.S. school-age population by the turn of the century, often are precisely those who need educational assistance most: they drop out of high school at higher rates and enroll in college at noticeably lower rates.

Arguments about equity aside, it is increasingly apparent that the nation can no longer afford to overlook these human resources. If labor market needs are to be met and economic growth encouraged, more of the children from traditionally underserved groups must graduate from high school and participate in postsecondary education. Adequate financial aid alone will not make this happen, but insufficient financial resources will constitute a serious barrier to equal participation by these groups. In an era of sharp fiscal constraint, this fact, too, greatly influences our judgments about how limited resources should be allocated.

Old Roles and New Responsibilities

Having looked at the current federal role in postsecondary finance, at evidence of shifting financial burdens, and at the context in which decisions about future federal responsibilities must be made, we now come back to our initial questions: What should Washington's response be to current concerns about financing higher education? What responsibility should the federal government take for new financing mechanisms? We present our answers within the framework of the burden-sharing model, examining whether, and how, the federal government should pick up more of the burden directly from families, encourage and assist parents and students with their shares, or both.

The most widely discussed proposals for new financing options, savings plans and tuition futures, emphasize assisting parents with their responsibilities. Most propose some kind of subsidy, usually a tax benefit, to create an incentive for parents to plan ahead and save for college. Almost certainly, such plans would provide most of their benefits to middle- and upper-income families, who can afford to save for their children's educations.

On the assumption that new federal resources will be scarce, we give a higher priority to improving the buying power of direct grant assistance for the financially needy than to providing tax benefits for the middle class. Demographic changes suggest that programs such as Pell Grants will come under increasing pressure. The need for grant aid will certainly grow to the extent that the nation is successful in efforts to encourage more students from traditionally disadvantaged backgrounds to continue their educations. We suspect that it will be all Washington can do to keep the buying power of Pell Grants at current levels. Should new money unexpectedly be available, however, we think that providing more of a guarantee of assistance (for example, by making Pell Grants a true entitlement at some higher level than today) for students whose capacity to bear the burden of college costs is limited is more important than providing federal incentives to families who have the capacity, if not the will, to pay for college.

In other words, we do not favor a major federal investment in savings and tuition-futures plans. Congress's recent enactment of a limited college savings bond plan goes as far as we think Washington should go in this direction. This plan, scheduled to go into effect in 1990, will allow parents a tax exemption for the proceeds of U.S. savings bonds if the bonds are used to pay for tuition and required fees (net of financial aid). Tax benefits are to be phased out, beginning with families with adjusted gross incomes of $60,000 and disappearing entirely at $90,000 (with income limits each year adjusted for inflation). The rules about who can benefit from the tax exemption and what education expenses are eligible are carefully circumscribed to keep federal subsidies limited.

The availability of these education savings bonds, coupled with the college savings plans adopted in a number of states, should satisfy the need for explicit public policies aimed at encouraging family savings for college. The task now is to popularize the program and maximize its potential as a catalyst for precollege saving and investment. We do not, however, favor further expansion of such federal subsidies, either through wider eligibility for savings bonds or through a federal tuition-futures plan.

The concept of tuition futures, pioneered in Michigan and under development in eight other states, has proven far more problematic than its sponsors originally indicated. The financial risks to government are uncertain and potentially high. The strongest argument for a federal plan, to avoid the balkanization of higher education that might result from multiple state plans, has lost force as states themselves have become warier of the concept and more inclined to enact savings plans instead.

Our comments to this point have reflected our preference for emphasizing current federal responsibilities for the financially needy rather than creating new financing mechanisms. In a similar vein, we think that attention should be paid to the way Washington encourages students to bear their share of the college cost burden, especially through student loans. The participation of students as partners in financing is crucial in maintaining access to higher education. Federal student loan programs (under which students now borrow $11 billion annually), together with the much smaller but important federal support for work-study, facilitate student "self-help" in the college finance equation. We have seen that the student-borne share of costs is growing, and we are concerned that the emphasis on loans versus grants has gone too far, especially for disadvantaged and low-income students. Yet there seems little likelihood that borrowing levels can be reduced in the foreseeable future; in fact, they are likely to grow.

We would therefore like to see some kind of insurance built into student loan programs to protect borrowers against the risk of low future earnings. The theory behind student loans is that education is in part an economic investment and that loans enable students to invest in themselves and the greater economic rewards that their education will bring. Although these assumptions undoubtedly hold true in general, there will always be individuals whose education does not pay off in the expected economic ways. Student repayment provisions could be adjusted to protect borrowers against this risk. This idea can only be suggested, not fully explored, here. But we suggest that this area would be a more appropriate target for federal subsidization if funds were available than some of the new financing tools under discussion.

Also important, but not possible to explore adequately here, is the larger issue of the structure and uncontrollable expense built into the federal student loan system. The government's cost exposure in Stafford Loans makes this program a shaky foundation for student assistance—and erodes support for grant programs. Rising default claims projected for the years ahead, combined with higher payments to lenders if interest rates rise, could generate another crisis-driven search for cost savings and could destabilize program operations, as students and institutions learned in the early 1980s. For the long haul, whether through restructuring or tightening of the current system, federal policymakers should consider reducing loan subsidies that are not directed toward needy students and stabilizing the long-term obligations that the government incurs when it guarantees loans to students and parents.

Having emphasized our judgment that the appropriate federal role in financing college should remain primarily the traditional one of lightening the burden of families of limited financial means, we turn now to proposals to reform dramatically the way in which grant subsidies to such families are given. Particularly, we refer to the proposals recently advanced by the Democratic Leadership Council and by Professor Charles Moskos in a report for the Twentieth-Century Fund to make federal student assistance contingent on participation in community or national service activities.[3] We cannot give our full analysis here, but we are wary of such proposals. Although advocates of national service may have worthy goals, a national service plan, in our view, cannot replace existing student aid programs. A critical roadblock is fiscal. Students who are not needy and those who are—who currently receive need-based financial assistance—cannot both be accommodated within the plans as currently described, yet the enlarged program that would be required by a "voluntary" plan open to all cannot be supported by the funds currently devoted to student aid. Moreover, some analysts have argued that educational opportunity would be restricted, rather than expanded, by a system that tied federal education benefits to mandatory national service.[4] There may be a role for the federal government in supporting some kind of smaller, more experimental undertaking, perhaps using education assistance as an incentive but not involving wholesale replacement of the existing student aid system. Here again, though, questions of budgetary trade-offs must be addressed head-on.

Finally, the federal government should look beyond narrow financing mechanisms as it assesses how best to carry out its responsibility to equalize educational opportunity in an era of limited resources and demographic change. So-called guaranteed-access programs, such as Eugene Lang's I Have a Dream Foundation model and the newly enacted New York State Liberty Scholarship program, include assurances of adequate financing for college as an incentive for young people to stay in school and acquire the proper academic preparation for higher education. But they also recognize the importance of individual guidance, tutoring, and encouragement in reaching at-risk youth. Perhaps the best and most equitable use of incremental federal funds in an era of fiscal constraint would be to support the federal TRIO programs, which bring such services to educationally and economically disadvantaged students.

Notes

1. D. Bruce Johnstone, *Sharing the Costs of Higher Education: Student Financial Assistance in the United Kingdom, the Federal Republic of Germany, France, Sweden, and the United States* (New York: College Entrance Examination Board, 1986).
2. Data in all three charts are taken from College Board, *Trends in Student Aid*, various editions (New York: College Entrance Examination Board, 1983-1988).
3. Democratic Leadership Council, *Citizenship and National Service: A Blueprint for Civic Enterprise* (Washington, D.C.: DLC, 1988); Charles C. Moskos, *A Call to Service: National Service for Country and Community* (New York: Free Press, 1988).
4. See, for example, Richard Danzig and Peter Szanton, *National Service: What Would It Mean?* (Lexington, Mass.: Heath, 1986).

13

The States' Role in Financing Higher Education: A Perspective

AIMS C. MCGUINNESS, JR.

The states have played—and should continue to play—a central role in the financing of American higher education. For the states to continue to promote creative and responsive innovation in higher-education financing, however, policymakers at the state level must recognize the changing terms of debate on the issues, they must understand and master the processes of reform, and they must take some major steps to exert leadership in meeting the evolving financing needs of the coming generation.

The Changing Agenda of Higher-Education Finance

The recent spread of new state tuition-guarantee and college savings bond plans across the nation is only one of several trends conveying a clear message: The terms of the debate about the financing of higher education are undergoing fundamental change. Because this is so, a discussion of the role of the states should begin with a recasting of the agenda for debate. At least five issues may rise to prominence in the next decade: the impact of financing decisions on educational quality, the emergence of state issues as a national concern, the cumbersome superstructure of the aid system, public concern about the affordability of higher education, and the effect of changes in financing for students and families on American higher education itself.

EDUCATIONAL QUALITY

Debates about financing higher education generally cannot take place now outside the context of the educational impact of one approach or another. Although in the 1970s it was common to hear alternative financing plans discussed mostly in terms of economic equity and efficiency, today's discussions are increasingly framed in terms of educational quality, which has reemerged as a national goal. For example, the higher-education community is increasingly aware that encouraging economically disadvantaged youth to pursue postsecondary education requires more than better-funded student aid programs or continued low tuition at public institutions. Equally important are efforts—once considered "ancillary"—to improve the quality of elementary and secondary education, to build students' self-confidence and self-esteem, and to instill in students and their families confidence that adequate financing will be available for postsecondary education.

Also affecting the issue of educational quality is the growing interest in higher-education circles in providing secondary students with a fuller range of choices to meet their educational goals. Where once secondary and higher education competed for limited tax resources, both camps now are identifying common goals that they can further by transcending traditional rivalries and boundaries, as high-school-oriented efforts such as Minnesota's Postsecondary Options program illustrate. Thus, topics for debate in the coming years may well include the question of whether we can develop financing alternatives that allow greater cooperation between the secondary and postsecondary sectors. For example, should the financing policies applicable to higher education be extended to the last two years of high school, so that families bear some of the costs, financial aid is made available, and students are given a wider range of educational options?

Further beyond considerations of equity and access, there is a growing awareness that the form of funding is not educationally neutral. That is, students may be steered in their educational and career choices by whether they receive aid in the form of loans, lower tuitions, grants, or opportunities for work or community service. On the negative side, fear of indebtedness can be a powerful deterrent to students' pursuit of higher education and can influence their choice of certain educational and career paths. In contrast, an opportunity to provide community service not only may help undergraduates pay for college but may spur achievement and broaden attitudes.

STATE ISSUES AT THE NATIONAL LEVEL

A second focus for discussion in the coming decade concerns the need to recognize that the issues of higher-education finance at the state level are inadequately recognized in the national arena. National discussions inevitably focus on technical matters that often make sense only at the federal level—for example, involving need-based student grants, work-study, and student loans. Yet any national discussion of financing alternatives cannot ignore the fact that the states collectively undergird more than $30 billion in support for higher education. Worthwhile discussions about the future financing of higher education thus must not take place without considering subsidy of public institutions, tuition policy, and state aid to private institutions. Given the sensitivity of the issues and the great variations in tradition and policy among states, it is difficult to raise these questions in a national context. Yet their collective importance must somehow be recognized.

THE UNWIELDY STUDENT AID SYSTEM

A third concern is that there is growing evidence that the complexity of the current student aid system is itself becoming a barrier to access and participation. The intricate application process, the highly technical process for determining eligibility, the proliferating provisions to curb fraud and abuse, and the ingrown nature of the professional student-aid community—all contribute to a public perception that the system has reached the limits of its capacity to deliver benefits efficiently and effectively. How can this be changed?

PUBLIC CONCERNS ABOUT COSTS

A fourth topic is that perceptions rather than facts about college prices and costs, about the availability of aid, and about the inability of income to keep pace with rising costs are becoming more powerful than ever in influencing student and family behavior. These perceptions clearly have motivated the current political interest in tuition guarantee and savings plans. Yet much misperception has been engendered by highly publicized statements by former Secretary of Education William Bennett, by less-than-clear responses from the higher-education community, and by a thousand other signals transmitted through the media. Correcting the misperceptions must go beyond developing new financing alternatives; it must involve effectively publicizing and marketing the alternatives. Thus, clarity, consistency, and confidence will be crucial to new proposals for the future financing of higher education.

THE IMPACT OF FINANCING CHANGES ON HIGHER EDUCATION

Finally, much of the debate about education has neglected to consider how various financing alternatives may reshape the nation's higher-education system. New alternatives for students inevitably have profound implications for institutions, for the higher-education system, and even for the nation's competitive position. In contrast to most other industrialized nations, the United States has a mixed public and private system of higher education that is heavily influenced by market forces. Yet traditional public and private roles are becoming blurred. Some privately owned institutions are now being heavily subsidized through publicly funded grants and loans to their students, whereas many publicly owned institutions are depending increasingly on private funding (e.g., revenue from tuition and fees, alumni giving, endowments, and philanthropic and corporate support). New financial alternatives will have profound effects on the socioeconomic, racial, and ethnic balance within different institutions, both public and private. They will also have serious effects on the capacity of different institutions—especially the traditional nonprofit private sector—to continue to compete and provide services to their students and communities. Thus, the demands for educational change, and even for institutional survival, in the next decade will press the U.S. system to exhibit more flexibility, innovation, and competitiveness.

If the issues regarding the future financing of higher education are viewed from this broader, revised perspective, it is difficult to conceive of financing alternatives that will not inevitably involve the states. In fact, it is clear that only by involving the states can many of the issues and interacting policies just mentioned be fully addressed. But what can be said about the capacity and willingness of the states to respond?

The Capacity of the States to Respond

The states have taken an important role in pioneering a number of innovative financing plans. These include tuition-guarantee plans, savings plans, and state-sponsored tuition-assurance plans, among others. State leaders were among the first to sense a change in the nature and terms of the financing debate and to recognize the limitations of relying on loans. Convinced that mere tinkering with traditional policies would not satisfy their constituents, state leaders were also among the first to take dramatic action by devising creative programs. Without denying the shortcomings of some of the new guarantee and savings proposals, one may remain convinced that the development of plans so far underlines the importance of state leadership in future financing efforts.

RECENT DEVELOPMENTS IN STATE-LEVEL FINANCING

Perhaps most important to understand is that the most promising alternatives have not leapt full-grown from the brows of their creators but have evolved through extensive dialogue and process.

The progress of the idea of tuition-guarantee and savings incentive programs across the country illustrates a pattern typical of the policy process for education reforms. A new idea is proposed in a single state. Then, with the help of sponsors who want to gain political recognition, the idea is given national publicity as a creative approach to a widely perceived need. At times this initial communication occurs at a national or regional meeting of state officials (such as the National Governors' Association; the National Conference of State Legislatures; and the Education Commission of the States, or ECS). Even before the initial idea is enacted, requests for copies of the bill are received by the initiating state from throughout the nation. If the timing is right, bills might be introduced in half the state legislatures within a few months—often with little change from the original proposal, except for the state's name and certain details relevant to the new state. Generally, such "Xeroxed" bills soon die or are killed in committee, but inevitably a few are hurried into law—especially if their sponsors have the legislative clout to suppress or sidestep debate. In most cases in which bills enter debate, however, the legislative process works well enough to provide for thorough airing of the pros and cons of a proposal. Opponents mobilize, alternatives are proposed, and often the issue is referred to a special study group charged with reporting to the next legislative session. A second round of debate then may lead to a law more carefully crafted and attuned to the needs and traditions of the specific state.

In the case of tuition-guarantee programs, the initial, most widely publicized action was taken by Michigan. The sponsors of the Michigan Education Trust (MET) saw a way to address a growing political challenge: they could allay the fears of families that college opportunities for their children were slipping out of their reach, yet could avoid new spending that would draw dollars away from other state priorities. The key to the attractiveness of the MET was, and is, that it promises "peace of mind." In the face of rising higher-education costs and a highly unpredictable and confusing investment environment, the program assures purchasers contractually that a college education will be available—provided, of course, that the beneficiary meets academic admissions requirements.

Aided by extensive publicity in the national media, the Michigan idea spread rapidly. An initial survey of legislatures in February 1987, two months after the Michigan plan was enacted, showed that forty states were discussing it and that thirty of them had considered actual bills.[1] Almost immediately, however, special studies, editorials, and other statements began to appear criticizing the plan. Some of the more familiar concerns were that the plan would deceive people into believing that the need for funding of student aid and other programs had been met and that low-income students would suffer as a consequence. In addition, critics charged that the plan would severely restrict student mobility because it was keyed to Michigan public institutions and would provide second-class benefits for participants who attended in-state independent institutions or out-of-state institutions.[2] Some defenders of the Michigan-type plans suggested that the schemes would serve as an indirect form of cost control because there would be pressure to keep future tuition increases down to continue the viability of the program. Yet, despite the best efforts of its sponsors, the Michigan plan itself remained burdened by complexities and ambiguities about refund policies, about federal taxability, and, above all, about who would bear the risk if the earnings of the trust were insufficient to keep up with increases in tuition costs.

By mid-1987, five states in addition to Michigan had enacted tuition-guarantee programs. The first was Wyoming, which, because its bill did not depend on a favorable federal tax ruling, was also the first to implement a program. The Florida legislature passed a plan after extensive discussion, but Indiana, Maine, and Tennessee enacted plans without much debate.

In the remaining states where the Michigan idea had been proposed, one of three sorts of action was taken. In the majority of states, the idea was tabled because of concerns about who would assume the long-term risks, uncertainties about an IRS ruling, or details of program design (e.g., how to make the program less restrictive for students attending private or out-of-state institutions). In a few states, the idea continued as a legislative proposal without action in the 1987 session. In the remaining states, special studies were initiated to examine the tuition-guarantee plan and other alternatives.

It was out of the special study and review process that some of the most creative and thoughtful proposals emerged. The most popular alternative to the Michigan plan was the Illinois college savings bond proposal, which emerged from an intensive effort to develop a compromise among four competing proposals before the Illinois General Assembly. In the Illinois model, state general obligation bonds were used as the basis of a savings incentive plan. By the end of 1987, North Carolina had enacted a plan similar to that of Illinois, and this new savings approach soon became the popular legislative alternative across the country, marking another beginning in the spiraling process of reform.[3] A glance at the states' current actions on tuition prepayment and savings plans shows an increasing complexity of alternatives under review. It also shows that the policy process has reached the stage of thoughtfulness and care across the nation for an individual state's unique circumstances. For example, Florida now has a multipart plan that includes two prepaid guaranteed-tuition plans, a four-year university plan, and a two-year community college plan (or "2 + 2" plan) and has provided for prepaid guaranteed dormitory contracts for purchasers of the four-year university plan.

Illinois, as noted, enacted the college savings bonds plan, the only one of four alternative financing plans passed by the Illinois General Assembly in

1987 that Governor James Thompson agreed to sign. The bonds may be used for any purpose, including any educational expenses, but in contrast to the Michigan program, there is no guarantee that the bonds will match future tuition costs. The program provides unlimited portability, but if the bonds are used for a public or private in-state postsecondary education, the state will pay a bonus of 0.25 percent of the interest. The first bond sale was in January 1988, and a second, in September 1988.

In still another alternative scheme, Kentucky established an educational savings plan providing a public trust with two funds: a program fund for savings and, to enhance the proceeds of this savings fund, an endowment fund to which both public and private contributions could be made. A student can benefit from the increased earnings from the endowment fund if the benefits are used at an in-state school. This is a savings incentive plan with no guarantee that earnings will keep pace with tuition increases.

In early 1988, Governor Mario Cuomo of New York proposed the Liberty Scholarships program, which has a target group distinctly different from other popular financing alternatives—low-income students. Drawing on Eugene Lang's I Have a Dream concept, the plan was designed to encourage high school students to stay in school and, in return, to assure these students of funding for postsecondary education. The original proposal was that seventh-graders who are from families with incomes up to 130 percent of the poverty level and who persevere in school would be guaranteed sufficient additional funding beyond other state, private, and federal assistance to attend a full baccalaureate program at a state institution or have that same amount applied to an independent institution. As passed, the program provides this guarantee to junior and senior high school students from families with incomes of up to $18,000. Awards will be made on a sliding scale. A partnership grant program for counseling was also added.

In Massachusetts, Governor Michael Dukakis proposed both a tuition-guarantee plan and a savings bond plan. Tuition certificates would have different values, depending on the tuition of the participating college the student chose to attend. The plan sought to provide the same peace of mind as the Michigan plan but reflect the differences in tuition between public and independent institutions. In modified form, this plan was not enacted in 1990, but whether it will actually go into effect is still unresolved.

What is of particular interest in all the plans under discussion is that most arose from extensive legislative debate or from special studies. In late 1987, ECS counted twenty-six states undertaking some special study of financing alternatives.[4] Some state study groups, such as the Massachusetts Task Force on Student Financial Aid and the New Jersey Committee on Student Financial Aid, began their work even before the Michigan plan was publicized.[5] But most groups were established in response to the Michigan plan, as legislatures, state higher-education agencies, and others sought to assess the pros and cons of various alternatives—from expanded student aid programs to savings bonds to tuition guarantees.

SHORTCOMINGS OF STATE POLICIES

Although in the past two years discussion of the broader dimensions of financing higher education has flourished, one must remain less than sanguine about the long-term results of this process in most states. State leaders still need to take deliberate steps to overcome a number of common shortcomings in the higher-education policy process. As a recent survey by the State Higher Education Executive Officers (SHEEO) documented, perhaps no more than five states have an "integrated" approach to financing higher education. In an integrated approach, state policies for operating appropriations for public higher education, tuition and fee levels, student aid policies and funding, funding related to private colleges and universities, and proposals for new financing alternatives (such as tuition-guarantee plans) are systematically considered in relation to state higher-education objectives.[6]

In terms of specific policies, such as setting public tuition and fees, states vary significantly in approach and degree of systematization. Of the forty-eight states responding to the SHEEO survey, thirty-two reported that they use a revenue model for setting tuition, meaning that tuition is set to generate all or most of the difference between what institutions believe they need and what the state government appropriates. The remaining sixteen use a formula approach, meaning that tuition rates or tuition revenue expectations are established by formal criteria. A few of the states using a revenue model use informal guidelines that have the same effect as a formula in giving some rationality and consistency to the tuition-setting process from year to year.

The annual survey of the National Association of State Scholarship and Grant Programs, conducted by the Pennsylvania Higher Education Assistance Authority, shows that aggregate funding for state student aid programs has increased substantially in recent years, but the character and levels of effort vary dramatically among states. The thirteen states that award the most dollars (at least $20 million annually) consistently award about 85 percent of the total dollars. These states have also accounted for most of the growth in state student aid funding since the early 1980s.[7] A study of state student aid formulas by the Washington Higher Education Coordinating Board found only one state (New York) that funded its programs on the basis of a statute specifying that entitlements must expand in coordination with population growth.[8] Seven other states (Arizona, Connecticut, Minnesota, Missouri, North Dakota, Ohio, and South Carolina) are employing or considering a formula approach.

The SHEEO survey found that twenty-seven states have some form of formal student aid policy, meaning that many states without formulas nonetheless have some policy basis for determining the funding for their student aid programs. At the same time, only seventeen state higher-education executives reported that financial aid policy is closely linked to tuition and state appropriations policy. Moreover, even if state policy asserts that increases in tuition and fees should be matched by increased funding for student aid, this funding requires legislative action that is not always adequate or forthcoming.

Furthermore, state responsibility for various dimensions of financing of higher education is commonly split between two or more state agencies. Even when the responsibilities are consolidated, the policies may not be carried out in the context of an overall policy framework. In many cases, entirely different agencies are responsible for making student loans (either state agencies or state-designated private loan authorities) and for administering the state need-based student grant programs.

Within state legislatures, the most common pattern is that issues related to financing higher education are considered by "money committees"—those concerned with appropriations, finance, or ways and means. Only a few legislatures—mainly in large states such as California, Florida, New York, and Texas—have substantive committees or appropriations subcommittees devoted explicitly to higher education. The more general pattern is for legislative education committees to focus on the elementary and secondary education system. Even worse, the tuition-guarantee and savings incentive proposals are often referred to banking and finance committees, which rarely handle substantive issues related to higher education. And it is uncommon for states, either at the agency level or within legislatures, to address the relations between the financing of higher education and that of elementary and secondary education.

Finally, political forces within states tend to restrict the movement of students out of state. In states with excess capacity in the public sector, politics militate against extending direct or indirect assistance to students attending private nonprofit or proprietary institutions. These forces also make it difficult for many states to address issues of financing higher education from a perspective beyond the needs and concerns of students attending in-state public institutions.

A NEED FOR STATE LEADERSHIP

The diversity of state approaches and the abundance of impediments to state action may cast doubt on the feasibility of taking a broader national approach to financing higher education based in any large measure on state initiatives. To such doubt must be added a sense of the extraordinary variation among states in economic health and fiscal capacity. Yet without leadership by the states, both individually and collectively, the nation will make little progress in the next few years on fundamental issues. Moreover, there are some good reasons to believe that the states, despite the obstacles, can make a vital contribution.

One point in favor of state action is that the prospects for new federal initiatives, especially those that require either new funding or reallocation of funding from existing programs, appear dim. The federal deficit is perhaps the biggest deterrent, but other factors are also likely to restrain federal action: intractable problems with existing programs (especially the Stafford Loan program) that will continue to drain resources and energies away from other programs and new initiatives, the entrenched interest-group structure around existing programs, and the legitimate priority of maintaining, if not increasing, funding of current programs. Making improvements in existing federal student aid programs and ensuring their adequate funding may be the most important and realistic federal roles in the foreseeable future. Beyond these areas, the federal government can have a powerful effect on state policy by prudent use of a few dollars at the margin through incentive or competitive funding.

Also, a strong argument can be made that the nature of the financing issues will demand collaborative action among a number of parties—the federal government, the states, institutions, public schools, and the private sector. If, as argued earlier, financing issues are intertwined with education issues, federal action without deep state involvement is unlikely to work. Also, if strategies to encourage the increased participation and success of economically disadvantaged youth depend on the availability of supportive educational and social services, effective federal strategies will depend on collaboration with states and other public and private parties.

The case of the movement for tuition guarantees and saving plans demonstrates the extraordinary capacity of the states for ingenuity in addressing perceived needs. Although this movement centered initially on the states, a surprisingly large number of states have reported that they prefer a federal, rather than state, approach to incentives for saving. This is not always or merely an argument to block state action but often represents a drive by states to develop similar or supplementary programs at the federal level.

Perhaps most important, despite the difficulties of fragmented policy processes and operations, the states may offer the greatest chance for efforts to make a comprehensive assessment of financing higher education. The Massachusetts Task Force on Student Financial Aid is just one example of several recent state initiatives that demonstrate the potential for this state leadership.

Steps the States Can Take

Recommendations for action by the states should be prefaced by the caveat that state traditions on critical elements of policy on financing higher education vary dramatically. Hence, initiatives should be tailored to the unique needs and traditions of the specific state. Yet even if the states cannot be served by a single, uniform model for financing higher education, they may be well advised to consider some general approaches that may be adaptable to their own situations.

CREATE AN INTEGRATED FINANCING MECHANISM

States should create a mechanism for integrating the diverse elements of an agenda for financing higher education over the next decade and beyond. There must be some way, for example, to ensure that legislative committees considering tuition-guarantee or savings bond proposals have information on how these will relate, if at all, to tuition and student aid policies. There need be no single best mechanism for financing for all states. One state might appoint an interim committee of the legislature; another might give the responsibility to the existing state higher-education board; yet another might create a special gubernatorial task force; and still another might undertake a privately funded statewide project.

Whatever form an integrated state effort for financing takes, it must define the goals that various alternatives are to serve. In addition, it must review all aspects of state policy affecting financing, including state appropriations to institutions, public tuition and fees; student aid, special programs for disadvantaged students, and, to the extent possible, connections with financing elementary and secondary education.

At the outset of its review process, a state should consider *all* the state's higher-education resources—both public and private—as available to meet student and state needs. The state should also frame the issues in ways that make sense to the general public and especially to parents and students. Much of the popularity of the Michigan and Illinois plans stemmed from the fact that they seemed to cut through the complexity of the student aid process, the confusion about prices and costs, the multiplicity of new financing schemes, and the ingrown nature of the financing community. That clarity should be preserved and enhanced in any financing process.

To the extent feasible, the criteria against which new financing alternatives should be assessed should be established in advance. Obviously this is not possible for states in which new proposals have already been made and are far along in development. In these cases, the key is to move the proposals into an arena—such as an interim study committee—where broader issues of impact can be examined.

EXAMINE AND EQUALIZE THE COST-BEARING RESPONSIBILITIES

Another major action states should take in the financing arena is to consider carefully the effects of the state's policies on the shared responsibilities for financing higher education among students, families, institutions, government, and the private sector. As the economist Michael S. McPherson has emphasized, paying for college should be seen from the perspective of shared responsibility among generations.[9] More by policy drift than conscious policy choice, the responsibility for paying for college has been shifting away from families and government to students and to the next generation—primarily through increased reliance on student loans to finance the increasing costs of college education. Each financing policy or alternative has direct implications in terms of who will bear the costs, and these implications should now be subject to conscious policy choices to foster balance and equity. Tuition-guarantee programs provide incentives for saving, but could shift part of the burden to the next generation of taxpayers or nonparticipant students who will have to assume the risks if the plan fails to meet its guarantees. Other savings programs without the guarantee tend not to shift burdens, but often do not have the same incentive to save as a tuition guarantee approach. Programs to encourage students to participate in community service programs at high schools and colleges also can be a means for students to assume some of the financing responsibility by working during their education rather than through loans after college. Low-tuition policies, especially at community colleges and the lower divisions of four-year undergraduate programs, give students and families confidence that higher education is accessible and reflect government underwriting of the social value of an educated citizenry. Student need-based grant programs and other aid targeted to low-income students reflect a commitment by government to provide aid when families and students cannot save and pay their expected contributions.

COORDINATE THE EDUCATION EFFORT

A third major action that should be on the agenda for the states is to strengthen the connections between financing policies and education priorities at all levels of the education system—both for higher education and for elementary and secondary education. The key issue is how a particular financing mechanism—low tuition, need-based grants, work opportunities, or loans—contributes or detracts from a particular educational goal.

Some specific questions should be asked about the utility of present and proposed efforts to integrate education priorities at various levels. For example, how can programs aimed at encouraging postsecondary participation of at-risk youth be coordinated at public school and higher education levels? Which efforts yield the most significant benefits: reform of middle-school education, early identification and support services for at-risk children, assurance of financial support for postsecondary education if the student does well in high school and graduates, continued support services once the student enrolls in a postsecondary education program?

Another question on integration of efforts is, How can the state relate its programs for financing higher education with strategies to restructure public education? Should students in the public schools be given more opportunities to choose not only among other public schools but among options such as early enrollment in postsecondary education (as in the Minnesota Postsecondary Options Program)? What incentives can be provided to attract and retain the next generation of teachers?

Could incentives for student community service be an element of the state's student aid policies? For example, if secondary students provide community service, could they earn credits toward financing their postsecondary education? Could incentives be established for college students to provide community service—including serving as mentors for at-risk students in the public schools?

Do the state's financing policies encourage progression of students through the education system and provide flexibility for choice of programs that meet unique needs—from secondary education to community colleges, from community colleges to senior institutions and beyond, from in-state to out-of-state institutions, and among both public and private institutions?

FACILITATE FAMILIES' FINANCIAL AND ACADEMIC PLANNING

In some respects, the problems of financing higher education are compounded by too much, rather than too little, information. Parents and students are flooded with promotions about postsecondary opportunities and sources of financing through the mail and media. As indicated earlier, some of the information from the national media about college costs has been misleading and has led to significant misperceptions about the financial accessibility of college. States can play an important role in organizing statewide information services aimed at encouraging early planning for college and providing information about both academic and financial issues. An alternative might be to tie such a program to a state incentive program (perhaps savings bonds) for college saving.

PROMOTE THE HIGHER-EDUCATION SYSTEM AS A WHOLE

In light of the changing educational needs of the nation's population and the intensively competitive world economic environment, states should be seeking to increase, rather than diminish, the flexibility, adaptability, and self-renewal capacity of their higher-education systems. Policies on financing higher education are keys to this effort. Each state should have a mechanism for monitoring the effectiveness of its system in terms participation rates, enrollment trends, income distribution of students, and trends in education outcomes.

BROADEN THE DEBATE ON ALTERNATIVES

The coming decade will provide an important opportunity for the higher-education community in the states to set the agenda and broaden the debate on the future financing of higher education. Governors are in a unique position, because of their relative independence from the complexities of the current financing system and their access to the media, to reframe the agenda and to call for a fundamental redesign of current policies. As argued earlier, the dynamics of the policy process make the chances of such bold leadership unlikely to emerge at the federal level. Although many may agree that nationwide, rather than state-by-state, solutions are essential, the states can goad the federal government to action by raising difficult issues and proposing bold alternatives.

Conclusion

This chapter has focused primarily on the policy process rather than on the pros and cons of a particular financing alternative. The emphasis has been deliberate. The past two years show that creativity in devising new financing alternatives is not wanting. The more fundamental issue is the lack in many states—and at the national level—of an agenda or policy framework through which the implications of policy drift or policy action can be assessed. Endless debates about technicalities, framed in terms of debates long past, will have little meaning to an increasingly frustrated and impatient public.

Notes

1. Aims C. McGuinness, Jr., and Jennifer Afton, *Survey of College Savings and Guaranteed Tuition Programs* (Denver: Education Commission of the States, 1987).
2. See *Invitational Conference on College Prepayment and Savings Plans: Proceedings* (New York: College Entrance Examination Board, 1988).
3. Courtney Leatherman, "States' Interest in Tuition Plans Grows; Focus Shifts Toward Savings Programs," *Chronicle of Higher Education*, September 14, 1988; see also Gwendolyn Lewis, *Trends in Student Aid, 1980-1988* (New York: College Entrance Examination Board, 1988).
4. McGuinness and Afton, *Survey of College Savings and Guaranteed Tuition Programs*, rev. ed. (1988).
5. See *Expanding Opportunity for Higher Education in the Commonwealth: Quality Access and Choice*. Report of the Task Force on Student Financial Aid, Board of Regents of Higher Education (Boston: 1988).
6. State Higher Education Executive Officers, *Survey on Tuition Policy, Costs and Student Aid* (Denver: SHEEO, 1988); see also Denis J. Curry, *Tuition and Student Aid Policies: What Role for SHEEO?* (Denver: SHEEO, 1988).
7. Kenneth R. Reheer and Jerry S. Davis, *NASSGP 19th Annual Survey Report, 1987-1988 Academic Year* (Harrisburg: Pennsylvania Higher Education Assistance Authority, 1988).
8. Shirley Ort, *Student Financial Aid Policy* (Olympia: Washington Higher Education Coordinating Board, 1988).
9. Michael S. McPherson and Mary S. Skinner, "Paying for College: A Lifetime Proposition," *Brookings Review* 4 (Fall 1986).

14

New Ways to Finance College Costs: An Institutional Budget Officer's Perspective

TIMOTHY R. WARNER

DATE: *January 15, 1992*
PLACE: *President's Conference Room, Elite University*
PROBLEM: *How to Balance the University Budget for 1992–1993*

Three administrators of Elite University sit around a cluttered conference table. The youngish budget director, Dave, is typing data into a NeXT II computer at one end of the table. The provost, Ben, is scratching his head, while the vice-president for finance, Joan, stares grimly out the window at a gray winter sky.

DAVE: We're still $3 million away from balancing this thing.

BEN: Well, we can't take a deficit budget to the trustees. Will you review our options again, Dave?

DAVE: *(In a wearied tone)* The options haven't changed, Ben. We can jack up tuition another couple of points. We can trim back on salary increases. Or we can squeeze down on the academic program in some way. Take your pick—one of the three or some combination.

JOAN: Aren't there any other options we could be pursuing? What about the utilities numbers? Have we pushed those people as hard as we can? Or how about financial aid? Have we checked our assumptions with the financial aid office?

DAVE: I think we've asked for more information in both those areas, Joan.

(A knock at the door. The financial aid director, Jim, enters, looking somewhat sheepish.)

JIM: People, I am pleased, though somewhat embarrassed, to report that my request for student aid funds was too high. This seems to be due to two factors. First, it appears that parental contributions are up by about 20 percent, a number I believe can be sustained. And, second, we have more people participating in the university's tuition prepayment program.

SAM: I'm surprised parental contributions are up so much. Our student body composition hasn't changed, has it? And the economy only grew by a couple of points this year. What's happening? How could families suddenly have more money to spend on college costs?

JIM: No, there are no changes along the lines you suggest. But do you remember those college savings plans implemented at the federal level a few years ago? Well, we're just starting to see the benefits of them now. It seems that parents have been saving under the plans, so they don't need as much financial aid from us as we'd anticipated.

JOAN: And that prepayment plan we started publicizing a couple of years ago is starting to pay off too. We're making money on that!

DAVE: *(Madly pounding numbers into his NeXT II)* Great! Those factors combined saved us $1 million. Now we only need another $2 million to balance the budget. What shall it be, Ben, salaries or tuition?

BEN: Well, I guess we'll have to raise tuition another couple of points to generate that $2 million. Oh, well, at least we didn't have to raise it three points. We got lucky with those savings and prepayment plans. Frankly, I'd forgotten all about them. . . .

(Curtain falls as the NeXT II's color monitor turns from red to gray.)

This scene may be a cynic's view of how some of the proposed alternative financing mechanisms may affect future college budgets. Yet it is probably not too far from the truth. At Elite University, there probably would be little consideration given to "rewarding" the savings efforts of families that participated in incentive-based savings plans. Elite University is committed to need-blind admission, and any additional parental contribution or outside source of funds immediately reduces the pressure on the institution to find money from its own resources to fund the student financial aid requirement. Also, it is unlikely that Elite would have instituted a prepayment plan unless it was *at least* a break-even operation.

Before we fully internalize that cynical perspective, though, we ought to take a more penetrating look at this budget-balancing scene to see if we can interpret it in a different, more positive, way. In this essay, I hope to show that the reactions of the budget makers at Elite University to alternative financing and payment mechanisms were not so callous as they might appear. In fact, I would argue that they were based on some clear institutional priorities and operating principles that historically have been in the best interests of the institution and its students. I believe that in any private selective college or university it is those goals, priorities, and operating principles that have helped shape how it thinks about new financing arrangements, whether those proposals are developed internally by the institution or externally by governments or private entities.

In this discussion, I will focus principally on my own institution, Stanford University, which of course bears only the slightest resemblance to Elite University. I am quick to recognize that what is good for Stanford may not be right for others, so I will try to point out how different institutions may respond. Still, my comments do address primarily the private-sector colleges and universities.

How Approaches to Alternative Financing Are Shaped

At Stanford, as at Elite University, the approach to alternative financing is likely to be shaped by a few fundamental priorities. Perhaps foremost among these is maintaining and enhancing the quality of the academic program. We are committed to attracting and retaining the best faculty in the country and to supporting the highest-quality academic programs.

Another fundamental priority is preserving the institution. We are in business for the long run. Consequently, any policy change or alternative must be considered in the context of the long-term viability of the institution. Perhaps more so than in other enterprises, short-term goals must be viewed in the context of the historic goals of the university.

Improving the quality and diversity of the student body is another priority at Stanford. For us, maintaining enrollments is really not a problem. Our question, rather, is whether we are enrolling the best students and achieving an acceptable—however defined—level of diversity.

Finally, we seek to meet the full demonstrated financial need of all our undergraduates. This is something that few schools are still able to do, but it is a key institutional policy at Stanford. Given the many problems of how need is determined, however, we may not know precisely any longer what it means to "meet full need." Nonetheless, under the existing methodology, we are meeting the full need by combining grants, jobs, and loans.

Although the goals of one institution may vary somewhat from those of another, before any institution can know what approach to take on alternative financing issues, it must define and order its own goals and priorities. Too often this apparently obvious point is not adequately thought through, or it is not considered thoroughly in the context of alternative programs as they come forth. That seems to be so whether the proposal is a seemingly attractive student financing arrangement or a new research program. The result of an incomplete review is often an inefficient use of institutional resources and a fragmentation of institutional purpose.

Usually, there is also a set of operating principles that the managers of an institution rely on to support their goals and priorities. At Stanford and institutions like it, four major principles stand out. First, there is a heavy emphasis on entrepreneurship. The incentive structure enforces it. Faculty members are rewarded for the new programs they develop and for the research grants they obtain. Staff members are continually pushed to find new ways to be more effective or to find new ways to generate more income from existing assets. It is also important to note that this kind of activity has to be balanced against the university's long-term financial health.

A second operational principle at Stanford and similar institutions is leverage. Seed money, research funds, gifts, and the use of debt allow an existing asset base to serve as a lever for greater productivity and greater programmatic depth and coverage. How colleges think about the use of leverage and how "leveraged" they are willing to become affects their approaches to new ideas, including alternative methods of financing the education of their students.

Third is the issue of flexibility. Even though most institutions have high fixed costs, they want to have the flexibility to respond to new ideas and to have some measure of control over their own destiny. Any financing mechanism or new way to pay college costs that constrains flexibility will be difficult to put over.

Fourth, colleges constantly ask themselves whether the market can provide services more cheaply and more effectively than they can do it themselves. There is an important operating principle that says we should not be running internal businesses when the market can do the job. So, to the extent that the new financing mechanisms involve or mandate the creation of new administrative structures and responsibilities, our scrutiny of them will increase.

A Review of Four Alternative Financing Mechanisms

Given the context of Stanford's institutional goals and the operating principles that support them, I would ask the following question: How has Stanford thought about the new ways to meet college costs and how likely are we and others like us to respond to these alternatives? To answer the question, I will review four principal types of alternative: loan programs; public service;

differential packaging; and a series of new options including tuition prepayments, guarantees, and savings plans.

LOAN PROGRAMS

Because enhancing quality and diversity are two of our major institutional goals, we have developed loan plans that enhance the ability of families to pay our charges. Our decision to move ahead on these plans, I must acknowledge, was also made because our competition had such plans. The first of our two plans is the Parent Loan Plan, in which we lend our own funds at something approximating a market rate for a secured loan. This program has been operating for about eleven years and has successfully provided parents a way of smoothing payments, typically over an eight-year period. It has provided loans to about a hundred new families per year and currently has an outstanding balance of about $10 million. This program is small, but meets an important need. Interestingly, rather than using funds leveraged from external sources, we have made this program an institutional investment. In keeping with the operating principle of trying to minimize the university's administrative burdens, the program is run by an outside agency. No institutional unrestricted funds are involved in the loans.

The second Stanford loan program is a new supplemental loan program in which a financial institution makes loans to our students and runs the program. The university provides the ultimate guarantee in the event of default. Given that Stanford's Perkins loan default rate is quite low and that we were able to contract with a strong servicer, this supplemental program is a good risk. Again, Stanford has not committed any of its unrestricted funds to this enterprise. The development and progress of this plan has prompted some discussion of turning the parental loan business over to a third party altogether and using leveraged funds more extensively to finance it.

Although there are a number of government-sponsored supplemental loan plans, I believe that an institutional loan plan can be advantageous for many schools, either on an individual basis or as part of a consortium. The SHARE program, in which Consortium on Financing Higher Education (COFHE) institutions are involved, is the kind of arrangement that has worked reasonably well. Such plans have the potential advantage of bringing the college and the family closer together in addressing financing needs. We have found that there is real value to that from the standpoint of public relations. It is not clear, however, whether this service increases enrollment or yield.

Another benefit of institution- and consortium-based plans over government-sponsored ones is that in the former, the institution can exercise some control over administration. The trade-off, of course, is in the greater commitment required to manage the plan. Another trade-off is the greater extent to which an institution will have to become leveraged through loan guarantees or through direct investment in the loans themselves.

It is clear that in Stanford's approach to loans, the operating principles of minimal administration and maximal leverage and flexibility are at work. Still, we have not used leverage as extensively as we might have done. For example, Stanford and many other institutions have not gone as far as the University of Pennsylvania's Penn Plan, which provides a variety of lending options, including prepayments and second-mortgage plans.

The Penn Plan approach probably is not suitable for Stanford's particular situation, because of the administrative costs, but it is somewhat surprising that other institutions have not adopted the model. Perhaps they do not see a marginal competitive advantage, or perhaps the range of lending options in the marketplace is already sufficient to meet the general demand. Moreover, there is little financial aid expense to be saved in running such programs. The intent of the original Penn Plan would have required students receiving financial aid to participate, which would have reduced the institutional scholarship requirement. But this feature was never fully incorporated into the plan.

The prepayment option clearly is an attractive one for most colleges, yet it has not been widely advertised. Although there probably is not a single college in this country that would not be happy to accept four years of tuition paid in advance, this option may not be as readily available as it might be, because universities are uncomfortable deploying it without other options that would make up a comprehensive package.

In sum, institutions must address two central issues in considering alternative loan plans. The first is that these loan plans are only supplemental financing mechanisms. Institutions cannot scrap their grant programs to create a large loan program, so any new loan program must compete for resources against grants and other priorities, and ultimately may result in a financial overextension for many universities. The second issue is how to integrate creative loan arrangements into other elements of a financial aid package, as the Penn Plan did. Obviously, alternative loan plans are not the sole answer to financing college costs, but they do give institutions a chance to play an important and useful role, if that role is considered carefully in the context of the priorities and operating structure of the particular institution.

PUBLIC SERVICE

At Stanford, a significant public service initiative is under way. Its focus is on providing volunteer opportunities to enrolled students and encouraging graduates to go into careers in the nonprofit sector. There has been—and remains—concern among students who are on financial aid that they are unable to participate in the community volunteer activities because of their need to work to fulfill the job component of their financial aid packages. The policy question then becomes this: Should the institution increase that student's scholarship or loan to accommodate this activity? That question quickly raises the more fundamental issue of why volunteer activity should be deemed more important than other things a student might do, such as taking another course, getting involved in a musical activity, or playing a club sport.

Essentially, the answer to the dilemma of volunteer public service is that institutional leadership must make a judgment about how much priority it should be given and how it should affect aid. At Stanford, after considerable analysis, we have made adjustments in aid packages, particularly to the amounts students are expected to contribute, to accommodate some public service activities and some research activities. We made the decision in the context of a complete review of our policies regarding self-help and student contributions. This review resulted in broad-based changes in self-help, in addition to those relating to public service. Even so, there has been legitimate criticism that volunteer work is not really "volunteered" if it means one's aid award increases in compensation. In effect, in such cases, students are being paid for volunteering.

Once a student graduates and takes a job in the public sector, the issue for the institution centers around loan forgiveness. Loan-forgiveness programs are intended to make careers in the nonprofit sector more attractive. Yet it is not clear that loan forgiveness will effectively tip the scale toward work in nonprofit areas. Moreover, there is no compelling economic justification for giving students who choose to work in nonprofit-sector careers a break. Many do quite well financially; perhaps they do not become wealthy, but often they are not so poorly off that they cannot handle student loan repayment obligations and begin to build an economic base for themselves. Thus, if colleges are interested in more rationally promoting careers in the nonprofit sector for their students, perhaps a restructuring of institutional loans along lines of graduated repayments would be suitable. Or institutions could employ the concept of low-income insurance. Either or both would be more appropriate than outright loan forgiveness.

DIFFERENTIAL PACKAGING

Of the four areas chosen for review, differential packaging may be the least interesting, in part because it is not a terribly new concept. The notion of requiring different self-help expectations from different groups of students has been in effect at Stanford and other places for years. Our philosophy on the issue is straightforward. Essentially, we require that students meet 25 percent of their budgets with a combination of loans and jobs, but we reduce that percentage for low-income students, the majority of whom are targeted ethnic minorities. Differential packaging reflects a commitment by Stanford to recruit targeted minority students. Lower loan and job expectations help to attract and retain these students. We have a similar policy for students given high academic ratings by the admissions office.

Differential packaging also reflects the principle of leverage in the sense that we are diverting part of our financial aid resources to a target group because we have chosen to keep our standard self-help expectation among the highest of all institutions with which we compete.

The use of merit aid for students who do not demonstrate financial need may be considered a natural extension of differential packaging. Its use is increasing as institutions seek to target their limited financial aid resources to particular groups or individuals.

TUITION PREPAYMENTS, GUARANTEES, AND SAVINGS PLANS

Stanford has watched with interest the proliferation of private and government-backed mechanisms to guarantee tuition or to promote savings for college. Our inclination, however, has been to remain on the sidelines of the new game. In fact, we seem to have put very little institutional energy into encouraging families to save for college. There are several reasons for this. First, savings incentives might result in tax breaks for the middle class, which could threaten the availability of government aid for lower-income students. Although there is no evidence that this has occurred in the past, the worry is immediately raised by people in financial aid and government relations whenever middle-class subsidies are discussed.

Another reason Stanford has remained on the sidelines with respect to these plans is that they might require changes in the needs-analysis system, which for most college and university managers is so difficult to understand that it has been left to the high priests and gurus of financial aid. That attitude, although understandable, is unfortunate, because the methodology has a significant impact on budgets.

A third reason is that the specific proposals made to date fail to offer genuine assistance to students, seem to present liabilities, or at best offer no tangible advantages to the institution. For example, saving for college is something needing promotion among younger families, and these families do represent our future customers, but whether we should take on the responsibility for selling savings plans is an open question. Will such involvement commit us to heavy administrative obligations? Even if the answer is no, strong enough to ignore the plans unless they represent some threat of making our market position deteriorate. Thus, we will allow institutions that are more pressed to meet enrollment levels to experiment as they choose. I would argue that this is shortsighted on our part, but it does reflect the very fortunate market position in which highly selective institutions operate.

Although Stanford and some other institutions may remain somewhat standoffish about the new programs, all institutions ought to be considering the key issues surrounding the plans and what role colleges and universities can play in relation to them.

Several issues are important. First, for many private institutions there is the worry that any government aid to the middle class comes at the expense of aid to the disadvantaged. Yet there is also the concern that without such government-subsidized savings incentives or some other form of aid to the middle class, those families will not have the wherewithal to attend private college. The threat to the private colleges is that as the differential grows between public and private college prices, families will opt for the public sector. Thus, private colleges have an internal dilemma when it comes to arguing about where government aid dollars should be directed. The dilemma is that the *desire* to achieve diversity comes up against the *need* to maintain enrollments. Private colleges no doubt will continue to argue both for aid to the disadvantaged and for subsidies for the middle class. But in an environment in which aid is not likely to grow, their dilemma will continue.

For Stanford, starting our own guarantee plan or participating in any savings or guarantee plan has significant public relations implications. One can be as clear as possible that tuition guarantees do not amount to admission guarantees, but until our record has been clearly established on this point, it remains a worry. For any plan to appeal to selective colleges, thorough consideration of this problem will be necessary.

Another concern is that any plan that does not leave the institution free to set its own prices will not get much support. That is one of the real problems with the Massachusetts plan. For us to agree that $1,000 invested in a plan today will buy the same portion of tuition ten years hence removes some of our institutional flexibility to set prices. Without other guarantees, that is a risk. Participation of some individuals under such terms also puts undue pressure on nonparticipants to make up shortfalls—through increased tuitions or reductions in financial aid or cuts in programs—if the plan fails to deliver returns that match general tuition increases at the institution. If a plan produced a contribution toward college costs, of course, it would probably work, but if it locked in a price without giving the institution some flexibility in controlling the investment pool, most institutions would be wary of it.

A final question about the new plans is to what extent they favor the public sector over the private. Private colleges and students can be hurt by guarantee plans that explicitly or effectively restrict choice to public universities. Diversity of choice should be protected.

What to Do

First, institutions need to think through their positions on middle-class subsidies. In a provocative paper, "The Great Sorting: The Inertia of Inequity in American Higher Education," Robert Zemsky documents the stratification along racial and income lines that has persisted over the past twenty years in

U.S. higher education.[1] Little has changed in that period in terms of our ability to enroll substantial numbers of minority and lower-income students. As Zemsky notes, "There is little reason to believe that increased aid is likely to solve the problem. . . . The larger problem is that there are too few minorities in the pipeline." Zemsky then goes on to ask, "What kinds of programs and responses can higher education commit to reshaping primary and secondary education?" Perhaps the larger issue is not about tax breaks for middle-class savings or finding more ways to get students involved in public service. Rather, the effort ought to be to get more minority and low-income students into the higher education pipeline.

Second, colleges and universities ought to come together to see if better private-sector savings products can be developed that would provide higher returns than are currently available. There is no reason why the private sector should not pursue alternatives for middle-class savings while public resources are directed toward the issues of minority and low-income constituencies. The COFHE group, in fact, has recognized, and is now studying, this aspect of the problem. Universities such as Stanford have achieved average total returns on endowment of about 9 percent, after inflation, over the past ten years. It may be reasonable to assume that universities could achieve comparable results under alternative plans. Even though such private alternatives might not be as attractive financially as some of the government-subsidized plans, they should certainly represent valuable options for families, especially considering that the current offerings to middle-class families of the for-profit sector are taking away part of the returns in profits.

Private-sector colleges and universities should consider consortial arrangements carefully. A principal worry is that a plan have enough flexibility and portability so that choice will not be affected unduly. This means that the consortial group must be large enough to offer students a realistic range of choice among institutions. Moreover, there are financial risks. To the extent that colleges need to become investors in the consortium by committing start-up money, those funds will be at risk until the operation has proved itself. And, as suggested earlier, if investment returns are intended to guarantee tuitions and the returns to the university fail to match required increases, the participating colleges will have to tap other sources of income to make good on their commitments. Despite these risks, however, consortial arrangements have potential and should be explored.

Third, universities such as Stanford have been lax for too long in promoting the idea of saving for college. That does not mean that we should necessarily begin lobbying for tax breaks, but it does suggest that if some simple plans, when begun early enough, do work for our future constituency, we ought to commit some resources to promoting them. But unless the needs-analysis system can be changed to reward the savings efforts of families or to penalize those who had the capacity to save but did not, the full effectiveness of savings efforts will never be realized.

Conclusion

Institutions such as Stanford have been trying a few new things to help families meet college costs, but we certainly have not taken an active or pioneering role in recent years. Rather, the private institutions have been looking to government or to entities in the private sector for ingenuity or assistance while going on about the business of raising money for financial aid or just doing very little at all. All those positions may be appropriate, but we can do more, and in the long term, it is certainly in our interest to do more.

Some things clearly work. For example, the Penn Plan or some variant of it that helps families smooth out the costs of college attendance can provide a really useful kind of "one-stop shopping" for college financing. Not every school will want, or can afford, to provide financing options such as second mortgages, but the model can be adapted or developed by a group of schools that could not consider it individually.

Regarding savings plans and tuition guarantees, colleges should approach these ideas with "an open mind but not an empty head," as a former Stanford provost used to say. What may look like a great way of helping families save for college may also be a formula for constraining an institution's ability to chart its own financial course in the future. Nevertheless, taking a critical look at savings plans does not mean that colleges should remain paralyzed. Saving is important, and colleges can promote it in useful ways. In fact, as part of this effort, we ought to be moving actively to change the needs-analysis system to reduce some of the disincentives to savings it now contains.

Consortial arrangements may offer the greatest promise for developing new savings and tuition-guarantee products—if they can be developed on a scale large enough to preserve students' latitude of choice.

Finally, issues about how families pay for college are of great importance to private institutions. Regardless of how those issues are approached, colleges will need to be clear about their own priorities and the operating principles they will employ to ensure the greatest probability of success.

Note

1. Robert Zemsky, "The Great Sorting: The Inertia of Inequity in American Higher Education," discussion paper prepared for the College Board Study of Admission to American Colleges and Universities, July 15, 1988.

15

The Role of Employers in Financing Higher Education

ERNEST A. LYNTON

An overall assessment of the financing of higher education should consider the emerging role of employers. Employers already finance a substantial portion of formal instruction provided by colleges and universities, primarily by prepaying or reimbursing tuition and fees for regular courses taken by their employees. Moreover, employer sponsorship of postsecondary education is being promoted by a secular shift in overall patterns of education and work. That is, the traditional practice of completing undergraduate, and even graduate, education before beginning permanent employment is declining, and an earlier interweaving of career employment and education is increasing. In engineering and management, for example, it is now the norm to pursue master's level education and part-time employment in the field simultaneously; the opportunity cost of pursuing a full-time graduate program in these fields has simply become too large. In general, mixing of education and career employment is becoming increasingly common, and thus a fresh look at employer-assisted education is warranted.

Types of Employer Assistance

Increasing involvement of employers in facilitating education for their employees is more than a matter of convenience for students or philanthropy on the part of employers. Developing and maintaining a highly skilled and productive work force has become a focus of national interest and of self-interest on the part of employers. Hence, employers have developed an array of financing arrangements for higher education, discussed below.

TUITION AID PROGRAMS

Most large enterprises provide some form of tuition prepayment or reimbursement for courses employees want to take. Most plans are open to all employees, usually after six or twelve months of employment. Payments often cover fees as well as tuition, and sometimes also books, supplies, and other education-related expenses. Most often, payment is provided after a student successfully completes a course. Although some employers limit education benefits strictly to job-related subjects, others pay tuition for all but sports programs, provided that the courses are offered by an accredited or otherwise recognized institution.[1]

Tuition assistance plans constitute one component of a larger system of training and education sponsored by employers for the enhancement of their employees' skills. Most corporate education is provided as in-house instruction specifically designed to increase employees' job skills and intended principally for the employer's benefit.[2] Under tuition assistance plans, however, courses generally represent standard offerings of institutional catalogs, chosen at the employees' initiative and for their personal benefit. It is these courses that represent direct financial support for the regular instructional activities of colleges and universities.

In the late 1970s, total expenditures for employer-financed employee education and training were between $30 billion and $40 billion. At that time, a Conference Board survey of companies with 500 or more employees, comprising about 32 million individuals, indicated that about 11 percent of the total expenditure, or close to $4 billion, went to tuition and fees for regularly scheduled courses taken by employees either after hours or on released time. About 1.3 million employees (4 percent of the total surveyed)—mostly nonmanagement and lower- and middle-management personnel—were involved in such activities.[3]

More-recent surveys of employers' educational assistance do not provide explicit figures of total expenditures, but do suggest similar participation rates. Census Bureau data show that in 1984, adults took a total of 10.2 million courses paid for by employers. Total employer expenditures for all tuition reimbursements are probably still in the $3 billion-$4 billion range, and employer expenditures on regularly scheduled higher education are certainly upward of $2 billion. Employer spending thus constitutes a significant portion of the $23 billion total tuition and fee revenues of all institutions of higher education. Looked at in another way, expenditures of this sort place employer spending in roughly the same class as Pell Grants ($4.5 billion) and university scholarships and fellowships ($4 billion).[4]

It is remarkable to note the magnitude of employer contributions in light of the low rate of employee participation in such plans (i.e., about 4 percent). In fact, many workers do not know that tuition assistance is available to them; others need guidance in defining their educational goals and strategies. Conversely, in a few companies that furnish their employees with systematic information and guidance about educational opportunities, participation in tuition aid plans is much higher than the national average. Thus, there appears to be great potential for expansion.[5]

One problem in tapping employers as a source of higher-education expenditures, however, is the tax status of tuition aid benefits. The basic policy issue, whether tuition payments are taxable as income, affects both the extent to which employees will take advantage of tuition aid plans and the extent to which employers will offer such benefits. The latter point, employers' willingness to sponsor education, is an issue because of the employers' responsibility for withholding income for tax purposes. The issue is difficult because employers might have to make complex and speculative decisions on which courses qualified as "related" to job responsibilities and therefore as exempt.[6]

On the tax issue, two statutes or regulations apply. Section 127 of the income tax law exempts from taxation as income up to $5,250 in tuition and fee benefits received annually by an employee.[7] This section was introduced as a temporary measure in 1978, lapsed in 1987, and was restored—but only retroactively for undergraduate courses for calendar year 1988—as part of the tax code correction bill passed in the final hours of the 100th Congress. Thus, the income exemption has again lapsed. Organizations such as the American Society for Training and Development (ASTD) have lobbied for renewal, but the higher-education community has not targeted the issue, and prospects for a broad-based exemption from tax are not strong.

Although the general exemption for education payments by employers has lapsed, Treasury Regulation 162 remains in force. This stipulates that employer payments for job-related courses are not taxable income.

COOPERATIVE EDUCATION AND PAID INTERNSHIPS

Cooperative education programs and paid internships constitute less-direct but nonetheless important ways in which employers can finance higher education. The stipends workers earn during the work periods of their education often constitute all, or at least a substantial portion, of the financial support students need to pursue their studies. This pertains not only to undergraduate programs but to professional programs. In law, for example, many students finance much of their educations through lucrative summer internships in law firms. Employer payments to interns and to participants in cooperative education and other work-study programs are clearly taxable income, however.

There are no comprehensive studies indicating the aggregate participation of undergraduate and graduate students in all sorts of paid internships, cooperative educational programs, or other programs alternating work and study. Probably the number of co-op education students is around 230,000, according to the Research Center on Co-op Education at Northeastern University. A recent Conference Board survey cited 73 percent of responding corporations as indicating they participated in some sort of work-study program, with a median number of 10 students.[8]

The importance of this category of employer financing transcends purely monetary issues. Systematic interweaving of study and career employment can have far-reaching advantages. First, if the simultaneous work and learning programs are accompanied by ongoing dialogue between educators and employers, the result, bridging the gap between theory and practice, will be a substantial benefit to the educational process. A further advantage is that distributing the advanced components of education over a longer period reduces the problem of intellectual obsolescence and allows more-effective adaptation of curricula to rapid technological and other changes. In short, academic programs combining work and study have significant pedagogic and practical advantages.[9]

In short, there are substantial educational and social reasons to increase the number of academic programs that combine work and learning systematically. Yet little attention has been paid so far to the policy implications of this aspect of employer financing, and there has been no examination, for example, of the feasibility of encouraging co-op and internship programs by providing tax advantages to employers.

Combination of work and education also can help to offset demographic and other factors. For example, as noted earlier, employers in high-demand fields such as computer science and engineering have already devised part-time master's degree programs because of a shortage of suitable employees. This was a reflexive reaction to market forces. But, with the decreasing number of highly trained young people in the work force, it is possible that in the next few years, employers who traditionally hire students as graduates of four-year colleges may begin to systematically intensify their quest for employees. For example, they might try to recruit individuals after their sophomore year, with promises to support their completion of their undergraduate degrees part-time at company cost and on company time. The desirability and policy implications of such tactics should be examined carefully, because they have major implications for individuals, for academic life, and for the degree of financing of higher education by employers.

NEW KINDS OF APPRENTICESHIP PROGRAMS

If apprenticeship programs have been given any attention in this country, it has been as part of secondary vocational education or as a postsecondary entry into certain crafts and some categories of manual labor. Furthermore, apprenticeships consist mostly of on-the-job learning by example and imitation, with little or no formal instruction. In contrast, West Germany and other European countries have a very successful system of combining classroom instruction, systematic skill development, and on-the-job training into work-and-learning programs of three to four years that extend into the postsecondary levels. Participants in this "dual system" are employees, and most of the costs of their education and training are borne by employers collectively through their chambers of industry and commerce.[10]

The appropriateness of such programs in this country should be explored. Research into the impact of automation on skill requirements at lower occupational levels increasingly indicates the value of skilled low-level technicians, the "blue-and-white-striped collar" workers who know "why" as well as "how." Their education should extend into the postsecondary level.

EMPLOYER PAYMENTS OF EDUCATIONAL BENEFITS UNDER COLLECTIVE BARGAINING

District 37 of the American Federation of State, County, and Municipal Employees pioneered a collective-bargaining agreement with New York, in which the city paid a certain amount per employee per year into an education fund overseen by a board of union members. The fund supports educational programs provided by the union as well as offerings of regional colleges and universities developed under contract. More recently, the United Auto Workers negotiated, first with Ford and then with General Motors, a contract that calls for contributions on a per-hour basis for each worker to a "retraining" fund. At Ford, this is called the Strategic Education Training Program (STEP). An important component of the STEP program is the College and University Option Program (CUOP), which is intended to facilitate the reentry of workers into higher education.[11] In this area, there is again a dearth of quantitative information, but the magnitude of educational funds collected through employer payments of benefits probably exceeds $100 million annually. Much of this finances special programs provided by universities and colleges that are not part of their mainstream offerings. Nevertheless, these funds can be used for employee participation in regular higher education and could come to represent a substantial component of employer financing of higher education.

VOLUNTARY CONTRIBUTIONS BY EMPLOYERS

During the past ten years, corporate giving to colleges and universities increased from less than $0.4 billion (1976-1977) to more than $1.8 billion (1986-1987). In addition, corporations spend about $100 million each year for direct scholarship support, as distinct from awards disbursed by academic institutions themselves. The rate of growth of corporate funding has slowed, however. After ten years of 15 percent yearly increases, gifts grew by only 7 percent in 1985-1986 and 1986-1987. Equipment and gifts of property constitute about 20-25 percent of the corporate donations.

MANDATORY CONTRIBUTIONS BY EMPLOYERS

A number of European countries have national policies regarding the financing of continuing education. Some education systems are wholly state-financed, whereas others are supported in part by employers.[12] For example, in 1971, France promulgated a statute that forced employers to contribute a certain percentage of payroll or some similarly prorated amount to France's National Education and Training Fund. Any direct expenditures by employers on training and educating their own workers could be used to offset payments into the central fund.[13] In West Germany, all private-sector enterprises are dues-paying members of regionally organized chambers of commerce and industry that oversee and finance the dual system of apprenticeships, mentioned earlier. Whether such statutory obligations could—or should—be imposed in this country is highly questionable.

EMPLOYER INVOLVEMENT IN EDUCATIONAL LOANS

A minor and indirect, but not negligible, component of employer financing of higher education is employer involvement in educational loans. A number of organizations involved in brokering such loans have special programs through which employees (and often their spouses and children) are eligible for loans, with employer participation. For example, United Student Aid Funds (USAF), a nonprofit corporation based in Indianapolis that annually processes over $1 billion in guaranteed student loans, has a program entitled Help America Learn. Employees of participating companies and their immediate families are eligible for guaranteed loans without paying the customary guarantee charge. The company pays a one-time charge on each loan of about 3-5 percent of the face value. The loan is guaranteed by USAF, not by the company. Presently about 150 companies participate in this scheme, and the loan total is about $35 million.

The U.S. Chamber of Commerce has a somewhat different program, CONSERN. Chamber members can participate in the program for an annual fee that is about $1 per employee, but not less than $25 and not more than $15,000. Employees then have access to ConSern loans, which are not guaranteed. About three thousand companies participate, and the annual loan total is about $30 million.

Conclusions

This brief overview of actual and potential modes by which employers fund college and university instruction has sought to draw attention to the topic and to indicate that it should be considered more systematically as a long-term policy matter. The role of employers is clearly important, even if one looks at financing issues only from an operational perspective—that is, if one simply asks, How will higher education be financed? From that perspective alone, one can see a number of crucial policy issues related to employers' involvement that will affect higher education. Obviously tax policies are foremost here; they will serve either as incentives or disincentives to employer participation. At the procedural level, the availability of information and guidance on suitable educational opportunities is important. Experience has shown that participation is highly correlated with an adequate advising system, and this will remain so whether the advisement is provided by employers, by the state, or by a consortium of educational institutions.

The issue of employer financing becomes more complex and more important if the social role of higher education is considered. In this context, these questions about the role of employers are paramount:

- Given the growing economic importance of a skilled labor force, should direct employer contributions to education be increased?

- Should governmental and other policies encourage the increasing interweaving of education and work? If so, how can employer financing of this be enhanced?

- Should governmental and other policies encourage lifelong and recurrent participation by individuals in organized instruction to maintain competence on the job in the face of rapid technological change? If so, how can employer financing of such activities be encouraged?

It is time to pay more attention to all these matters.

Notes

1. For a description of tuition plans, see, for example, Paul E. Barton, *Worklife Transitions* (New York: McGraw-Hill, 1982).
2. Ernest A. Lynton, *The Missing Connection Between Business and the Universities* (New York: ACE/Macmillan, 1984). See also Nell P. Eurich, *Corporate Classrooms* (Princeton, N.J.: Carnegie Foundation for the Advancement of Teaching, 1985).
3. Seymour Lusterman, *Education in Industry*, Report no. 719 (New York: Conference Board, 1977).

4. American Society for Training and Development, *Employee Educational Assistance* (Alexandria, Va.: ASTD, 1985); Conference Board, "Corporate-University Relations Programs," *Perspectives* 14 (1988), pp. 11–16. See also Seymour Lusterman, *Trends in Corporate Education and Training*, Report no. 870 (New York: Conference Board, 1985).

5. See Barton, *Worklife Transitions*, p. 9.

6. American Society for Training and Development, *Taxation of Educational Assistance to Employees* (Alexandria, Va.: ASTD, 1985).

7. For a description of the original provisions of Section 127, see American Society for Training and Development, *Taxation of Educational Assistance to Employees*.

8. Research Center on Co-op Education, Northeastern University, private communication, January 1988; Conference Board, "Corporate-University Relations Programs," p. 4.

9. Ernest A. Lynton and Sandra E. Elman, *New Priorities for the University* (San Francisco: Jossey-Bass, 1987).

10. Stephen F. Hamilton, "Apprenticeship as a Transition to Adulthood in West Germany," *American Journal of Education* (1987), pp. 314-45.

11. Information is available on this program from CAEL/Joint Venture Center, 226 South 16th Street, Philadelphia, Pennsylvania 19102.

12. See, in general, Henry M. Levin and Hans G. Schuetze, eds., *Financing Recurrent Education* (Beverly Hills, Calif.: Sage, 1983).

13. See Pierre Caspar, "French Law on Continuing Vocational Training," in Levin and Schuetze, eds., *Financing Recurrent Education*.

16

The Role of
Philanthropy in
Higher Education

ROBERT L. PAYTON

The role of philanthropy in addressing the problems of financing higher education is insufficiently recognized and poorly understood. As a result there is overemphasis on governmental ("public") solutions, on the one hand, and on marketplace ("private") solutions, on the other. Higher education, like most other facets of society, continues to behave as if the United States were a two-sector rather than a three-sector society. I argue in this essay that the third sector, philanthropy, has been displaced by a new and self-serving professionalism.

Philanthropy should not be equated with money. Many in higher education think little, if at all, about philanthropy and then think of it simply as a source of funds and hence necessarily as a weak third to funds from government and funds from private sources (especially tuition income). I use the word as an umbrella term to include the principal forces of voluntary action for public purposes: voluntary service, voluntary association, and voluntary giving and fund-raising. Voluntary initiative is a source of ideas and influence, an alternative when government and marketplace fail or go astray. That is the most important role of philanthropy, and it is a role that few scholars have attended to seriously if at all. The moral aspect of philanthropy, its most distinctive characteristic, also has declined in importance and is barely visible in the present environment.

Background

Voluntary action by voluntary associations, usually brought into being by farsighted individuals, was the means by which most colleges and universities were organized. Building a college was the means hundreds of communities used to make themselves attractive to new settlers. The story is recorded in the classic study by Merle Curti and Roderick Nash, *Philanthropy in the Shaping of American Higher Education.*[1] There was a familiar coalition of local government, business interests, and religious organizations behind the creation of hundreds of colleges. Cooperation of the three sectors was taken for granted. No one of the sectors could have managed without the others.

What is most important about the history of American higher education is that the social purposes of education were clear and understood. Colleges were created to serve as an important resource for community development—political, economic, cultural, and moral. Economic development was primitive and uneven; the tax base was narrow; resources available for tuition were limited. Unless people added voluntary contributions of service, goods, and money, the colleges would have failed in even greater numbers.

The importance of benefactors often was crucial to institutional development. Thomas Hollis played an active role in the religious disputes within the Harvard faculty and used his influence to bring science ("natural philosophy") into the curriculum. Joseph Sheffield helped to bring engineering education into Yale, as Joseph Wharton brought business education into the University of Pennsylvania. A variety of church leaders and philanthropists (George Peabody and Matthew Vassar are examples) brought higher education to blacks and to women.

On balance, the emerging system of higher education was pragmatic, pluralistic, and generally high-minded—as well as public, private, and philanthropic.

The Research University

The story of the land-grant university is too familiar to require any discussion here, except to point out that private philanthropy is evident early in the history of public institutions as well as private. The names and faces of great financial benefactors appear prominently, along with war heroes and political leaders, on campus buildings, in somber portraits, and even in statuary. Gifts for libraries, museums, and other collections for study of research; gifts for scholarships, professorships, lectureships; gifts for endowments, for general support, and all too often for deficits and fiscal crises—all these instances of voluntary giving have left their visible and tangible traces. We know much less about the role of voluntary service, but the histories of most institutions include references to the role of individual trustees who played a crucial role in institutional survival as well as development.

The era of the land-grant university, with its emphasis on public service, is still celebrated in the commercials at the halftime breaks of intercollegiate football games. Less attention is given to the yielding of that model to the hegemony of the so-called research university—the hundred or so universities that dominate American higher education. Private universities, many founded by great philanthropists (Johns Hopkins, the University of Chicago, Clark University), made common cause with public universities (the University of Michigan, the University of California) in stressing science-based research conducted by academic specialists. American higher education has been dominated for fifty years by the research-university model. The institutions are almost indistinguishable in terms of "public" and "private." What is essential to them is the priority they give to research. Alas, the model itself was a voluntary initiative, unexplainable by a two-sector perspective on American society.

The research university's growth to dominance is interwoven with the extraordinary growth of science and the confident expectations of the new social sciences. Each of these movements influenced the nature of the new professionalism. The professions came together with the research universities. The clearest illustration, of course, is medicine. The broad community-based social purposes of the college movement of the early years were supplanted by the agenda of the professions and their new institutional base in the universities. What we now live with is the result—a growing gap between society's view of the purposes of higher education and the uses of the universities by the professionals who dominate them.

One aspect of the decline of the role of philanthropy is evident in the diminished moral role of universities. Intellectual requirements (highly pluralistic and relativistic) of the secular research universities have replaced the moral requirements and teachings of the religiously affiliated colleges. The private professional interests of science-trained academics have supplanted the private professional interests of theology-trained academics. The strong involvement of the churches in American higher education as a source of funds and as a guiding influence has all but disappeared. The irony is that higher education has abandoned religion, but the American public has not. In fact, religious organizations still represent approximately half of the total philanthropic activities of the third sector.

The notion of philanthropy is important to these reflections because there is also a strong philanthropic dimension to the traditional notion of professionalism—the professional's moral obligation to keep the interests of the client paramount. The diminished voice of religion in the life of higher education, and especially in the research university, removes one of the few organized voices for teaching philanthropy as a way of life.

The importance of voluntary community service is obvious in other essays in this volume. Best known are Campus Compact and Campus Outreach Opportunity League. Several important initiatives are under way to link undergraduate course work to the voluntary experience. Some would require voluntary service, despite the oxymoronic quality of the idea, because public or community service is seen as a social good. The philanthropic aspect is central to these appeals, but is seldom made explicit.

The argument, then, may be summarized at this point as contending that the role of voluntary action in higher education has been of great historical importance but has become obscured in recent years. The research university, itself a product of voluntary initiative and philanthropic contributions, is a model that attends primarily to government and the marketplace. The research university is the creature of the professional academic, more concerned about professional needs and interests than about the social purposes for which colleges and universities were created. The professions are decreasingly guided by philanthropic values and increasingly dominated by marketplace values. Business corporations and government agencies are willing conspirators. Research-university-trained grant makers in foundations and research contractors and grant makers in corporations and government agencies join with their academic counterparts. The grant-making function has been captured by the ideology of the new professionalism.

That grossly oversimplified and overstated critique reveals disenchantment with all three sectors. It understates the importance of the community college movement, for example—a movement that owes little to philanthropy except some local and occasional voluntary leadership. The challenges to the present professional hegemony come in various forms, ranging as widely as former Wisconsin senator William Proxmire's popular Golden Fleece Awards to Young Turk rebellions in medical and legal education. Intellectual attacks on the professions as exclusionist, sexist, and racist have shaken the confidence of the professions as well as the public.

The rising criticism of the most powerful and arrogant of the professions, medicine, portends similar criticism of the professionally dominated universities. William Bennett as Secretary of Education was one of the most popular and influential members of the Reagan cabinet. His attacks on higher education were overstated and oversimplified. Interestingly, however, he used his office to articulate a position better expressed from the vantage point of voluntary action. And it is to voluntary initiative that we must turn if the problems of higher education are to be addressed: the self-serving professionalism already discussed, continuing restrictions of access, the absence of consensus about the content and achievement of learning, the loss of a clear sense of the public purposes to be served by higher-educational institutions, the insupportable costs.

The New Agenda

My own worldview has been influenced by involvement in higher education since 1946, as a student, administrator, and now faculty member. The dominant image of the role of the university in my generation was the GI Bill. Suddenly, hundreds of thousands of people who had never thought of the possibility—even of the desirability—of higher education found themselves on college and university campuses. The core value of American higher education was to be the core value of American democracy—opportunity for everyone, regardless of origin. The thrill of that sense of new opportunity has long been lost. The children of GI Bill veterans take higher education for granted. The struggle for access for new generations of excluded students often finds the students themselves uninterested.

The rise of public institutions has dramatically lessened the relative importance of the private institutions. Tuition assistance schemes have been valuable, but the public sector of higher education simply has claimed a far larger share of the market. Private colleges have turned to the government for subsidies and to business for marketing strategies and techniques. Voluntary assistance for students in financial need has grown, but is only a small fraction of what is needed. Some of the most interesting financial aid experiments, of course, have been introduced by private colleges and universities (Washington University and tuition-rate guarantees, for example).

The conflict of the value of access with the value of intellectual standards remains the central issue of the debate. While the debate goes on—at Stanford, for example—the community-college movement continues to address the problem realistically. Access wins. The community college is the traditional means to bypass the selectivity screens. The community college provides the feeder system for the public institutions and many private ones.

The most dramatic new initiative, of course, is Eugene Lang's personal promise to pay the college costs of a class of underprivileged students. His idea has spread in its own form through the work of what is now the I Have a Dream Foundation. More important are the public variants being introduced, in New York, for example. There has seldom been a clearer case of private voluntary initiative influencing public funding policy.

A group of faculty members at Washington University worked for two years to publish *The Purposes of Higher Education*.[2] The book, actually written by philosopher Huston Smith, was representative of the efforts to restate the needs of general education: What are the values that make the university a community of learning? The degree of consensus thirty years ago was far greater than it is today, fragile as it was even then. The cultural, as well as intellectual, fragmentation revealed by the continuing debates at Stanford and in such esoterica as deconstruction and antifoundationalism are beyond the comprehension of the general public (and of their political representatives). Know-nothing counterattacks are increasingly frequent and effective.

The most influential forces seem to be those classed as politically conservative, largely based in autonomous foundations and think tanks—that is, in the tradition of voluntary action. Thus far the political alternatives to the

Heritage Foundation and others on the Right have not been equally successful in using voluntary action. Perhaps it is because the Left has been so wedded to governmental categories in its thinking. Over the years since World War II, of course, some of the most influential innovations in higher-education finance have come from, or have been sponsored by, philanthropic foundations.

The general public assumes that higher education serves public purposes. I have argued that higher education has been diverted from its public purposes to excessive attention to, and concern for, its inner-directed professional needs and ambitions. The university's mission to serve the needs of the society is an affirmation of philanthropic value. The American university, in its original conception, is neither a tool of government and politics nor a tool of corporations and self-interested technical experts. The loss of a sense of mission and purpose—the loss of the first principle of voluntary association for the public good—leaves the public without a way to conceptualize higher education. Higher education gradually moves toward a governmental role— toward being nothing very different from every other bureaucracy. Or it moves toward a marketplace role—toward selling its services to those that can pay for them.

It is no wonder, then, that the rising costs of education are seen as increasingly burdensome. Legislatures increasingly avoid their responsibilities to maintain public higher education and force public universities to become increasingly dependent on private philanthropy. I interpret such a practice as a clear political reading by legislators on what the public now thinks of higher education: less than it did twenty-five years ago, and declining. Even the great achievements of science are no longer sufficient to engender enthusiasm. The costs of Big Science are larger than ever, and the single-minded pursuit of vast projects puts all other organized learning in jeopardy.

Rediscovering the Three Sectors

Much is made of the fact that American higher education is a mixed economy. Public funds flow into private institutions; private funds flow into public institutions. Federal, state, and local governments play roles in setting the limitations that colleges and universities must accommodate. Federal social policies are increasingly intrusive in the lives of institutions. Affirmative action is the most publicized, but the use of the courts as an arbiter of academic policy, even in promotion and tenure cases, is now taken for granted. The needs of private colleges and universities for public subsidies for tuitions has made many of them "quangos"—quasi-autonomous nongovernmental organizations. The lure of public subsidies was the lure of assured income—with public subsidies, we won't have to devote so much time to fund-raising, and we can concentrate on our real work, went the rationale—but this has led to great disappointment. Public sources have proved as fickle and unreliable as the most unpredictable benefactor. The gradual and reluctant recognition of the need to raise money from private sources, although deeply resented by many, is the clearest evidence of the rising importance of private philanthropy as the source of marginal improvement.

It is possible, of course, that the mixed economy in higher education, so attractive to pragmatic, pluralistic, and high-minded Americans, is not the panacea it promised to become.

Consider two examples. First, the university medical center is a research center, a center of private medical practice, a social welfare agency, and an educational facility. It draws its funds from all available sources. As the medical center has grown larger and more complex, its financial needs have strained even its extraordinary resource-generating capabilities. There are more-frequent charges that the model is not working very well. Patients are dissatisfied, physicians and other medical staff are dissatisfied, and costs threaten the system, as well as many of the institutions within it.

The second example is that of intercollegiate athletics. No part of the university makes more blatant and aggressive use of marketplace values and techniques. No higher-education activity seems more inconsistent with institutional purpose and mission. Yet even university presidents banded together have been powerless to resist it. A century of excess simply has led to greater excess. There are now powerful proathletics constituencies with no other interest in higher education than that.

From this emerges my own tentative conclusion: Voluntary action in higher education has become almost exclusively concerned with money. Volunteers are used almost exclusively in fund-raising. Volunteers are people who buy tickets, support booster organizations, provide equipment for laboratories—and do not get in the way of the professionals who are running things. Trustees are recruited for their financial influence and business acumen. The important distinction between business practices and business values is often lost sight of—by university administrators quite as much as by business-based trustees. As Hofstra University economist Harold Wattel expressed it, "A university is an educational institution with business problems, not a business enterprise selling educational services."[3] Public universities do not have the power to tax, although they would like nothing more, and are in fact dependent on those who control the allocation of tax revenues.

I have tried to argue that the mission of higher education has been lost sight of as professional and marketplace values have crowded out philanthropic values. Intrasystem goals now come first. But philanthropy, properly understood, sees money in its proper perspective. Thus, the financial needs of American higher education must be reevaluated in the perspective of the fundamental mission of the institutions.

Notes

1. Merle Curti and Roderick Nash, *Philanthropy in the Shaping of American Higher Education* (New Brunswick, N.J.: Rutgers University Press, 1965).
2. Huston Smith, *The Purposes of Higher Education* (New York: Harper and Row, 1958).
3. From a private conversation with the author.

Index